DARING
to
DREAM

A HANDBOOK FOR HOPE
IN THE TIME OF TRUMP

MIROLAND IMPRINT 17

Canada Council **Conseil des Arts**
for the Arts **du Canada**

ONTARIO ARTS COUNCIL
CONSEIL DES ARTS DE L'ONTARIO
an Ontario government agency
un organisme du gouvernement de l'Ontario

Canadä

Guernica Editions Inc. acknowledges the support of the Canada Council
for the Arts and the Ontario Arts Council. The Ontario Arts Council
is an agency of the Government of Ontario.

We acknowledge the financial support of the Government of Canada.

DARING
to
DREAM

A HANDBOOK FOR HOPE
IN THE TIME OF TRUMP

Angelo Bolotta

MiroLand
publishers

MIROLAND (GUERNICA)
TORONTO • BUFFALO • LANCASTER (U.K.)
2018

Connie McParland, series editor
Michael Mirolla, editor
David Moratto, cover and interior book designer
Kristiina Paul, photo researcher
Guernica Editions Inc.
1569 Heritage Way, Oakville, ON L6M 2Z7
2250 Military Road, Tonawanda, N.Y. 14150-6000 U.S.A.
www.guernicaeditions.com

Distributors:
University of Toronto Press Distribution,
5201 Dufferin Street, Toronto (ON), Canada M3H 5T8
Gazelle Book Services, White Cross Mills
High Town, Lancaster LA1 4XS U.K.

First edition.
Printed in Canada.

Legal Deposit—Third Quarter
Library of Congress Catalog Card Number: 2018943219
Library and Archives Canada Cataloguing in Publication
Bolotta, Angelo, 1951-, author
Daring to dream: a handbook for hope in the time of
Trump / Angelo Bolotta. -- 1st edition.

(MiroLand imprint ; 17)
Issued in print and electronic formats.
ISBN 978-1-77183-341-7 (softcover).--ISBN 978-1-77183-342-4 (EPUB).
--ISBN 978-1-77183-343-1 (Kindle)

1. Social history--21st century. 2. Social problems. 3. World politics--
21st century. 4. Social action. 5. Government accountability. 6. Political
participation. 7. Social psychology. 8. Critical thinking and media literacy.
I. Title. II. Series: MiroLand imprint ; 17

HN18.3.B65 2018   302   C2018-902790-8   C2018-902791-6

DARING to DREAM

A HANDBOOK FOR HOPE IN THE TIME OF TRUMP

Acknowledgements

To Alissa, Alanna, and Mara

My wish is that each one of you experience the peaceful joy that comes with seeking truth and doing justice. In our artificially complicated world, there can be no greater gift than the satisfaction that comes from the realization that what you have done has made a difference in the lives of others. Know that your love and support have greatly helped me to become the person that I am today. In the life journey before you, remember to stay on the high road, regardless of the immediate cost. Believe me when I tell you that you will never regret it, when looking back.

To my many colleagues, students, and friends

Thank you for your support and encouragement throughout the years. Know that I learned much from our encounters and the honest sharing of ideas. This dialogue has been so important in shaping the contents of this handbook.

To young dreamers everywhere

Thank you for daring to dream. Thank you for recognizing that much can be changed for the better. Do not be disillusioned. Continue to dream in glorious colour. Stay focused on the prize and do not be afraid to work hard to make it happen. It might take longer than you expect. But then, evolution has long produced more lasting results than revolution. Do not let power and privilege crush or manipulate your dreams. All real power is latent. As any honest leader will tell you, the minute you have to resort to force, you have effectively lost power, not gained it. Never be afraid to speak truth to power and justice to privilege.

Preface

I vividly remember the events of October 1962, as if it were only yesterday. I remember almost two weeks of escalating tensions, bringing the world again to the brink of war. I did not understand exactly what was going on, but it became abundantly clear that what was happening, in the adult world, was not good.

I remember running home from school terrified one afternoon, while repeatedly looking up to the sky to see if Russian missiles were going to rain down on me, before I could make it safely home. I imagined pointed ballistic missiles striking me right on the top of my head. I was only eleven, so I did not have a grasp of adult realities like nuclear Armageddon and the material permanence of death.

I remember going through 'civil defence' drills in elementary school which consisted mainly of one thing: In the event of a nuclear attack, we were instructed to hide under our desks and pray silently. Only silent prayer was allowed because we had to listen for further instructions from our teachers. Much as I trusted the Sisters of St. Joseph, who ran our school, I was not totally convinced of the soundness of this defensive strategy, based on what my elders had told me about the bombardments they experienced during World War Two. These new bombs were supposed to be much more accurate, powerful, and deadly!

I was a new Canadian, having immigrated to Canada from Southern Italy, with my mother, seven years earlier. I was happy in my new home. We had many relatives in America. I remember being riveted to the flickering, second-hand television set that my father had brought home one day. We lived in the basement of my father's barbershop. Unlike some of my American relatives, we did not have a bomb shelter and we did not have the room to build one. Every inch of basement was already occupied.

My father had spent twelve years serving his country during various wars —starting in North Africa and ending with World War Two. Each time he completed his obligatory military service, a new conflict would break out and he would be recalled to active duty. He did not talk much about his experiences of being under bombardment by enemy forces, but it did not take a rocket scientist to figure out that these new Russian missiles would be very different.

I remember watching flickering images of the youthful American president and a much older and meaner looking leader of the communist Soviet Union. They were playing a deadly game of nuclear chicken. It was not difficult to interpret the adult words we overheard, the fear on their faces, and the abrupt silence once we came into the room. The issue was the placement of Russian nuclear missiles in Cuba, a stone's throw from the United States. The communist dictator of Cuba had requested these nuclear missiles to deter further aggression from the Americans.

The Cuban Missile Crisis was eventually averted when the Soviet Union backed down on its plan to bring missiles to Cuba, so as not to confront an American naval blockade. In the end, reason prevailed over emotion and hard cold facts triumphed over conflicting ideology and escalating rhetoric. The cold war between democratic and communist ideals continued but never again escalated to this breaking point. This, of course, is my adult understanding of what transpired, based on subsequent experienced knowledge, careful reflection, and emotion-free hindsight. My understanding at the time was that the Russians had changed their minds and no missiles would be coming at me, for the time being.

Fast forwarding to the present day, I see in my two adult daughters many of the fears, anxieties, and tensions I experienced about the fate of humankind on our planet. This anxiety has increased exponentially since Donald Trump acquired the mantle of leadership in America.

My daughters live in a world of renewed hostility. Russia's 'strongman for life' becomes bolder each time international protocols are successfully abused. The unstable dictator of North Korea is flaunting his newly acquired capacity to fire missiles capable of carrying nuclear weapons. He has threatened to use them against the United States. The American president has responded with equally aggressive rhetoric. A new game of nuclear chicken appears to have emerged. My daughters live in fear that, this time, logic and reason may not prevail. They fear the doomsday clock is rapidly approaching midnight.

I cannot allay my daughters' fears, any more than my parents were able to protect me from "God-less communists bent on world domination." But, I can focus their critical thinking to help my daughters sort through the hype, misinformation, and loaded rhetoric, often prevailing in today's post-modern, digital world. In fact, it has become increasingly more important to process information carefully in our digital age.

Critical thinking may help uncover concealed realities about our human journey on this planet. This careful, probing, and thorough kind of thinking may help my daughters to read between the lines of the various media messages they are constantly being presented. This too is a kind of bombardment that requires careful consideration. Critical thinking will help people become more effective truth seekers, in an increasingly more complex and convoluted political world. My focus will not be on what to think, but rather, on how to think to become a discerning and contributing citizen locally, nationally, and globally.

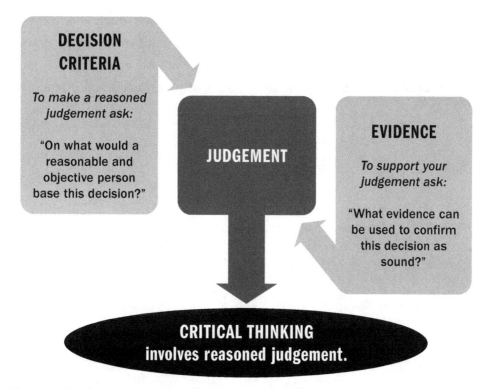

DECISION CRITERIA

To make a reasoned judgement ask:

"On what would a reasonable and objective person base this decision?"

JUDGEMENT

EVIDENCE

To support your judgement ask:

"What evidence can be used to confirm this decision as sound?"

CRITICAL THINKING involves reasoned judgement.

Reasoned judgement requires choosing appropriate criteria to base your decision and solid evidence to support it. Complex and important decisions require sound critical thinking skills.

By sharing these reflections, I hope to pass on the experiences of my life journey to help illuminate the way forward. I hope to help my daughters to make more informed decisions, to keep their sense of humour, and to become more discerning truth seekers in an increasingly more politicized world. I hope to help them temper fear with logical and reasoned optimism, and to help them realize that the light at the end of a long dark tunnel need not be a fast approaching train.

The following pages do not reflect the results of exhaustive empirical research and strict academic analysis. Rather, the contents represent a personal, reflective, and hopefully humorous account. My hope is based on the experience charged belief that there is more good than evil in our world, and that benevolence will invariably prevail over malevolence. As an educator and lifelong learner, I have relished my calling as a voice of hope and promise, enabling young people to recognize opportunity, even when it comes cleverly disguised as an unsolvable problem or a difficult crisis.

In responding to my daughters' fears, I am simultaneously speaking to all those who share their concerns and reluctance to assume the responsibility of moving our troubled world forward and leaving it in a better state for future generations. Mistakes can be painful, but they can also trigger learning and growth, as long as discernment, honesty, and altruism prevail over their opposites.

—AUGUST 20, 2017

The Journey Forward

Think clearly,
Care deeply,
Laugh loudly,
Dream boldly,
Act wisely,
And this too shall pass,
As the winding road,
Of human progress.

While attending a fundraiser four years ago, my eldest daughter, Alissa (left), won a family portrait. When the photographer asked what it was like being the only male in the family, I told him a bit about my experience and the rest is history.

Of all the photos taken that day, this was the one the family unanimously chose as the official portrait. I know my girls all love me because they voluntarily took off their spiked heels to pose for this unusual portrait. Otherwise, the whole experience could have been very painful. (Courtesy of Ken Schultz Photography).

Contents

CHAPTER ONE

ONE CIRCUS DIES, A NEW CIRCUS BEGINS— LONG LIVE 'THE GREATEST SHOW ON EARTH'

IN JANUARY OF 2017, just as Ringling Brothers and Barnum and Bailey officially announced the winding down of their 146-year-old circus business, with great fanfare, the most televised circus in American history moved into Washington, D.C. The first act of this new circus occurred only one day after the inauguration of the new president, ring master and principal performer. In a bold-faced lie, newly appointed White House press secretary Sean Spicer angrily denied all evidence to the contrary and proclaimed the honest truth to be that the Trump inauguration received "the largest audience ever to witness an inauguration, period, both in person and around the globe."

Without substantiation, it was implied that conspirators had posted doctored aerial photos of the Trump inauguration and the record setting 2009 inauguration of president Obama. 'Discerning' Americans were expected to believe that the National Park Service must have 'doctored' photographs to make the new president look bad. Logically, a feeble rationale could be fabricated to explain this alleged conspiratorial behaviour. The National Park Service could be accused of opposing the new president because it was feared that he planned to allow the desecration of America's national parklands to extract natural resources and to better exploit the parklands' previously untapped economic potential.

For example, instead of wasting money looking after a huge and dangerous hole in the ground, why not convert the Grand Canyon into the world's largest and most profitable landfill project? This would simultaneously promote capitalism, create jobs, and address the environmental problem of what to do with the tons of garbage generated in America every day. It could be argued that the National Park Service had a vested interest in conspiring to maintain the status quo, and therefore, stood in the way of "making America great again."

> *"There are no facts only interpretations."*
>
> *"All things are subject to interpretation. Whichever interpretation prevails at a given time is a function of power and not truth."*
> —FRIEDRICH NIETZSCHE

According to Sean Spicer, the truth demonstrated by comparing two inauguration crowd photos was actually 'fake news' created by the *Fake News Media*, with the explicit intent to deceive the gullible American public. Luckily, the new president's legion of supporters was not that gullible, leaving only Trump's critics mired in the gullible camp. This was a slap in the face to honest and respected professional journalists everywhere. Trump is reported to have gotten directly involved in demanding the removal of the Park Service photos and the name of the employee posting them.

In the coming days, 'Fake News' would come to be defined as any media messaging that did not wholeheartedly endorse and support the new president, his musings, or his *agenda de jour*. Interestingly, I found no evidence to corroborate Sean Spicer's interpretation of the facts in the crowd size debate. At least not from traditionally reliable news services, with stellar reputations for reporting truthfully. Therefore, any conspiracy would have had to be widespread and masterfully executed. It is a fascinating insight into the human condition to observe how people often see in others the very faults they choose to ignore in themselves.

At the risk of sounding Freudian, this pattern of behaviour can either be intentional or subconscious. The deliberate act often reveals an arrogant narcissist in denial. The more unintentional behaviour may reflect insecurity or ignorance.

In any event, neither cause is indicative of quality character traits. Should a narcissist occasionally recognize small personal faults, he will usually take great comfort in finding those same traits to exist in others, in what is often determined to be a much higher degree. So, chronic liars will see many others as bold-faced manipulators of the truth, while rationalizing their own actions as little white lies made necessary by difficult circumstances.

Perhaps the most cynical and manipulative use of fault finding is the deliberate accusation of rivals and critics as demonstrating the very behaviour being used and concealed by the accuser. Regrettably, this practice has become more prevalent in recent times and its frequency of occurrence can further obscure the truth and erode trust. Trump has shown himself to be a master of this technique.

This underhanded technique has been deviously perfected to maximize distraction. In our post-modern digital age, crafty manipulators expertly do the very thing that they accuse their enemies and rivals of doing. They are banking on the fact that the disillusioned and the ignorant will be easy to persuade.

Figure 1.1: Trump's Inauguration Day in 2017 (right) compared to Obama's record breaking Inauguration Day in 2009. (left: Emily Barnes / Stinger / Getty Images, right: Lucas Jackson—Pool / Getty Images).

Notwithstanding the artistic breakthrough called Photoshop®, where digital photographic images can be easily manipulated or enhanced, the difference in crowd size between these two National Park Service photos indicates an over-whelming 1:3 ratio. This is not even close to comparable. Any doctoring of the original image would not require this much exaggeration to make the desired point.

To claim the 2017 inauguration as "the largest audience ever" requires the liberal use of what Trump surrogates (and well paid staffers) subsequently began calling "alternative facts." During a January 22 interview on *Meet the Press*, Kellyanne Conway (an advisor to the new president) defended the White House press secretary's obviously false statements as providing the American people with "alternative facts." This became the new term for favoured falsehoods. Under scathing attack from veteran journalists, Conway later clarified her choice of words to mean "additional facts and alternative information." This confirms that there are many ways for a wordsmith to frame a lie.

Given improved technology and millions more people living on our planet in 2017, compared to 2009, it would be difficult to refute the potential for a larger audience around the globe. But potential does not constitute reality. Just like alternative facts, alternative information, and alternative 'truths' do not constitute an objective reality. For example, using a high-powered magnifying glass, I am alternatively able to detect two portly figures, in the 2017 photo. These figures bear a striking resemblance to Jimmy Hoffa and Elvis Presley. But still, I cannot confirm or deny their support of the Trump presidency.

Figure 1.2: Adaptation of a popular meme circulating the Internet following the ridiculous crowd size debate. (left: Emily Barnes / Stringer / Getty Images, right: Lucas Jackson—Pool / Getty Images, inset: age fotostock / Alamy Stock Photo).

Equally tongue-in-cheek, others have discovered a sea of supporters proudly wearing their white hooded robes. Unfortunately, without enhancing the original photo, the legion of white robbed supporters become invisible against the white floor they are standing on. Coincidence? I think not! This white floor mat was meant to deliberately conceal crowd size—an obvious conspiracy to discredit the new president and his loyal staff.

If nothing more, this crowd size discrepancy and the controversy generated is a clear indicator that what we have taken for granted for many years now needs closer examination and more focused reflection. The escalating politicization of official messaging may have finally crossed into blatantly dishonest and overtly manipulative territory.

> "The press doesn't stop publishing, by the way, in a fascist escalation; it simply watches what it says. That too can be an incremental process, and the pace at which the free press polices itself depends on how journalists are targeted."
>
> —NAOMI WOLF

When is the truth no longer the truth?
How can thinking be manipulated to confuse or conceal the truth?
When is an alternate truth more reliable than the actual truth?
Who ultimately gets to define truth? Does winning an election allow the victor to selectively redefine the truth?
What role do evidence, logic and reason have in the truth-seeking process?

The more we ask ourselves these critical questions the more we can break free from the manipulation and trickery of those who would sabotage or exploit our democratic, economic, and social freedoms and dreams for their own personal gain. Perhaps the

> *"The sad truth is that most evil is done by people who never make up their minds to be good or evil."*
> —HANNAH ARENDT

most sinister and cynical of exploiters are those of wealth and privilege who cavalierly profess that simply by enabling their personal goals to come to fruition, automatically the dreams of millions of others will be made possible.

That the successful Trump campaign slogan, "Make America Great Again" resonated with a large number of disenchanted and disillusioned Americans confirms a sad reality. The poor health of the American Dream is a matter of undeniable public record. This malaise is both chronic and acute. It has been a long time in the making and has the potential to be fatal. If left untreated, or if many citizens continue to pretend that nothing is really wrong, fatality can be the eventual outcome.

Those in positions of power and privilege may have a vested interest in keeping the myth of the American Dream alive, simply to keep those being disadvantaged loyal to the cause. A disillusioned, disenfranchised, and explicitly marginalized majority will eventually cease to buy the hype that the American Dream is alive and well.

For proud Americans to turn to a politically inexperienced, cynical, anti-establishment candidate, claiming that America is broken and only he can fix it, reveals the limited options available to voters in 2016. The logic used by Trump to court working class and ethnic votes is remarkable, especially in light of his condescending treatment of visible minorities and his propensity to profit from the employment of vastly underpaid foreign workers, at the expense of American jobs.

On both occasions, the eventually successful candidate apparently failed to complete his train of thought. In these impromptu departures from the scripted speech, Trump failed to share one final detail: "What have you got to lose? Well, vote for me and I will show you what you have left to lose."

> *"You're living in poverty, your schools are no good, you have no jobs, 58% of your youth is unemployed—what the hell have you got to lose?"*
> —DONALD TRUMP
> AUGUST 19, 2016 IN
> DIMONDALE, MICHIGAN

> *"Our government has totally failed our African American friends, our Hispanic friends and the people of our country. Period. The Democrats have failed completely in the inner cities. For those hurting the most who have been failed and failed by their politician—year after year, failure after failure, worse numbers after worse numbers. Poverty. Rejection. Horrible education. No housing, no homes, no ownership. Crime at levels that nobody has seen. You can go to war zones in countries that we are fighting and it's safer than living in some of our inner cities that are run by the Democrats. And I ask you this, I ask you this—crime, all of the problems — to the African Americans, who I employ so many, so many people, to the Hispanics, tremendous people: What the hell do you have to lose? Give me a chance. I'll straighten it out. I'll straighten it out. What do you have to lose?"*
>
> —DONALD TRUMP
> AUGUST 22, 2016 IN AKRON, OHIO

Trump's contempt for America's current reality is nothing short of alarming. "I could stand in the middle of Fifth Avenue and shoot somebody and I wouldn't lose voters," he proudly boasted during a campaign rally in Sioux Center, Iowa in January of 2016. This cavalier statement may have confirmed the loyalty he sensed from his hard-core supporters, but it simultaneously called to question whether he could comport himself in a 'presidential' manner. In retrospect, it reflected an accurate assessment of the degree to which an increasingly large number of Americans had grown disillusioned with their politicians, and how desperate they were for any alternative.

Trump's propensity to use such a violent metaphor betrayed his insensitivity to the issue of escalating gun violence in America. If this was just an attempt at humour, then at very least, it showed poor taste and an alarming tendency to carelessly use suggestive and dangerous hyperbole in his messaging. In reality, since his support base was not appreciably diminished after the comment, then he was absolutely correct in his assessment of the widespread disillusionment of American voters.

Not surprisingly, while in office, Trump's propensity to court violent rhetoric did not waver. On July 28, 2017, while speaking to a group of law enforcement officials in Long Island, New York he openly encouraged officers, "don't be too nice" with the suspects and thugs being arrested. In damage control mode, after the backlash, he later claimed this to be a joke. Given serious concerns across America regarding the excessive use of force by some police officers, sometimes leading to the death of their suspects, it is unconscionable for a president to truthfully consider this a laughing matter.

Any president who claims for himself the right to say and do anything he wants, regardless of appropriateness or consequences, empowers his electorate to behave in similar fashion. This can only create problems for America down the road. In one year, America has already become a much meaner and more cynical place. In addition, instead of improving active listening skills, Americans have shown a marked tendency to ignore and dismiss those with different views, without bothering to listen,

> *"The great enemy of the truth is very often not the lie —deliberate, contrived, and dishonest —but the myth —persistent, persuasive, and unrealistic."*
>
> —JOHN F. KENNEDY

let alone investing sufficient time to reflect on the significance of what is actually being said. This growing political intolerance can also impede the process of discernment and truth seeking.

During Trump's tumultuous first year as President of the United States (POTUS), he has revealed an aggressively contrarian spirit. When strongly advised not to do something by his closest advisors, he often did the very thing he was being warned against, sometimes just to prove that he, and only he, could pull it off successfully. Orchestrating the firing of FBI deputy director Andrew McCabe, two days prior to his official retirement—so as to jeopardize his pension—cannot be seen as anything less than a cold-hearted, partisan, and vindictive move to punish McCabe and intimidate other civil servants by publicly demonstrating the foolishness of provoking the wrath of this POTUS. Too often, truth can be forced to the periphery by political expediency. In the crafty world of Donald Trump, accusing rivals of the very trickery you are engaging in serves to confuse gullible onlookers. And so, accusing reliable sources of providing 'fake' news while your own supporters promote a narrative of favourable lies and deceit is considered an act of genius, because people of questionable intellect would be fooled into thinking exactly the way you wanted.

An Experience Worth Noting:
Conveniently Fabricating Truth to Suit the Occasion

★ ★ ★ ★ ★ ★

Figure 1.3: The village of Carpanzano, Cosenza in August of 2003. (Photo courtesy of the author).

While growing up in my village, there was an illustrious citizen whom villagers often referred to as "the guy who became a lunatic to avoid going to war." Carpanzano, the village of my birth, was nestled securely on an ancient volcanic plug in the mountains of Calabria, on the way to the vast plateau and forests of La Sila. Since the middle ages, peasant farmers and well-to-do landowners lived together in this small village. Carpanzano was originally settled by people from the Cosenza area, who were fleeing Saracen raiders and Norman invaders.

If memory serves correctly, this particular citizen was nicknamed *Rico the Fox*. He came from a family of peasant farmers who worked the fields owned by wealthy landlords. As share croppers, each year his family was required to divide their harvest into thirds. One third would be used to pay taxes, one third would go to the landlords, and the remaining third would be what his family was left to live on. They were also bee keepers, known for producing a honey of superior quality. Rico was a close friend and schoolmate of my uncle (zio) Antonio. As neither classmate could be even remotely considered a scholar, they often skipped school together. They were both drafted into the Italian army, just as the Second World War effort was beginning a steady decline.

Almost immediately, Rico began acting out in public. Instead of helping his family with the daily chores of subsistence farming, he would climb trees around the village and scream out obscenities, for no apparent reason, like a crazy person. Ultimately, he was declared unfit for military service. Along with his steady companion, a goat he proudly introduced as his "fiancé," he was often seen dancing down the streets of the village after receiving his exemption from military service. For all intents and purposes, Rico did avoid going to war by altering the truth.

My uncle, on the other hand, was drafted into the army and eventually sent to the Russian front for combat duty. On the bitterly cold train ride to the Russian front, zio Antonio suffered a severe case of frostbite. As a result, the index finger on his right hand was permanently deformed and immobile. This complication may have saved his life, because he was declared unfit for duty and sent home. The rest of his battalion fought the Russian army and most were killed.

Rico's troubles really began after the war had ended. With peace having been finally restored, government authorities could now devote more time and resources to the provision of social services. In his case, the authorities wanted Rico placed in an insane asylum. It was reasoned that he would be better cared for in an institution and not present an additional burden to his poor family. Given the sad state of mental asylums in Italy, this represented a tragic turn of events for Rico. All of a sudden, going to war might not have been the worst thing.

What was now needed was a small miracle. He had to be declared sane to avoid being institutionalized. He had always insisted on his complete sanity. This was a key part of his public persona during the war years. As he saw it, insane people are often the last to see themselves for what they are. But the villagers were never quite sure of his state of mind. He did have an explosive temper and this often got him into trouble. Villagers liked to tease and mock him to try to solicit the volcanic eruption of his volatile temperament. Without television, this passed as affordable entertainment.

Some local children and teens went out of their way to steal figs from his family's prized fig tree. This tree was easily accessible from the roadway, so a quick getaway was possible. They took great delight to see him chasing after them wielding a big stick and swearing profusely. One day he boldly put up a large sign on the fig tree that proclaimed: "Be warned! One of these figs has been poisoned." This proved an effective deterrent because many villagers were not completely sure of his actual state of mind.

As his public behaviour calmed down, he was eventually declared sane. This was met with a small celebration among friends and relatives. However, this new truth also proved problematic. Local youths again started to raid the family's fig tree. Once again, he put up a large sign to warn that one of his prized figs had been poisoned. But this time the theft continued unabated. In fact, one local smartass put up a counter sign indicating that, "Now, two figs have been poisoned." Ultimately, sanity prevailed and the poisoned fig strategy/bluff was abandoned by all sides.

Figure 1.4: Things may not always be as the mind perceives them. This interesting three-dimensional artwork, winner of the 2014 Venice Chalk Festival, in Florida, was photographed in 2015.

And so, in life, all human beings have occasion to interpret, embellish, and outright fabricate what passes for 'truth'. In truth, we all see the world from our own personal frame of reference or experience base. When we do this, it can say more about ourselves than it actually says about the world we perceive around us. Some fabrications result from unintentional misinterpretations of facts and realities. These can be considered the result of human misperception. Others are deliberate misrepresentations intended to deceive. Each 'new' truth we fabricate can bring about its own set of complications or consequences. The more a 'new' truth is riddled with inaccuracies and inconsistencies, the more the complications and unintended consequences it can generate. Often, one false statement can easily generate the need for additional misrepresentations of the truth, down the road, to help sustain or re-work the original.

Humans are regularly challenged to build a perceived truth around them. This truth influences the way they see and respond to the world. In turn, this professed truth influences how the world sees each builder. A person of integrity mindfully avoids convenient fabrications because of the debilitating effects on the fabricator. Such a person prefers the most accurate and morally responsible representations of reality possible.

A person of keen intellect avoids truth fabrication because of its proclivity towards escalating recurrence. This leaves only self-serving persons of limited integrity and limited intellectual capacity to embrace truth fabrication as a convenient way to influence others. The most callous of these self-serving individuals have no moral qualms about weaseling out of what was actually said earlier as "your misunderstanding (and therefore, fabrication) of what was actually said and meant."

One benefit of telling the least adulterated truth is that you do not have to worry as much about remembering the specific particulars you have told others. But do not expect that the truth will always "set you free" as the Bible (John 8: 32) proclaims. In reality, the truth can also be inconvenient. It can create a moral imperative to take action to help ensure that least adulterated truths prevail over the injustices created by those fabricating convenient (and often self-serving) alternative truths.

The Trump experience provides Americans with a challenging test of their discernment and resolve. The *Washington Post* has tracked and documented 2,001 false or misleading claims during his first year (355 days) in office. This represents a staggering 5.6 questionable claims per day directly made by the American president. Half of these questionable claims included statements that were found to be false once the facts were actually checked. Regrettably, this pattern has had minimal negative impact on the size of his core support base.

Ironically, Trump used convenient fabrications to avoid the military draft and going to war. Yet today, he insists on questioning the patriotism of professional football players who dare to protest that "Black Lives Matter" during the playing of the pre-game national anthem. Some might see this as hypocritical. Now, what does this actually say about Trump, and what does this say about those who perceive hypocrisy?

The Parable of the Self-Absorbed Circus Impresario

★ ★ ★ ★ ★ ★

Fact finding and truth seeking are essentials for living in our post-modern digital age, where information is exchanged instantaneously, truth has become subjective, and alternate facts have been lauded as 'objective' realities for 'discerning' minds. The following parable helps reveal some of the dangers.

The Greatest Circus, Ever!

Figure 1.5: By editorial cartoonist Paul Sharp. (Courtesy of CartoonStock.com).

Trump's Budget at Work

Figure 1.6: By editorial cartoonist Pat Bagley. (Courtesy of Cagle Cartoons).

A billionaire misogynist spent his charmed life wrapped up in himself. He loved himself so much that he felt the world was God's gift to him. He travelled all over the land looking for the most powerful spotlight to shine on himself. This would allow everyone and everything to bask in his presence.

He finally decided to take over the greatest circus in the land, with the brightest spotlight in the world. He hired and fired staff until he found people that would follow his strict instructions, including staying totally out of the spotlight. In fact, he was the only one allowed under the bright light. This, he explained, "was to prevent others from hurting their eyes."

As a marketing genius, he charged no admission into "the peoples' circus," only a stiff exit fee. He saw it as a great public service to offer people a nice diversion from their ho-hum lives. As ringmaster, he told great stories (mostly whoppers) about his courage and genius. As a magician, he used scantily clad female assistants, which he personally certified as 'solid 9s' after thorough manipulation. This was something he felt entitled to do given his celebrity status. While the audience was distracted by fireworks and colourful puffs of smoke, the assistants picked their pockets clean. With no money to pay the exit fees, they became a captive audience.

After all the smoke finally cleared, the audience got to see the magician make an illegal immigrant disappear. As a daredevil, he had himself shot out of a cannon to soar through the air, free as a bird. He found this so exhilarating that he flew several times a show. In fact, he loved flying so much that he started to grow bright orange feathers. He even started to tweet constantly like a songbird. As a birdman, he tweeted day and night. Occasionally his tweets even made sense. This left his captive audience longing for the day he would finally decide to flock off.

He finally did leave the peoples' circus one day, but not without a final surprise. While people were distracted by the noisy circus, HUGE budget cuts were quietly administered to public schools, healthcare, the arts, scientific research, and the environment. In the end, somebody had to pay for the greatest circus ever!

CHAPTER TWO

CONNECTING DREAMS, REALITY, TRUTH, AND 'ALTERNATIVE FACTS'

THROUGHOUT HISTORY, DREAMS have been instrumental in advancing human potential. Dreams have provided the motivation to try something different, to go against the grain, to step out of one's comfort zone, to look beyond existing obstacles or constraints, and to dare to take calculated risks. All of this is done in the hope of finding or making something better. The motivation to adapt the available opportunities in life to the betterment of self, loved ones, community, society, and ultimately, humankind, often begins with a simple dream. In the process of making dreams reality, great insights into the self and into the human condition are simultaneously gained. The dreams we dare dream while wide awake are often the most powerful.

It has often been said that "the dream never dies, just the dreamer." This may have been true at one time, especially for the most noble of human dreams. Sadly, this may no longer be true in today's post-modern world. Nor will it be true in the 'golden age of the transnational corporation' that will follow. In this new world, dreams can be effectively killed by those in positions of privilege and power. If the advertising industry can effectively manipulate consumer wants on behalf of clients willing to pay for their expertise, then dreams can also be manipulated or misdirected over time. Perhaps one of the most sinister forms of manipulation is the façade of individual autonomy in the midst of covert control. In other words, a person is made to believe that their thoughts, dreams and perceptions are their own, while in reality they are greatly influenced or directed by others.

Great nations were built on noble dreams. One of the most notable examples was the American Dream. This revolutionary 'American' dream empowered a passionately free populace to seize the reins of their own destiny and to build

> "Nothing happens unless first a dream."
> —CARL SANDBURG

considerable wealth and prosperity through hard work, fair play and love of truth, justice, liberty, and the individual pursuit of happiness. The highly-individualized approach that emerged (blending democratic government and a free market economy) has become affectionately known as "the American way."

The 'Canadian' way is a second example of new world dreams leading to nationhood. Curiously, everywhere else in the world where English and French interests met, the result most often was conflict, war, and destruction. In 1867, French and English immigrants and their descendants peacefully agreed to build a new nation together. This new nation would become an ongoing experiment in collaboration and compromise among diverse cultures and interests.

The Canadian constitution reflects a more collectivist spirit than its American counterpart. Where the American dream focused on the 'individual pursuit of happiness,' the Canadian dream instead focused on 'peace, order and good gov-

> "When something is important enough, you do it even if the odds aren't in your favour."
> —ELON MUSK

ernment.' Under this Canadian model, individual rights and freedoms were protected but tempered by a social conscience and an eye toward the common or greater good. Throughout human history, differences have been a source of division and conflict. The 'Canadian' dream goes against this historical pattern. In multicultural Canada, citizens are challenged to embrace diversity as a source of innate strength. According to Canadian writer John Ralston Saul, this notion of national identity will require constant attention, hence the "permanently unfinished" nature of the noble Canadian enterprise.

And so, despite their imperfections, the two neighbouring nations of free dreamers attracted large numbers of immigrants from around the world, by inviting them to share in the dream of a better life. In America, a 'melting pot' strategy was used to naturalize newcomers into the American way of thinking, living and dreaming. A plaque on the pedestal of the Statue of Liberty in New York Harbour, the port of entry for many new arrivals to America, boldly proclaimed:

Give me your tired, your poor,
Your huddled masses yearning to breathe free,
The wretched refuse of your teeming shore.
Send these, the homeless, tempest-tossed to me,
I lift my lamp beside the golden door!

—EMMA LAZARUS, 1883

(EXCERPT FROM *THE NEW COLOSSUS*)

The American Dream was nurtured and passed on to successive generations. For many years, America stood out as a beacon of hope and promise, a place where those willing to work hard were free to accomplish great things. Many other nations looked to America as a model for functional democracy, free enterprise and rugged individuality. Friends and allies, like the Canadian neighbours to the north, began to appreciate America's growing presence and steadfast vision. In the case of America, the whole was always seen to be worth more than the sum of its individual parts. An economist might say that there was great *value added* in the American brand.

In Canada, almost a hundred years younger than its American neighbour, the original issue of distinct cultural differences among its three founding nations (Indigenous, French and English) led to the natural evolution of a *multicultural mosaic*. In this inclusive nation, newcomers were invited to bring the best that their native culture had to offer to contribute to the evolving Canadian identity. This sharing of cultures generated a healthy tolerance for differences and respect for a common humanity within

> *"Canada is a nation that works better in practice than in theory."*
> —STÉPHANE DION

this diversity. In the Canadian vision, cultural diversity was to be celebrated and respected as a national resource and a living tribute to the human family. Since differences can often be a source of division and conflict, Canadians are required to look well beyond the obvious differences, to ultimately recognize and build on common values, beliefs and dreams for the future that is being constructed together.

In both nations, citizens are encouraged to dream big, like their ancestors did when they first arrived. Newcomers are invited to integrate the dreams that motivated their immigration. Then, all are encouraged to work hard to make their dreams become reality. This is the hope and promise connected to both American and Canadian dreams. But, many unexpected things can happen on the long and winding road from dream to reality. Some experiences serve to reinforce and embolden the original dream. Others have the capacity to divert, confuse or distort the original vision.

Today, we may well be on the cusp of a radical shift in how Americans approach their dream or in the very dream itself. Some of the harshest critics argue that the dream is dead, or at very least, on its deathbed. In effect, a growing number of Americans demonstrate increased concerns about where their country is headed.

Fundamentalists and conservatives argue that the original dream has been polluted and compromised. Progressives and liberals claim that the dream has been rigged to favour those with great wealth and power, at the expense of the others. Social reformers lament that, despite the progress made in approaching racial equality in America, the anchor principle of "freedom and justice for all" remains an elusive dream in many respects, often falling victim to racially motivated intolerance, fear and distrust. Populists are sick and tired of what they perceive as being lied to and failed by career politicians. In growing numbers, this populist movement advocates a purge (or "draining of the swamp") to replace all professional politicians who have become self-serving leeches on the public purse. In this highly polarized and divisive environment the ongoing honest dialogue, negotiation and compromise needed to refocus the American dream are less likely to occur.

Domestically, social and economic inequalities continue to prevail. Race relations in America continue to require a more honest and equitable treatment than is presently afforded. Too often, communities assume credit for achievements in race relations that are far from a sustainable reality. The most frustrated social reformers might argue that instead of addressing deep seated racial intolerance, bigoted people have simply learned to be more guarded and subtle in their ways. Regrettably, some of these bigoted individuals and groups feel empowered and supported by the rhetoric emerging from the *Twitter storm* that is the Trump messaging machine.

The adjacent quote, dating back to one of the cradles of democracy and classical philosophy, provides an interesting benchmark from which such messaging can be meaningfully assessed. The resulting assessment is substantially less flattering than the huge A+ rating Trump consistently reserves for himself and his musings.

> *"Strong minds discuss ideas, average minds discuss events, weak minds discuss people."*
> —SOCRATES

Regrettably, in our digital age, attention spans and voter memories have become increasingly shorter. Therefore, political controversies do not have the staying power they once did. The critical question is:

What happens to political accountability when controversy comes and goes so quickly?

This question becomes especially more serious when elected officials are successful in setting the bar of acceptability lower and lower with successive controversies, effectively desensitizing the electorate.

Economic inequalities and the widening discrepancies between social classes in America, the persistent shrinking of the middle class, and the obscene incomes of the privileged class of corporate executives continue to pit *Main Street America* against Wall Street. In this adversarial environment, it becomes more difficult for elected politicians to strike a healthy balance. In the process, distinct winners and losers often emerge. In a healthy and sustainable economy, Main Street needs Wall Street, and vice versa. An honest partnership is needed to fuel the growth and prosperity desired by and for everyone.

> *"American business would be run better today if there was more alignment between CEOs' interest and the company. For example, would the financial crisis of 2008 have occurred if the CEO of Lehman and Morgan Stanley and Goldman and Citibank had to take a very small percentage of every mortgage-backed security ... or every loan they made?"*
> —AUBREY MCCLENDON

When leaders of powerful corporations are seen to exploit circumstances for personal gain, when quick profiteering is favoured over more sustainable and socially responsible alternatives, when corporate executives continue to receive astronomical raises, bonuses and stipends in the midst of massive layoffs, declining productivity and worsening recession, ultimate accountability appears limited. One such example occurred during the subprime mortgage crisis that launched America and the rest of the global economy into the *Great Recession* (2007–2010). Government bailouts were needed to save large American financial institutions from falling victim to their own greed and reckless decisions. At the same time, many of the executives responsible continued to receive healthy rewards.

When corporate executives are seen to receive large bonuses while laying off countless workers, the conclusion that big business is in conflict with working class America is not difficult to reach. If obligations to corporate shareholders constantly force other stakeholders to the periphery, then there can be no denying that the economic system is rigged to favour some at the expense of others. The shrinking middle class and the widening income gap between wealthy and other Americans is further evidence that current economic realities are not sustainable. The president himself has historically contributed to unemployment in America by preferring to import goods for his companies from cheaper off-shore suppliers in order to maximize profits. In his defence, he claimed to be doing only what current laws allow. He went on to conveniently blame bad decisions by incompetent predecessors for America's economic decline. A clear distinction was never seen to be made between what the individual can do (by law), and what the moral individual should do in good conscience.

In addition, when the very rich are seen to be paying substantially less taxes than lower wage earners, relative to percentage of overall income, the irrefutable question of tax avoidance resulting from privilege can no longer be ignored. Ultimately, trust is further eroded and the relationship between Main Street and Wall Street becomes increasingly adversarial. Ultimately, this relationship becomes incapable of creating the necessary win-win outcome, resulting in greater poverty in the midst of extreme affluence—the very antithesis of the American Dream.

On the international scene, since the Trump administration came into office, a growing number of foreign nations and allies have begun to question whether today's America is stable and trustworthy. More significantly, enemy powers and rivals have taken advantage of America's current instability and political turmoil to test its resolve. North Korea's communist dictator has boldly accelerated missile testing and boasted about his nation's emerging capacity to strike North American targets with nuclear weapons. Chinese companies and Russian rocket scientists have been instrumental in supplying North Korea with the equipment and technology needed. China, North Korea's largest trading partner and neighbour, has done little independently to rein in the rogue missile testing program.

Iranian ships have boldly confronted American military vessels patrolling in the Persian Gulf. Russian submarines, exploring Arctic waters in search of natural resources, have ventured deeper into American and Canadian territories than ever before. Russian fighter jets have deliberately come dangerously close to

American planes while on military manoeuvres. With Russia's protection and support, Syria's besieged dictator has used chemical weapons on his own innocent civilians, in spite of repeated warnings from the American government. Surprisingly, the retaliatory air strike ordered by the American president (on Syrian air fields) came one hour after Russia had already been warned of the impending strike. The weakening of America from within can embolden those forces seeking a new world order—one where America is forced from centre stage and to the periphery.

Drastic cuts to public education, sometimes in favour of charter schools in select communities that can afford quality education, are another clear game changer. Since today's students will become tomorrow's citizens, the more American students continue to lag behind foreign students in international tests, the greater the danger that dreams may be compromised in the increasingly more competitive world that awaits them.

A great paradox of our times is that the richest and most powerful country became the last of the economically developed and affluent nations to provide affordable health care to its citizens. The Clinton administration tried but was unable to deliver on this promise. The Obama administration finally succeeded in 2010. This required considerable effort, given a Republican majority in the Senate. Many opponents argued that it was forced on the American people.

Since this was a first attempt at a very complex program, involving millions of patients, as well as large and powerful insurance and pharmaceutical companies with vested interests, there were bound to be problems with *Obamacare*. This left plenty of room for future adjustment and improvement. Overall, the notion of affordable health care for all Americans was seen as a step in the right direction by a substantial number of Americans, many of whom could not afford medical insurance before. For some uninsured Americans, becoming seriously ill meant choosing between declining costly health care or forfeiting their life savings to pay medical bills. So much for building on dreams!

"Repeal and replace *Obamacare*," became one of the most popular slogans of the Trump election campaign. Trump promised supporters that it would be a quick and easy process because *Obamacare* was a soon to be "bankrupt" failure. After the election however, nothing proved to be further from the truth. Trump had promised to kill the Affordable Health Care Act in favour of making better choices available to the American consumer. This was based on the premise that the consumer would be able to pay for the new choices made available. It is economically doubtful that any replacement legislation, where insurance and pharmaceutical companies have far greater leverage, will be equally affordable for low income Americans.

I suspect that the deep seated thinking by proponents of this political reversal is the arrogant notion that "forced" *Obamacare* should have never happened in the first place. When consumers cannot afford adequate coverage, they only have themselves to blame. Living in the richest and most powerful nation on earth, it could be argued (especially by champions of smaller government and lower taxation) that opportunities have been squandered by making poor choices.

> *"Today [2016], the top one-tenth of 1 percent owns nearly as much wealth as the bottom 90 percent. The economic game is rigged, and this level of inequality is unsustainable. We need an economy that works for all, not just the powerful."*
> —BERNIE SANDERS

When replacing *Obamacare* proved much more difficult than first imagined, the president's team focused on repeal without replacement and then repeal without details. These Trump tactics were found so unsupportable by sufficient numbers of Republican law makers that both initiatives failed. After six awkward months in office, even with a Republican majority in the Senate and the House of Representatives, the president's "repeal and replace" health care tactics did not prevail. Trump immediately focused his attention on starving *Obamacare* of adequate funding so that it would become the "bankrupt failure" he had always claimed. Thus, orchestrating a self-fulfilling prophesy.

The political and economic systems originally built to serve all Americans can now be seen to favour some at the expense of others. Some social reformers might even argue that these systems have become tools of oppression. This reflection from Senator Sanders crystalizes the sad reality about the distribution of power and wealth in America and in the global economy. Government appears complicit in favouring or at least enabling the rich elite.

The rapid accumulation of individual wealth can be a sign that others are being exploited or disadvantaged. In a free market economy, effective regulation is often lacking to protect consumers from excessive profit taking. The abuse of market dominance by successful entrepreneurs and corporations has also not been effectively regulated. Since power and privilege will always have the capacity to sway government policies favourably, citizens must be constantly vigilant to ensure that every government is seen to hold the common good above the interests of the elite.

The notion of self-regulated individualism is as inconsistent with human nature as the notion of automatic improvement through socialization. Excessive profiteering and the maldistribution of wealth and power are natural by-products of unbridled free enterprise capitalism. Inefficiency and declining productivity are natural by-products of unbridled socialism. Moderate, balanced, or multi-dimensional approaches are often more fruitful than their extremist or highly partisan counterparts.

Although some benefits have trickled down to the rest of society, a disproportionate amount of wealth and influence remain concentrated in very few hands. Too much power in too few hands has most often proved worrisome throughout human history. A system of checks and balances is needed to help ensure that power is not abused. This becomes increasingly necessary when power and privilege are being constantly concentrated in fewer hands. One need only look at the Russian model, under Vladimir Putin, to see the results of a corrupt system where rich oligarchs (including mobsters) are rewarded for doing Putin's dirty work.

This all needs to change if dreams of our collective well-being on this planet are to prevail. Goodness and justice cannot triumph over darkness and injustice without enlightened human intervention. All forces acting against the common good need to be held in check. Prayer alone will not make it so. Individually and collectively, we need to willingly activate the beauty and goodness in our dreams.

> "*The future belongs to those who believe in the beauty of their dreams.*"
> —ELEANOR ROOSEVELT

An Experience Worth Noting:
Separating Fact from Inference and Opinion

★ ★ ★ ★ ★ ★

While working on my Bachelor of Education degree at the University of Toronto, I took an interesting course from Dr. Ralph Dent from the Educational Psychology Department at the Ontario Institute for Studies in Education. He introduced me to an activity that proved very useful throughout my teaching career. In this activity, each participant was provided with a copy of 'The Story' and then required to answer a series of short questions about the story. The only instruction was to avoid inferences and assumptions and to stay completely focused on the pertinent facts of the story to answer each question honestly and correctly. Students were then required to assess and correct their own work, as each question was taken up via class discussion.

Try the following activity for yourself, to test your own ability to clearly distinguish between statements of fact and fabricated inferences. Once you complete the activity, see page 259 for the correct answers. This will help to determine the effectiveness of your own thinking.

SEPARATING FACT FROM OPINION

The purpose of this activity is to test your ability to separate fact or direct observation from inference or opinion. Read the story and then assess the 10 statements that follow to determine whether each is true or false. If you cannot determine whether a statement is true or false, relative to the facts presented, check the *Don't Know box*. You must not draw any inferences, make unsubstantiated assumptions, or form any opinions.

THE STORY

A storekeeper had just turned off the lights in the store when a man appeared and demanded money. The owner opened a cash register. The contents of the cash register were scooped up, and the man sped away. A member of the police force was notified immediately.

	True	False	Don't Know
1. A man appeared after the owner had turned off his store lights.	☐	☐	☐
2. The robber was a man.	☐	☐	☐
3. The man did not demand money.	☐	☐	☐
4. The man who opened the cash register was the owner.	☐	☐	☐
5. The store owner scooped up the contents of the cash register and sped away.	☐	☐	☐
6. Someone opened a cash register.	☐	☐	☐
7. After the man who demanded the money scooped up the contents of the cash register, he ran away.	☐	☐	☐
8. While the cash register contained money, the story does not state how much.	☐	☐	☐
9. The story concerns a series of events in which only three persons are referred to: the owner of the store, a man who demanded money, and a member of the police force.	☐	☐	☐
10. The following events were included in the story: someone demanded money, a cash register was opened, its contents were scooped up, and a man sped away.	☐	☐	☐

Figure 2.1: Learning activity worksheet adapted by the author.

Over the years, I have used this adapted version of the activity with high school students, university students (at faculties of education), and in professional development workshops for practicing teachers. Regardless of the age of the audience, invariably, participant scores were consistently low. The most common participant scores range from 3/10 to 4/10. Needless to say, such low scores regularly generated heated discussions. I vividly remember one particular occasion when I was accused of manipulating the whole exercise to skew the outcome. I resorted to invoking *Teacher's Prerogative 22b*. Students were told this fabrication expressly stated that, "Regardless of the circumstances, when in doubt, remember that the teacher is always right!"

Nina, a very bright student, spontaneously responded with a loud, "How can you even say that? What about facts?" I congratulated her, smiled, and suggested she remember her exact words whenever she encountered anyone claiming a monopoly on knowledge or rightness. Nina went on to become a very successful lawyer in downtown Toronto, not that I had anything to do with that. After some reflection, Nina and her classmates recognized that they had inferred things about my instructions (oral and written) regarding the activity.

This consistent performance pattern reveals how difficult it is for people to clearly and consistently distinguish between statements of fact and statements of inference or conjecture. It would appear that we humans are genetically disposed to make assumptions, draw inferences, and form opinions. To be more effective processors of information, people must be more mindful of the important distinction between fact and conjecture. This applies when assessing their own words, as well as those of others.

The Trump experience provides discerning Americans with a clear test of their ability to separate facts from fabrications. This president's demonstrated propensity to make false and misleading claims requires discerning citizens to regularly seek out facts for the verification of claims, to recognize inferences and opinions as distinct from factual accounts, to use appropriate criteria to base their judgements, and to use evidence to support their conclusions.

Returning to the dilemma left hanging at the end of the previous *Experience Worth Sharing*, the lingering question of Trump's presumed hypocrisy requires fact checking, perspective taking, inference testing, and ultimately, critical judgement based on reasoned criteria and supporting evidence. In the polarized politics of today, this kind of clear and deep thinking is becoming increasingly rare. Since this thinking takes considerable time and effort, busy citizens often abdicate this responsibility.

Regrettably, with few effective mechanisms to hold elected representatives accountable for their words and actions, some devious politicians have resorted to purely self-serving strategies. For these unscrupulous individuals, when facts are inconvenient, they are merely replaced with more favourable alternative facts, often with no apparent basis in objective reality. Statements of opinion are passed off as statements of cold, hard fact. To be more convincing, these questionable statements are repeated often. When elected officials behave in this calculated manner, they betray the responsibility of leadership entrusted to them by the people. Too often, this type of politician forgets that they have been elected to serve all of the people, and not just the core supporters who voted for them.

It is up to the people to accurately assess the political situation and then to take appropriate action. Without taking back the power entrusted to these un-scrupulous political leaders, noble dreams of personal and collective progress and fulfilment can be easily compromised.

Critical Thinking Checkpoint One

★ ★ ★ ★ ★ ★

Reflect on the following probing question to apply your critical thinking skills. Consider organizing your thinking around two distinct question parts, focusing on the presidency and on American society.

Will Trump's propensity to misrepresent facts and conveniently lie ultimately have a positive or negative effect on the office of the President of the United States and on American society?

JUDGEMENT CRITERIA On what would a reasonable and objective person base this decision?	MY DECISION
☐	
☐	
☐	
☐	
☐	
SUPPORTING EVIDENCE What evidence can be used to confirm this decision as sound?	**RELIABILITY** How do I know my sources are objective, accurate and trustworthy? Can I find other sources to independently corroborate the facts?

The Parable of the Diamond Studded Shoes

★ ★ ★ ★ ★ ★

Fact finding and truth seeking are essentials for living in our post-modern digital age where truth has become increasingly more subjective. In essence, a post-truth reality can be more easily propagated. The following parable exposes some of the stakes involved if the post-truth world is allowed to flourish and all truth becomes a fabrication of the selfish mind.

The Eternal Welcoming

"Or, as we call it, Alternative Heaven."

Figure 2.2: Courtesy of editorial cartoonist Pat Byrnes.

A billionaire misogynist once bought himself a pair of expensive handcrafted leather shoes, with a string of 100 diamonds embedded into each sole. When asked why he would do this during a serious economic recession, he never answered. He just smirked and thought to himself: "I do this because I can and you can't. This indisputable truth clearly separates winner me from loser you."

Walking down the street the next day he was alarmed at what he almost stepped into. As he examined the scene, he quietly thought to himself: "This looks like bullshit.

It smells like bullshit. It feels like bullshit. It even tastes like bullshit. Am I ever glad I did not step in it with my new shoes!" As the new shoes got quickly scuffed and worn, the grated diamonds lost their sparkle. This would have caused most people to rethink their fabricated truth. But this billionaire was too smart for that.

Sitting contemplatively on his gold-plated toilet, he blamed cheap Indian leather, shoddy Chinese workmanship and inferior African diamonds as the key alternative facts, and only true reality, that mattered in the end. He wrote off the full cost of the shoes as a legitimate business expense and received a healthy tax break for his troubles. Once again, he did this because he could. The billionaire never bothered to distinguish between what he could do (legally) and what he should do (morally). And so, his charmed life continued without missing a single step!

CHAPTER THREE

WHEN BULLSHIT BAFFLES BRAINS, NONSENSE TRUMPS TRUTH

SOME TRUTHS ARE self-evident. One might say that they can, therefore, speak for themselves. The reality about the importance of water and oxygen to the human body is one such self-evident truth. Regrettably, most truths cannot speak for themselves; therefore they require an orator to interpret and articulate them. When venturing into fields incorporating various shades of grey, like politics, government, and economics, careful and precise articulation is essential.

One of the anchor principles of the American Dream has long been the belief that truth will ultimately prevail over its opposite. This deep-rooted belief has become an important element of jurisprudence. British, American and Canadian legal systems were all based on the premise that, through a respectful and orderly adversarial process, opposing sides each present their strongest arguments and refute the arguments of their opponent. In doing so, truth and justice will ultimately prevail.

Today, many are becoming less convinced that truth and justice prevail. In fact, for many critical thinkers, the justice system is seen as becoming increasingly more prone to breakdowns spawning injustice. These injustices are not limited to cases involving racial profiling and discrimination, although a disproportionate number of cases may fall into this category. The notorious O.J. Simpson murder trial, in 1995, is one glaring example.

In the Simpson case, a "dream team" of diverse, high profile lawyers were able to secure a not guilty verdict after, for all intents and purposes, Los Angeles police officers attempted to frame a guilty man. Defense attorney Johnny Cochrane's eloquent retort "If the glove does not fit, you must acquit," became the mantra for an African American community still seeking payback for the acquittal of four Los Angeles police officers, after the brutal beating of a helpless Rodney King in 1991. In spite of the existence of compelling video-taped evidence showing the beating, all four officers successfully claimed they were merely subduing a suspect who was resisting arrest.

The riots that followed the original acquittals lasted for six days and resulted in 53 deaths, over 2,380 personal injuries, some 7,000 fires, and considerable damage to 3,100 local businesses. The lament of African Americans (racial profiling, police brutality, poverty, and lack of economic opportunity) often goes unheard in inner-city America. In a subsequent federal trial, ordered to address the Rodney King beating, two of the four officers were each convicted and sentenced to 30 months in prison.

> "A riot is the language of the unheard."
> —MARTIN LUTHER KING JR.

For some in the local African American community, since the law allowed white police officers to get away with beating a helpless black man, then why not acquit a black celebrity who allegedly killed his white wife and her white friend. As if two wrongs ever could make something right! After the Simpson verdict, one of the jurors openly admitted that the jury's conclusion was fair payback for the Rodney King beating. Notwithstanding its nobility, how can the American Dream withstand this kind of racially motivated injustice and contempt for human life on both sides of this racial divide?

The same principle of truth and justice ultimately prevailing was seen to apply in government matters. Debate by opposing political interests was intended to lead to negotiation, compromise, and ultimately, a consensus or composite solution which better served the common or greater good. In a democracy, free and open debate by elected representatives is intended to generate ideas, negotiations, options, and ultimately laws that reflect the will of a substantial majority.

> "You can fool all of the people some of the time, and some of the people all of the time, but you cannot fool all of the people all of the time."
> —ABRAHAM LINCOLN

This is not to say that a majority is automatically right and just in its position solely by virtue of its size. As is becoming increasingly clearer, a sizable segment of the population can be bamboozled or manipulated by crafty and self-serving politicians and their surrogates. President Lincoln saw this strategic manipulation as capable of achieving occasional universality, but lacking the capacity to achieve permanence.

According to traditional belief, in time, truth will prevail and the selfish intentions of elected politicians will be exposed and ultimately condemned. When laws are seen to be broken, the people will get some justice by voting these scoundrels out of office. Scoundrels must also be prosecuted to the full extent of the law. But Lincoln's scenario was articulated long before the advent of television, mass media and the multi-million-dollar advertising industry. For a long time now, television, and advertising have been effectively used to influence popular thought and individual behaviour.

Advertising campaigns have helped businesses promote their interests and increase both market share and profits. If corporate giants did not receive a substantial return on their hefty investments, why would they insist on spending millions of dollars annu-

> "The advertising industry's prime task is to ensure that uninformed consumers make irrational choices, thus undermining market theories that are based on just the opposite."
> —NOAM CHOMSKY

ally on advertising budgets? They spend millions in order to earn tens of millions in additional profit. Through advertising, consumer wants can be effectively manipulated, brand preferences effectively established, and conspicuous consumption increased.

In the political arena, the same analogy applies. Why would candidates spend millions of dollars in partisan advertising during election campaigns, if they did not expect to be rewarded at the polls? The constant bombardment of a set political message can influence voter thinking over time. The mantra has become that if people see, hear, and read something long enough they start to believe it. This is even more prevalent when message recipients are uninformed or politically polarized towards a more extreme manner of thinking. Unless one takes the time to look closely into media messaging, to consider whether sources can be trusted to be honest and reliable, the tendency is to start accepting all messaging perceived as favourable, despite inherent biases, assumptions, and errors.

> "Until you realize how easily it is for your mind to be manipulated, you remain the puppet of someone else's game."
> —EVITA OCHEL

The American political scene today is a highly polarized environment. As such, there is a tendency to automatically dismiss (without critical thought) what is not perceived to favour or support one's own views and interests, or what is being postulated by an "opposing" camp. In reality, since all political parties and the ideologies driving them are human constructs, all parties and their platforms are limited by their design. Political parties are all prone to error, misrepresentation, and bias. As a result, no political party can ever justifiably claim to hold a monopoly on truth and righteousness. The same can be said for individual candidates. Each will have strengths and human limitations.

All political messaging requires critical analysis to better understand the full implications of the text being presented. The critical thinker needs to reflect on pretext, context, and subtext to effectively read 'between the lines,' thereby constructing a fuller and more realistic understanding. When free individuals decline this opportunity to think deeply about the political messaging received, they forfeit their ownership share in the political process, and can easily become prone to manipulation by experts. This becomes a personal loss as well as a blow to the democratic dream of ultimate power resting with the people. These people effectively become disenfranchised while still appearing to be engaged in the political process.

Both politically and economically, power has been systematically shifted away from voter/consumers and to paid manipulators and their ultra-wealthy patrons. Regrettably, critical thinking skills are not emphasised enough in public education, to the detriment of the holistic development of learners as discerning consumers of often questionable information.

The absence of critical thinking can lead people to gullibly accept, as absolute truth, what is presented by others in support of their own views or favoured agenda. Without sober reflection, how can any claim of a more truthful and objective understanding be justified? Anything can be rationalized but not everything can be justified! This distinction is important when choosing between loaded alternatives, each skewed in favour of a particular bias on current issues, priorities, and available options.

The end result of all these changes in the political arena and in the thinking applied to it has been to weaken the safety valve articulated by President Lincoln, in a manner that does not serve democratic ideals. Professional manipulators can now fool more people and for a much longer period of time. In response, voters must become more discerning consumers of the 'truth'.

The advent of the Internet has further complicated matters. Be it insight or brain cramp, righteous or malicious, profound or profane, we live in an age where every thought can be instantly blasted into cyberspace. Regrettably, public schools do not seem to give sufficient priority to the development of media literacy skills. This would enable voter/consumers to better assess the media messaging they will be bombarded with daily, throughout their lives.

To reduce the risk of manipulation, today more than ever, voter/consumers need to be media savvy. They need to understand five fundamental realities about media messaging. They need to ask critical questions about message content and implications to acquire a richer and more functional understanding and to discern what can safely be believed.

Voter/consumers need to invest the time to probe beyond the explicit message to uncover what is implied, assumed and suggested. Just like the beer commercials that associate a desired lifestyle with their beverage brand, political messaging often contains subtly suggestive implications that may or may not correspond to objective reality. Often these more subtle or hidden parts of the message need more reflection than is currently being afforded to them by increasing numbers of busy people. If you ever catch yourself shopping for something nice, on a day when you are feeling down, you should ask yourself how you came to associate consumerism with happiness. In a political context, one might ask how discerning voters came to associate the reopening of long closed coal mines, moth-balled coal furnaces, and rusted out factories with sustainable growth and progress.

The text of a message represents what is explicitly being said or presented. Reading **text** requires a logical kind of thinking sometimes referred to as "reading the lines." Reading **pretext** requires anticipatory or proactive thinking, focusing on what is already known about the source and subject of a particular message to access prior knowledge and to extrapolate objective or intent. This could be referred to as "reading ahead of the lines."

Reading **context** requires relative or relational thinking, focusing on the relevance or currency of the message. Why this? Why here? Why now? Why to me? Understanding context requires understanding cause-consequence relationships, as well as the related issues and ideas that give the message its currency. This kind of thinking can be described as "reading around the lines."

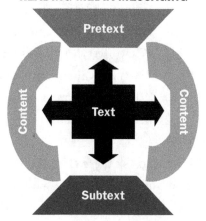

READING MEDIA MESSAGING

Pretext

Content · Text · Content

Subtext

Figure 3.1: Reading Media Messaging.

Finally, reading **subtext** requires critical thinking (informed by all previous thinking) to determine the significance, merit, and potential impact (benefits and costs) of what is being advocated. This ultimate kind of thinking involves "reading between the lines" to make a judgement based on sound criteria and supporting evidence.

Adapted from the *Center for Media Literacy*, the following five realities need to be applied to every media message received by voter/consumers:

1. All media messages are deliberate constructs. They are the result of design rather than accident.

2. Media messages are fabrications that creatively employ language, symbols and suggestion to achieve a desired effect.

3. Different people experience the same message differently, depending on their background, personal experience, and/or frame of reference.

4. Media messages have embedded values, points of view, and biases. A critical thinker cannot afford to focus only on the text of a message. It is important to read between the lines to uncover any unstated pretext or subtext.

5. Most messages are crafted to gain profit and/or influence. Influence is power.

With the above considerations squarely in mind, discerning voter/consumers must ask the following critical questions in order to make a sound judgement regarding and relative to incoming messages:

1. Who created this message? How reliable and trustworthy is this source of information?

2. What techniques were used to attract and hold my attention?

3. How might others understand this message differently than me?

4. What lifestyles, values and points of view are being promoted? What lifestyles, values, and points of view are being omitted or diminished?

5. Why was this message sent? What is being sold? How is my thinking being influenced?

Those who ask these critical questions will be less likely to fall victim to manipulation and deceit. Those who accept a message, after this scrutiny, have consciously bought in. This mindfulness is essential in a functional democracy. Critical thinking is very helpful in the truth seeking process.

Critical thinking is equally helpful in neutralizing the politics of fear. Fear mongering has become a growing element of American politics, especially since the deadly terrorist attacks of 9/11. But the culture of fear prevalent in America today predates the collapse of New York's Twin Towers. Fear of increased criminal activity and disorder, fear of outsiders, fear of economic decline leading to unemployment, fear of foreign influence on the American way of life—all these long-standing fears are added to growing worries about terrorist attacks on American soil.

Manipulating fear has proven to be an effective tactic in political campaigns, especially by candidates seeking to unseat incumbents or political veterans. It is not surprising that pre-election polls found Trump supporters to be disproportionately fearful. The Trump campaign was able to work this emotional bias to full advantage. Fear makes people want to be protected, regardless of the cost. Sometimes even police state tactics are considered acceptable if they will get the job done. Regrettably, this can be a slippery slope.

> *"Countless innocent American lives have been stolen because our politicians have failed in their duty to secure our borders and enforce our laws."*
> —DONALD TRUMP
> (AUGUST 31, 2016)

Fear makes people eager to hold on more tightly to what they have and value. Fear can make people wary of what is new, unfamiliar, or different. Fear makes people long for the relatively tranquil times of the past. Nostalgic longing for "the good old days" can cause people to emotionally and selectively redefine goodness. Often the bad or problematic elements of the past are overlooked. When substantial brain capacity is invested in worry, fears, and negativity, less bandwidth remains available for critical, progressive, and creative thinking. Fear mongering can distort reality and compromise potential.

Hope is a natural antidote for fear induced paranoia and paralysis. The 'politics of hope' involve a commitment to the revitalization and realization of laudable dreams. Hope needs to be built on realistic goals and small steps forward, where nobody is deliberately excluded or left behind. Hope needs to be grounded in the reality of what the next achievable growth step can be. Otherwise it remains a dream.

> *"May your choices reflect your hopes, not your fears."*
> —NELSON MANDELA

Ignorance, Apathy, and Arrogance, Oh My!

★ ★ ★ ★ ★ ★

The original democracies of the world were small Greek city states, where all free citizens knew each other well. To further simplify matters, only free males were allowed to submit their names as candidates for public office. Then political leaders, officials, and magistrates were chosen by lottery from this group of candidates. There was no need for formal elections. In such an environment ignorance and apathy were not affordable commodities. Free citizens needed to remain active and engaged.

> *"... most people, most of the time, don't give politics a first thought all day long. Or if they do, it is with a sigh...., before going back to worrying about the kids, the parents, the mortgage, the boss, their friends, their weight, their health, sex, and rock 'n' roll.... For most normal people, politics is a distant, occasionally irritating fog."*
> —TONY BLAIR

Fast forwarding to present day mega democracies, millions of voters are free to cast their votes to choose their elected representatives in the democratic decision making process, or to vote on significant propositions by referendum. In theory, the model still works. In practice, growing voter ignorance and apathy have become serious problems, as politics becomes increasingly more remote and confusing for a growing number of busy citizens.

When voters conclude that their one ballot will not make a significant difference, in a ballot box stuffed with the votes cast by thousands of other individuals, then apathy can easily set in. Voters concluding that there is no appreciable difference between competing candidates can also be prone to apathy. This apathy can be a by-product of voter frustration and fatigue.

When candidates are seen to continually make great promises, based on what is claimed as personal conviction, and then deliver only what is most politically convenient and opportunistic, apathy can be the end result. These apathetic voters may not bother to vote at all, thus abdicating their democratic right to others. In many elections, voter turnout is quite low relative to the power and privilege afforded to winning candidates.

Unscrupulous candidates, and their opportunistic strategists, can exploit this apathy. Strategists have learned that specific candidates can benefit from keeping specific groups of voters at home on election day. This predatory practice is based on speculation, often supported by careful polling. The speculation is that opponents stand to lose more votes than their candidate if a targeted group abstains from voting in large numbers. This tactic appears to be one of many manipulations attempted during the 2016 election cycle, as specific ethnic groups were deliberately targeted. The tactic can backfire if voter sentiments shift from apathy to anger.

In Canadian politics, a particular strategy exposed after the 2011 federal elections involved the use of real-person and automated phone messaging or *robocalls*. These calls were used to misdirect voters, determined to be non-supporters, to the wrong voting stations. It was arrogantly assumed that frustrated voters, as well as those with a limited command of the English language, would not bother going to the correct station to vote. Where this happened, the suppression of unfavourable votes could effectively be achieved. After the election, individual junior campaign workers were implicated but insufficient evidence existed to hold candidates and party leaders accountable. In the end, only one junior staffer of the Conservative Party of Canada was convicted on one count of violating the Elections Act. The Conservative Party did lose the next election but not exclusively for this reason.

Political ignorance is another mitigating factor becoming increasingly more widespread in America and beyond. The political world is confusing at the best of times. If the only incentive to stay informed is to cast a crucial vote, once again this theory does not hold up in today's mega democracies. The odds that one vote will decide the outcome are comparable to the odds of winning a mega lottery. Perhaps this is why the purchase of state sanctioned lottery tickets is sometimes referred to as a tax on ignorance and stupidity.

> *"Even more than most others, the awful 2016 election cycle has highlighted the dangers of political ignorance. Data has long shown that voter ignorance is widespread on both sides of the political spectrum. A high percentage of the public is often ignorant of even very basic information, such as which party controls Congress, which officials are responsible for which issues, and how the federal government spends our tax money."*
> —ILYA SOMIN

The decision to remain politically ignorant, in favour of investing precious time and energy elsewhere, is quite rational. But this practice is not justifiable in a functional democracy. To make matters worse, under-informed voters also do a poor job of evaluating what they do know. Instead of being objective truth seekers, they often default to serving as 'political fans' for their candidate, party, and ideology of choice. Rarely do they bother to sort truth and fact from hype, misdirection, and outright fabrication.

Most fans tend to emotionally over value what comes from their favourite sports team, artist, or political party and candidate. They then under value or disparage anything coming from opposing camps. It is helpful to remember that the word fan is an abbreviation of the word *fanatic*. Until Americans are able to recognize their own fanaticism and bias, there will be little hope of reversing the current trend towards intense partisanship and almost 'tribal' polarization in American politics today.

Interestingly, in legal matters, ignorance of the law is not excusable. The accused are found guilty even when they did not know that their behaviour broke the law that binds us together in civility. In the economic world, the principle of caveat emptor (*let the buyer beware*) has been part of the dynamic of commerce since Roman times. The onus is on consumers to become informed and aware before buying. Since politics involves the craft of persuasion, all voters must be truth seeking consumers of political messaging. In politics, a similar principle is needed to deal with the problem of growing ignorance. Those who believe that government should play a large role in a democratic society need to embrace the principle that the quality of voter truth seeking and decision-making is of paramount importance. When ignorant voters entrust great power to the wrong people, there is potential for great disservice.

It is worth noting that, notwithstanding what an arrogant politician or strategist may think, ignorance does not automatically constitute stupidity. Stupidity requires feeble-mindedness and the absence of wisdom or common sense. Often forgotten in bitter partisan politics, stupidity is reserved for the idea and not the person expressing it.

> *"Everybody is ignorant, only on different subjects."*
> —WILL ROGERS

Limiting and decentralizing government is one option in dealing with voter ignorance. But this may be akin to throwing the baby out with the bathwater. Since it becomes next to impossible for free citizens to govern themselves, the rationale that good government is so important to a democratic society that it needs to be limited seems, at very least, peculiar. By the same token, the notion that governments alone should decide how big they need to become and who exactly should be stationed at the public trough is equally suspect. As is the notion that simply voting out scoundrels is a sufficient remedy. Far more accountability is needed.

Voter education is paramount. There also needs to be a culture shift in politics to clearly articulate the qualities desired in political officials and then to create a more responsible vetting process for potential candidates. It is equally important to ensure that those ultimately elected will serve the greater good and not just their own interests. To achieve this, there needs to be clear confirmation of the public's *voglia* (what Italians call the willingness to make something happen). The 'something' in question here refers to nothing less than the revitalization of the democratic dream and process. This would require American citizens to realize the dysfunctional nature of current political practices. Then they must recognize and value what is at stake and embrace the moment of opportunity and promise before them, to affect progressive thinking and positive change.

> *"Culture eats strategy for breakfast."*
> —PETER DRUCKER

To revitalize this dream, there needs to be a full-frontal assault on the culture of entitlement that permeates the current political landscape. To reclaim a metaphor used most successfully by a recent presidential candidate, we need to *rehabilitate* the swamp. Replacing one set of swamp creatures with another is not "draining" the swamp. It is merely exchanging those who have made a career out of benefitting personally from the political swamplands, with a new group with their own vested interests. This replacement strategy has been tried numerous times in the past with limited success.

Like swampland, the seat of government for and by the people is a necessary safeguard. It must be noted that swampland is among the most fertile and useful ecosystems once unpolluted and rehabilitated. Swampland serves a key role in purifying land, air, and water. Ecologically speaking, swamp rehabilitation requires the removal of contaminants. Politically, swamp rehabilitation needs to focus on the removal of entrenched parasites and predators feeding on the public purse with a profound sense of entitlement. Most often, limited public service can be seen coming in return. These are the politically arrogant in our midst. Not all career politicians and public servants are arrogant, but an alarming number are, given the nature of their proclaimed "vocation to serve."

This arrogance comes, in part, from the quality of character of those attracted to politics under the present culture and climate. This arrogance also comes from cynical *politicos* (elected officials and bureaucrats) that judge the electorate to be substantially ignorant, unaware of what truly serves their best interests, and therefore, ripe for manipulation. Ultimately, this arrogance comes from a privileged feeling of superiority relative to the ignorant and malleable masses these professional *politicos* are supposed to serve. Among the most arrogant of *politicos* are those insisting that they know what is in the best interest of their electorate, more than the electorate itself.

Too often, in recent political campaigns negativity has trumped positivity. In many cases, candidates prefer to attack the perceived shortcomings of rivals, instead of promoting the relative strengths of their own position, beliefs, or political platform. These *attack ads* have become increasingly more common and mean spirited in American political campaigns. To a lesser extent, this practice has emerged in Canadian politics as well. The inherent problem with this practice is that negativity is a destructive rather than constructive force. So instead of building upon something, thought and energy are invested in tearing down opposing ideas, as well the rivals proposing them.

Another practice gaining popularity among professional politicians is the avoidance of specific details in favour of "quick hit" slogans and buzz words that are constantly repeated. This strategy is most effective when those receiving the messages start to assume truth without doing any confirming research. Regrettably, for some uninformed voters, if they hear something often enough they just assume it must be true, often without anything remotely resembling a *sniff/touch/ taste test* (see page 28) for verification.

Avoiding disclosure of relevant facts and details, is another shrewd manipulation tactic gaining momentum. When new laws, programs, and initiatives are being proposed as better alternatives to what currently exists, or when new approaches are being proposed to address new problems, often crucial details and logistics are deliberately not disclosed. This may be done to 'un-complicate' the dialogue, but often there can be another agenda at work.

Once the specifics of what exactly is being advocated have been articulated by a politician, campaign, or political party, the risk of exposing inherent flaws, inconsistencies, or omissions increases exponentially. This can provide valuable ammunition to political rivals. Therefore, in today's political arena cards are increasingly played very close to the vest. This increases the need for objective (non-partisan) news media, employing responsible journalists, to uncover key facts for busy voters. Regrettably, some news media and influential owners of numerous local television stations today are far from objective or non-partisan. They often become part of the problem, rather than the solution to message pollution.

Candidates who stand on points of personal conviction may be more comfortable with the political strategy of full factual disclosure, even given the inherent risks. Conversely, those engaged in the craft of leadership by convenience are generally far less comfortable sticking their necks out because their political platform is subject to change, depending on which way the prevailing winds are seen to be blowing. Regrettably, in the post-modern political world, leadership by conviction is too often replaced by self-serving leadership by convenience. This will be explored further in the next chapter.

It is interesting to note that, during the presidential elections of 2016, the successful populist candidate provided almost no details regarding how exactly America would be made great again, how the "clean coal" industry would be revived and sustained, how long-lost manufacturing jobs would be repatriated, how the political swamp would be effectively drained, how the replacement of *Obamacare* would be designed to better serve low income Americans, how the Great Border Wall would be paid by Mexico, etcetera, etcetera. The only prevailing message seemed to be that previous elected officials were incompetent and had failed the American people.

Once in power, this president demonstrated a marked preference towards tweets, campaign style rhetoric, and photo ops. Stakeholder consultation, bi-partisan negotiations, consensus seeking dialogue, substantive meetings, and the careful analysis of details were considered pointless.

Without this homework, the complex implications of what is proposed as obvious improvement to a broken America cannot be sufficiently understood. Clearly, a judgement has been made that there is more political mileage in style rather than substance in America today.

The alternative conclusion might be even more alarming. Long-standing issues rarely demonstrate the simplicity of a cleanly black and white world. This president may not be capable of the complex thinking and attention to details (and complicating factors) required to effectively address major political issues.

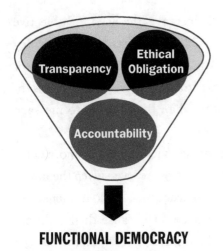

FUNCTIONAL DEMOCRACY

Figure 3.2: Three anchor principles safeguarding functional democracy.

Otherwise, he might not have boldly pronounced that his bright son-in-law would almost single-handedly solve the bloody conflict in the Middle East. This conflict has confounded numerous diplomats and political leaders for generations. Past efforts to broker peace in this volatile region have been abject failures. No pressure Jered Kushner! No pressure at all! This should be a walk in the park for you. Mind you, as a savvy New Yorker, I'm sure you have often ventured into Central Park in the dead of night!

To alleviate current levels of dysfunction, a reformed culture of politics must prevail, at all levels of government. This reformed culture should be anchored on the three principles of ethical obligation, transparency and accountability:

ETHICAL OBLIGATION must permeate the relationship between citizen and elected official. Honest and respectful representation is a democratic right of all citizens in a functional democracy. This right would apply not only to how supporters are treated by elected officials but equally to how non-supporters are treated. In return, responsible citizens have an obligation to become informed before voting. This is required to justify (and not rationalize) their choice. Voter ignorance can never justify dishonest or disrespectful treatment. In addition, voters have an ethical responsibility to let elected officials know when they have stepped out of line.

For every elected position, there should be a clear public articulation of expectations, code of conduct, and fiduciary duties. Candidates for office must accept these requirements and then be held to this standard both during the campaign and while in office. The actions of surrogates, aids, and staffers must also be seen to meet these standards. Before being declared the winner, a candidate should be obligated to earn at least 50% plus one of verified eligible votes and not be found in default of any ethical obligations. In this way, no candidate can benefit directly from voter abstention or manipulation. Run-off elections, with lowest vote earners removed, may be required to earn sufficient votes.

TRANSPARENCY (or full disclosure) serves as another important anchor principle. Every candidate needs to articulate a personal vision for the position they are seeking, including core beliefs, major goals, and preferred strategies to achieve them. Furthermore, candidates need to disclose any personal holdings and affiliations potentially causing a conflict of interest between personal goals and public duties. In the case of federal and state (or provincial) leaders, documents must be filed to disclose personal assets, business interests, and revenue streams.

Trump's refusal to submit income tax documents (and his subsequent lame excuse) should have disqualified him from seeking the presidency of the United States. His diverse personal holdings and world-wide business activities created significant potential for conflict of interest. An impartial judicial hearing may be needed to identify assets constituting conflict and the adequacy of any blind trust established to mitigate this conflict. Even with this transparency, individual integrity cannot be guaranteed, but at least a modicum of due diligence is reflected.

ACCOUNTABILITY is the ultimate anchor principle. Without rigorous accountability, transparency and ethics hold little meaning and provide little positive impact. Some critics argue that it is already challenging enough to find credible candidates to step forward today. Adding requirements and conditions will only discourage more individuals from entering politics. Admittedly, this is a serious concern. But since so many candidates appear to enter politics today for questionable reasons to begin with, this unfortunate reality needs to be investigated fully in the subsequent chapter.

To help maximize accountability, every candidate should articulate specific 'success criteria' to be used by the public to assess achievement at the end of one's term in office. This assessment would yield valuable information, regarding the merits of returning this individual to public office. In addition, throughout the mandate, citizens can refer to these articulated success criteria to provide descriptive feedback to politicians, advisors, and strategists. Success criteria should be subject to annual review to keep them current.

The practice of simply voting unacceptable politicians out of office does not provide sufficient protection. There also needs to be a more rigorous accountability after terms have been served by elected officials. When the personal incomes and assets of politicians are seen to increase substantially more, on an annual basis, while in office than before, these extra revenues need to be investigated and confiscated if found to be "fruits of a poison tree," to use a classic legal term. This determination would require a thorough and impartial judicial process.

Income levels immediately after completing a public service might also prove a meaningful comparison. This is not to say that all bribes and kickbacks are direct and easily detectable. Once detected, illegal activities must result in appropriate punishments, not merely slaps on the wrist. In addition, when an elected politician is proven to have engaged in inappropriate conduct, the individual politician must be seen to pay directly for any transgressions and not the public purse. Using public funds to pay for personal transgressions may provide compensation to victims, but it does not hold the elected official sufficiently accountable for inappropriate conduct.

These are just some potential remedies gaining attention in light of recent experiences. Perhaps the greatest legacy of the Trump presidency will be the collective will to ensure that the political system will never again be exploited so blatantly by a candidate and his camp. Much objective dialogue is required to find a workable set of solutions to the "perfect storm" that allowed Trump to acquire the presidency. Complex problems are seldom fixed with singular strategies.

Education and culture shifts are essential. Regrettably, education and culture shifts require a lengthy gestation period and time is not exactly a luxury given current levels of dysfunction and disservice.

Apathy, complacency, and ignorance are qualities complicit with giving the nation and the national dream away. There are two distinct levels to this harmful complicity. At the basic level, apathy, complacency, and ignorance can result in casting a vote counter to the public interest. At a more harmful 'advanced' level, duped voters become active supporters and visible promoters. These actions enable the acquisition of votes within one's sphere of influence.

Before openly supporting and promoting a candidate, it is essential to do the requisite homework to ensure that you know who and what you are voting for. All who supported and assisted the politician in acquiring power share the responsibility for any abuse of that power. All who worked for the politician without disclosing what they knew about abuses are also complicit. All share in the lost credibility and betrayal of the public trust. Regrettably, voter memories have become increasingly short over time. This is where a free and impartial press is needed to serve as guardians of the collective memory and public consciousness.

So, it often comes down to this. In the end, bullshit can baffle brain power. Since the American presidential election of 2016, this sad reality has been further refined. The new reality has now become:

Bold faced and mean spirited lies can trump truth and goodness.

But, only if citizens allow it to happen.

Discerning citizens must be constantly on guard, so as not to be placated by empty promises and unsubstantiated claims from self-serving politicians. In the current political arena of bold faced lies and mean spirit,

> *"Why are we having all these people from shithole countries come here?"*
>
> —Donald Trump
> (January 11, 2018)

it is essential to constantly ask the following critical questions:

> *What facts can I find to substantiate this claim?*
> *How do I know these facts are accurate and true and that my sources are*
>   *trustworthy?*
> *What criteria can I use to make a sound judgement about this claim?*
> *What evidence can I use to support my judgement?*

Citizens without sufficient discernment can easily become confused, misdirected, and manipulated into becoming the puppets of someone else's game. As in Canada, immigrants helped build and strengthen the American nation, contrary to the strong opinions of racist, xenophobic bigots. These immigrants were often brought in to do the difficult work that native Americans did not want to do. The irrepressible immigrant spirit contributed greatly to America's collective character. The hundreds of thousands of illegal children, smuggled into America years ago by hopeful family members, are just one example of contributing immigrant groups. They proudly, if not publicly, carry the *'dreamer'* name. Evidence shows that they are not the rapists, drug pushers, muggers, and thieves that bigots profess.

An Experience Worth Noting: Trumping Nonsense with Sensibility

As a principal of program for the Toronto Catholic District School Board, I was responsible for coordinating the social studies program, as well as resources supporting the assessment of student achievement. My duties included working with high school department heads and elementary school resource teachers to provide professional development for classroom teachers. It was always invigorating to deal with teachers eager to add to their teaching repertoire and effectiveness. But it was equally frustrating to deal with mediocre teachers totally resistant to change. In time, I developed an effective disarming strategy. Those with limited constructive information to share often demonstrated a propensity to pontificate unequivocal conclusions, while offering limited evidence and factual support to back their bold claims. They betrayed themselves by speaking mostly in generalities void of specifics.

On one particular occasion, while facilitating a PD workshop for high school teachers, I recall being confronted by a gruff, veteran teacher regarding the assessment strategies that were being presented. The topic was assessment strategies that improve learning. The elements of risk-taking, revision, and redemption were being discussed as "three R's" that can effectively motivate improvement in student learning. Teachers were encouraged to use '*second chance assessment*' to motivate students to redeem an earlier limited achievement through focused additional effort. The advantages of using most recent, most consistent achievement were discussed, instead of exclusively using running averages to determine report card grades. Specific examples were used to demonstrate how grading can be made more accurate and educative. Effective studies research and the conclusions of leading researchers were used to confirm the effectiveness of these strategies, as tools to improve student learning.

This particular teacher openly confronted me by saying that I was just "repeating the party line that bureaucrats at the Ministry of Education told me to repeat." It was then further postulated that I was doing this "to keep my job and avoid returning to the classroom." The teacher went on to proclaim that what was being advocated would result in the continued "watering down of academic standards."

My response was to return to the slide listing leading education researchers and confirming the benefits of the strategies being promoted. While this slide was on the screen, I thanked the teacher for expressing an honest opinion and asked, "Have we ever met before?" When the teacher indicated no prior contact with me, I commented on how quickly a detailed judgement had been formed about me and my motives. I then asked what actual evidence or research could be shared to back up what was being stated so passionately and dogmatically. No such evidence was provided except for "over twenty-five years of classroom experience." The snickers and muffled laughs of colleagues were quite revealing.

Next, I asked when was the last time the teacher had discussed assessment with someone from the Ministry or consulted the official policy document on student assessment. In a convoluted manner, the teacher finally admitted to limited knowledge of the policy document, no personal contacts at the Ministry, and limited professional reading. Common sense was the teacher's only claimed asset.

I asked when was the last time the teacher had worked with school colleagues on reviewing and updating assessment practices to improve learning. The teacher's response was, "All the time." To force a move from the vague to the specific, I quickly asked, "Who did you work with most recently and what common sense did you contribute to the result?" With many colleagues in attendance, the teacher was hard pressed to come up with a single specific example of collaboration or contribution. I asked if any colleagues could help trigger the teacher's memory, but there were no volunteers.

Finally, I explained that since many of the happiest days of my career were in the classroom, I had no fear of returning there at the earliest opportunity. To close, I thanked the teacher for sharing an opinion even though little was provided to corroborate it. Before returning to the program, I invited a follow up discussion regarding academic standards after the workshop, but this teacher was among the first out the door. After the workshop, a delegation of colleagues came to me to thank me for the strategies and materials shared, and to apologize for their colleague, who was described as a "fossil" and a "loner."

Almost a decade later, much of what was being advocated in this workshop was specifically articulated in the Ministry of Education's policy document entitled *Growing Success: Assessment, Evaluation and Reporting in Ontario Schools*. After much consultation, this key document was finally published in 2010.

The Trump experience provides discerning Americans with a similar opportunity to separate nonsense from substance, and to help ensure that facts and evidence ultimately triumph over generalities, empty promises, and misleading claims. Discerning consumers of the truth must be able to detect bullshit regardless of how it is branded, packaged, and promoted. In reality, some of Trump's messaging does not even pass the bullshit test, because it often lacks even minimal substance. Perhaps a more accurate descriptor might be *verbal diarrhoea*.

Figure 3.3: This mural of a Trump inspired poop emoji, complete with swarming flies, appeared in New York City's Chinatown. The work of anonymous street artist Hanksy, it was suddenly removed prior to Trump's inauguration. (By photographer Terese Loeb Kreuzer, courtesy of Alamy Stock Photos).

In complex matters, Trump often prefers to speak in generalities, often providing gross simplifications of complicated realities. This reveals either a lack of appropriate preparation, a misunderstanding of inherent complexities, or an ignorance of their significance and full implications. Armed with this superficial understanding, he is absolutely scathing in his criticism of the "failures" of predecessors, and absolutely glowing in self-praise of everything he is, promises, and does. His self-professed intellect and ability are the very definition of wonderful and ingenious. Trump sometimes appears to become sucked in by his own public persona. He is confident he can make things happen just by wishing them into existence, often offering little explanation or supporting evidence other than a terse, "Wait and see."

What Trump does not believe in or understand is dismissed as absolutely useless. What he proposes or believes is absolutely wonderful and beyond question. It is up to discerning citizens to accurately assess these matters as far removed from absolute, and then to take appropriate action. By not taking action, Americans are complicit in the damage done to their fragile democracy. According to Trump, much of the damage to America is done by immigrants from "shithole countries" and "Democrats." How convenient!

The Parable of Happiness

★ ★ ★ ★ ★

Like many others, I always thought it was happiness that money could not buy. Reflecting on the following post-modern day parable exposes the flaw in our collective thinking.

Figure 3.4: Photography and poster art by the author.

A billionaire misogynist once used his money, notoriety, and craftiness to attract beautiful young women, as well as the occasional porn film starlet. When this proved boring, he used his wealth, craftiness, and notoriety to acquire great power. But exercising this power proved to be much more difficult than acquiring it.

In exercising his new power, the billionaire revealed a remarkable absence of things money cannot buy. So, he surrounded himself with like-minded individuals and political opportunists equally interested in seizing the moment. Together they set out to exploit the vulnerable and the gullible. The billionaire bullied and intimidated all who exhibited "foreign" qualities, including all those who saw right through his façade and challenged his credibility.

The people's frustration, at his unbridled abuse and incompetence, often orchestrated as diversion, made him very happy! And so, he happily basked in the spotlight he so craved. When it got too hot, he simply went on vacation to one of his many lavish properties. Those, after all, are things money can buy!

LEADERSHIP BY ~~CONVICTION~~ CONVENIENCE: WHEN SELF INTEREST TRUMPS PUBLIC SERVICE

THERE WAS A time in American history when the effectiveness of leadership was measured by the growth a leader inspired in others. The character traits of good leaders were seen to transfer to those being served. In the formative years of the American Dream, leaders were courageous visionaries from a group of British American colonies who resorted to revolution to free themselves from tyranny and oppression. The second sentence of the 1776 *Declaration of Independence* succinctly

> *"If your actions inspire others to dream more, learn more and become more, you are a leader."*
> —JOHN QUINCY ADAMS

professes their collective conviction: "We hold these truths to be self-evident, that all men are created equal, that they are endowed by their Creator with certain unalienable Rights, that among these are Life, Liberty and the pursuit of Happiness." Subsequently, this articulation became an anchor principle for other nations seeking or redefining their own freedom.

Regrettably, the issue of legalized slavery was not recognized as running counter to the vision of a truly free society. For some in early America, slavery and the cheap manual labour it provided was an economic asset. As a moral and social contradiction, slavery contributed greatly to the political impasse leading the young nation down the path of civil war. By the spring of 1861, America found itself caught up in a brutal civil war, with slavery as one of the key points of contention in a bloody North/South conflict. Each side demonstrated great conviction for their cause.

Today, more than 150 years after the civil war and the end of slavery, full equality of personhood, social treatment and economic opportunity is yet to be achieved across America. Over time, this racial divide has been ameliorated but never eliminated. In fact, some critics argue that most recently, a sharp U-turn has occurred taking the nation back towards stronger xenophobic and intolerant sentiments.

Hindsight is most often associated with 20/20 vision. This is why it is important to remember and revisit the past, not to dwell there, but to learn from past experience so as to avoid replicating errors. This retrospective reflection facilitates a deeper understanding of contemporary problems, issues, perspectives, and realities. A motorist who refuses to use the rearview mirror, because it only reflects what has already been safely passed, can count on more than the occasional surprise along the journey.

> *"Life can only be understood backwards; but it must be lived forwards."*
> —SOREN KIERKEGAARD

Retrospective thinking should inform critical, progressive, and forward thinking to enable the achievement of public goals. Social change requires reflection by citizens who care to make a difference through honest dialogue. This change process requires leadership focused on service and committed to address issues in a constructive manner that fosters learning, growth, and progress. A key question for discerning voters becomes:

> *"The best government is that which teaches us to govern ourselves."*
> —JOHANN WOLFGANG VON GOETHE

What personal growth does this political leadership develop or inspire?

The politics and collective decision-making of a community or nation can suffer greatly when collective memories are short. Given a short memory span, past mistakes can be easily forgotten and repeated. More importantly, the opportunity to transform past mistakes into future successes is compromised. The opportunity to focus the political agenda on collective hopes and dreams can easily be lost and the movement towards progress curtailed. This applies to both social and economic advances.

All political leaders and elected officials are prone to error. This is an undeniable fact of human existence. Discerning citizens and voters need to ask:

Do errors result from intentional actions and deliberate calculation? How do I know?

Errors that are recognized and freely admitted can lead to corrections down the road that represent significant progress. This can only happen if an atmosphere of honest dialogue prevails. Partisan bickering is always part of the problem and never part of the solution.

When elected officials are driven by conviction, there is a natural transparency in their actions and priorities. Much of what is said and done can be traced back to fundamental beliefs and anchor principles, with very few surprises. Leaders with nothing to hide always say what they mean, mean what they say, and promise only what they can deliver. They do not exaggerate claims, avoid problems, or over-simplify solutions. They are quick to acknowledge errors and omissions as learning opportunities.

However, when elected officials are more driven by personal convenience and opportunism, motives and strategies can be less transparent and more convoluted. Most politicians exhibit both qualities from time to time. Conviction drives ideological big picture formation and convenience provides pragmatic tactical effectiveness. The question for discerning voters becomes:

Which best reflects this politician's overall style, leadership by conviction or leadership by convenience? What evidence do I have to support my conclusion?

In recent years, there has been a shift in the qualities of leadership demonstrated by those willing to enter the political arena. Today, a greater number of politicians show a tendency towards leadership by convenience. Many of those attracted to politics are strong personalities with very defined interests and firm views of what needs to be done to achieve their goals. These interests can be carefully fashioned to bring considerable benefit and gain to the politician, making the headaches of political life more personally rewarding.

Sometimes these new leaders demonstrate a lack of flexibility regarding complex and multifaceted issues. Many prefer to surround themselves and work only with like-minded individuals, instead of collaborating with diverse people with different perspectives. Their vision is to lead from the front so that the people they were elected to serve can follow closely behind. Sometimes these new leaders demonstrate great charisma, but limited substance and personal integrity. We need to remind ourselves regularly, as active citizens, that we are treated as consumers by many politicians. That is, we are often sold the sizzle instead of the steak. The question for discerning voters becomes:

Can I see consistency between what this politician says and what is actually done? Can I see evidence of personal integrity at work?

The unabashed poster boy for the 'leadership by convenience' political movement may well be Italy's Silvio Berlusconi. Self admittedly, this billionaire media tycoon and entrepreneur entered politics, in 1994, to avoid prosecution for shady business practices. Later that same year, this same charismatic personality was appointed prime minister. For many Italians, he represented the fresh face of a political outsider (and very successful businessman) who was going to bring efficiency and accountability to a government bureaucracy out of control. He became the 'chosen one' to reform the struggling nation from top to bottom.

> *"I am forced to enter politics, otherwise they will put me in prison."*
> —SILVIO BERLUSCONI

Despite political controversies and personal scandals, he became Italy's third longest serving prime minister of the post-war era. One ongoing controversy arose after Berlusconi refused to sell off the business interests (a dominant media empire) considered to constitute a conflict of interest for a political leader. This controversy was accentuated by his solemn promise to divest himself of these assets upon entering the political arena, only to continually refuse to act on this promise later.

Berlusconi seized the opportunity provided by Italy's fractured and dysfunctional political landscape to quickly assume the mantle of leadership. During the divisive national elections of 2001, Berlusconi borrowed a page from the American playbook to help secure his return to power. He greatly impressed Italian voters by undertaking to sign a *Contract with the Italians*. This was a strategy copied from Newt Gingrich's *Contract with America*, introduced weeks before the American congressional elections of 1994. In his contract, Berlusconi promised five substantial improvements:

1. Simplify and improve Italy's convoluted and easily exploitable tax laws;
2. Cut Italy's stubborn unemployment rate in half;
3. Organize and fund a massive public works program; (Interestingly, no great border wall was involved in this program!)
4. Raise the minimum monthly pension rate;

5. Fight escalating crime rates in cities by increasing the size and vigilance of the police force.

Lastly, Berlusconi promised that he would not stand for re-election, if he did not deliver on at least four of his five promises. This creative political masterstroke effectively played to the fears of the electorate and he was returned to power. In the end, he delivered only on the promise to improve pensions. Both economically and socially, Italy continued to slide downward during his leadership. And yet, he presented himself several times subsequently for re-election as prime minister. Sometimes he would win or come close enough to fabricate a victory through coalition.

As soon as opportunities arose, Berlusconi used political coalitions and backroom deals to forge temporary partnerships enabling him to hold on to, or return to power. Often, deals were made with former rivals and ideological opponents. Like general Charles De Gaulle in France, Berlusconi used the political party as a strategic vehicle to secure power, rather than as a standard bearer for ideology and core beliefs. He changed party affiliation and invented new parties whenever politically convenient.

Berlusconi assumed the role of moderate, liberal, conservative, populist, jester, showman, neo-fascist, and reformer as needed. The only core principle of the *Berlusconism* that emerged over time was a prevailing spirit of entrepreneurial optimism, based on the belief that shrewd business interests will always find a way to prevail, even during difficult economic times. According to most critics, right from the start of his political career, Berlusconi's extensive ownership of and control over Italian media was a clear conflict of interest. He promised to divest himself of these controversial holdings but he subsequently thwarted every opportunity to make it happen. Instead, mass media were used to ensure that a favourable account of his actions was always presented to the Italian people.

Sex scandals, shady business dealings, poor judgement, arrogantly brash statements, and insensitive remarks that would have spelled the end of a political career in the past, did not substantially affect Berlusconi's core support base. Nor did this questionable behaviour alter his bold-faced calculation that for Italian politics he was by far the best of a sorry lot. In June of 2013, Berlusconi was convicted of paying for sex with a teenaged belly dancer. In August of 2013, Berlusconi was finally convicted of tax fraud. As a convicted felon, new anti-corruption laws barred him from holding public office for six years. He appears set for a political comeback in 2019.

The Berlusconi experience is a clear example of ego trumping ideology and, of opportunism and convenience trumping conviction and true vocation to public service. Berlusconi's cavalier and condescending treatment of most political matters betrayed his contempt for politics, politicians, and public service. A key question for discerning voters becomes:

> *What can be learned from the experience of others that can help me to make better assessments and decisions closer to home?*

Several interesting parallels can be drawn between Italy's Berlusconi and America's Trump:

- Both are successful billionaires and architects of a substantial corporate empire;
- Both took great care to develop their public persona, their corporate brand, and their close ties and influence over news media;
- Both love to be in the spotlight and to be the center of public attention;
- Both demonstrate a misogynistic interest in attractive young women;
- Both demonstrate little concern about the objectification and exploitation of women;
- Both were political new comers and rose quickly through the ranks;
- Both were seen as political outsiders with the capacity to reform the state and its bureaucracy;
- Both changed political party affiliations (at least twice) to further their personal aspirations;
- Both came to power riding a populist wave of political sentiment;
- Both demonstrate a remarkable propensity to make and shake off gaffes and misstatements;
- Both are prone to harsh language and disrespectful treatment of others, including condescending exaggerations and hyperbole to make their points;
- Both reject most criticism as conspiracies, lies, or fake news;
- Both promised but failed to effectively divest themselves of business interests potentially conflicting with public interests;

- Both used tax avoidance to full advantage, in the belief that wealthy entrepreneurs should be taxed at lower rates (regressive taxation), because they create jobs and incomes for others;
- Both demonstrated a preference to be polarizing and divisive with unsupportive members of their own party, and most especially with those considered political rivals;
- Both continued to experience substantial growth in their personal wealth while in office;
- Both demonstrate a cavalier attitude in the presence of, and in their dealings with, other world leaders;
- Both demonstrate a propensity to use bully tactics and intimidation in business and politics;
- Both demonstrate a profound contempt for details and inconvenient facts or truths;
- Both have an unabashedly extravagant lifestyle and tend to flaunt their great wealth;
- Etc.

Around the world and close to home, the current political arena appears ripe for the picking. Populist candidates have demonstrated a remarkable capacity to draw substantial public support from among the disillusioned. The 2017 presidential elections in France are one such example. Far-right candidate Marine Le Pen managed to become one of two final candidates for the presidency. She campaigned on an ultra-conservative platform promising to return France to the French people. This included taking back many economic, monetary, and law-making powers from the European Union (EU).

In addition, order and security were prioritized. Tight control over national borders, clamping down on the steady influx of foreigners, and a hardline position on the treatment of Muslims were all key parts of her political platform. Le Pen clearly benefitted from the fear and xenophobia resulting from numerous terrorist attacks in Paris, Nice, and Normandy. Russian interests have also been accused of using the Internet to disseminate information promoting support for Le Pen and her party. Allegedly, this was done with the intent to destabilize the EU and a key NATO ally. Her ultimately unsuccessful campaign was plagued by spending irregularities and judicial inquiries into the alleged diversion of EU funds.

EU funds were allegedly used to pay some of Le Pen's party workers for almost five years.

Several promising candidates now decline to enter the current political arena. Some have declined for personal and family reasons, seeing themselves as not being able to contribute the requisite time and attention. Others are discouraged

> "We are all faced with a series of great opportunities brilliantly disguised as insoluble problems."
> —JOHN W. GARDNER

because the problems that need to be addressed appear to be deep-rooted, complex, and often, irreversible. They decline the opportunity to serve because they assess the opportunity to make a significant difference to be limited. In the current reality, politicians motivated by conviction can often be dwarfed or sidelined by their ambitious counterparts, motivated by convenience and personal opportunity. Since all elected politicians are chosen to lead their communities, one critical question is:

How has this leadership transformed the community to date and what can be reasonably expected for the future?

One reluctant federal politician once confided to me that he could not afford to become engaged in the reform process because, "The system will get to me, long before I can ever get to change it." Over time, similar sentiments were expressed by politicians in all three levels of government. And so, it appears that a disproportionate number of those entering politics today demonstrate a conviction rhetoric but a propensity to act by convenience behind the scenes. This propensity is especially prevalent in those with aspirations to quickly climb up the political ladder.

Those who are not good at backroom dealings either do not enter the political area or do not stay long. This absence can leave the arena to political veterans passionately motivated by a single agenda or primary interest. Often these politicians have deep-rooted viewpoints with strict, non-negotiable conclusions regarding the public interest. The political arena is also left to self-serving politicians motivated by the power and privilege available through politics. With such qualities permeating the political arena, a polarized political landscape can emerge where the desire to do "the most good for the greatest number" can take a back seat to partisan ideology, demagoguery, and greed. A key question for discerning voters becomes:

What evidence is there of flexibility and objectivity in this political leader? Is there a demonstrated propensity to seek input and to validate the views of others?

In time, an elite political class can evolve with an overdeveloped sense of self-importance and entitlement. With the escalating financial costs of entering politics, as well as the costs of mounting campaigns to successfully persuade voters, many cannot simply afford to enter the arena unless they are independently wealthy or unless they have secured the support of wealthy backers to bankroll necessary expenses. Regrettably, people do not often give large amounts of money to political candidates without expecting something in return. A positive thinker, who optimistically sees the glass as half full, might argue that the expected return is simply honest leadership. A cynic might argue that the return is influence on the politician once elected to office.

One result of this connecting of wealth to politics can be to distance the political elite from the electorate. As this happens, voters may begin to look for fresh-faced alternatives promising sweeping reforms and a revitalization of the "power to the people" dream. If frustrated or disillusioned enough by the machinations of the political elite, increasing numbers of voters may be willing to try more extreme politicians and measures. Opportunistic politicians, able to accurately recognize the extent of this frustration, can use it to personal advantage. The following sales pitch will resonate with a large number of frustrated or disillusioned voters: "The system is rigged against you. I am not part of the exploiting class so I can fix the system. Give me a chance. What have you got to lose?" The key question for discerning voters becomes:

What evidence of self-importance and entitlement can I detect in this politician? Can I trust that my needs and interests will be looked after? Why?

Not all politicians are self-centred and malicious. Some have a genuine interest in making a difference in their communities and society. Others pragmatically oscillate between giving and taking. When a disproportionate number of 'servant leaders' are discouraged from the political arena, this vacuum can result in a leadership crisis.

Sometimes, elected representatives avoid dealing with serious problems, because they fear career damaging political fallout. For example, inaction or ineffective action may be the end result if self-interested politicians determine the electorate to be severely divided about the most appropriate course of action to take. When elected representatives determine the electorate to be substantially uninformed, their response can either expand the divide and disconnect between voter and politician, or alternatively help to bridge the gap through education and voter engagement.

Current impasses, and the quasi-tribal polarization evident in the political landscape, need not be a permanent condition. If the full potential of leadership is harnessed to serve the greater good, and not just partisan interests, the hopes for a return to functional democracy and the revitalization of the great American Dream can be effectively refocused. To achieve this transformation, the people must will it and work towards making it happen. We cannot expect that, given its righteousness, democracy will benefit from an *invisible hand* that will keep it honest and focused on "the most good for the greatest number." In the past, some of those raising concerns about the state of democracy in America were labelled not as critical thinkers but as "un-American." Rather than being deemed counter to American interests, this kind of critical dialogue needs to be encouraged to inform and engage the public consciousness.

This much-needed transformation cannot be accomplished by the political class alone. It will require the articulation of a code of conduct for political leaders and elected officials. This articulation would clearly outline public expectations to those considering entering the political arena. It will then require politicians to publicly accept the expressed standards of servant leadership. This same articulation could then be used to critically assess performance, using reasoned criteria and appropriate indicators for the level of service being provided (relative to expectations). This should effectively inform voters prior to casting the next vote. These improvements create potential for a more mindful and accountable political process. In this mindful process, three key critical questions are:

What can we rightfully expect from our political leaders and elected officials?

Does past experience, conduct, and performance sufficiently reflect community standards? How so?

Has this incumbent politician earned my vote? How so? Has this
newcomer earned a chance to assume the mantle of leadership? How so?

63

LEADERSHIP BY CONVICTION CONVENIENCE: WHEN SELF INTEREST TRUMPS PUBLIC SERVICE

Any alternative approach focusing on the above questions should provide an improvement over the current levels of dysfunction and manipulation. If these adverse conditions are seen to persist, then at least they can be attributed to conscious decision-making and not ignorance or bamboozlement. In the end, in any functional democracy, the people ultimately get the kind of leadership and representation they deserve.

Just like consumer spending, voting ultimately reflects the voter's world view. In a sense, every vote you cast is a vote for the kind of world and the kind of community you want. At very least, the Trump experience should have taught American voters to be very careful in what they wish for. Ironically, in a political arena marked by leadership by convenience, quite often the

> *"Every time you spend money, you're casting a vote for the kind of world you want."*
> —Anna Lappé

people must lead, rather than follow their elected leaders. Convenient leaders can be hypersensitive to shifts in popular opinion. Therefore, it is imperative that voters make their opinions known and respected. Democracy was never intended as a spectator sport. The democratic process was always intended as an active and participatory investment in building a civil and self-governing society.

Ten Key Questions Facilitating Discernment: A Summary List

1. What personal growth does this political leadership develop or inspire?
2. Do errors result from intentional actions and deliberate calculation? How do I know?
3. Which best reflects this politician's overall style, leadership by conviction or leadership by convenience? What evidence do I have to support my conclusion?
4. Can I see consistency between what this politician says and what is actually done? Can I see evidence of personal integrity at work?
5. What can be learned from the experience of others that can help me to make better assessments and decisions closer to home?
6. How has this leadership transformed the community to date and what can be reasonably expected for the future?

7. What evidence of self-importance and entitlement can I detect in this politician? Can I trust that my needs and interests will be looked after? Why?

8. What can we rightfully expect from our political leaders and elected officials?

9. Does past experience, conduct, and performance sufficiently reflect community standards? How so?

10. Has this incumbent politician earned my vote? How so? Has this new-comer earned a chance to assume the mantle of leadership? How so?

> *"Those who do not remember the past are condemned to repeat it."*
> —George Santayana

A Report Card on Political Leadership for Discerning Voters

★ ★ ★ ★ ★ ★

With over 40 years of service in public education the report card concept often comes to my mind as a tool to assess achievement and track personal progress towards identified goals, expectations, and performance standards. Most everyone can relate personally to the progress report card experience, with both positive and negative recollections. Lucky for elected officials, my career was not invested in medicine or health sciences. Otherwise I might be suggesting more radical strategies like mandatory psychoanalysis, gene therapy, brain surgery, or colon cleanses!

In our digital information age the report card strategy has the potential to yield useful information upon which to base future decision-making. Reports can be used to confirm a pattern of performance over time and to track progress towards achieving goals and expectations. The documentation involved can help refresh the increasingly short memories of the electorate, prior to making new decisions. The personal assessments of diverse voters can be tabulated to produce an objective composite of a particular leader's performance. Lastly, the report card strategy can help to make an often abstract and complex process more focused, concrete, and practical for decision-makers. If nothing more, this tool can help focus voter thinking on appropriate criteria on which to base an informed judgement.

SAMPLE REPORT CARD TEMPLATE

Elected Leader: _____ Position: _____

ASSESSMENT SCALE FOR OBSERVED LEADERSHIP					
Use the following scale to rate the **achievement** and **performance** of this elected leader while in office.					
Descriptor	Not passable	Limited but passable	Satisfactory / adequate	Very good / solid	Excellent / outstanding
Demonstrated Proficiency	Unacceptable	Minimal	Basic	Proficient	Advanced
Achievement Level	**0**	**1**	**2**	**3**	**4**

Complete one of the following tables for each of the following assessment criteria:

Integrity	Commitment to Service	Humility
Ability	Emotional Intelligence	Flexibility
Transparency/Honesty	Fairness	Growth Mindedness

Assessment Criterion:	Achievement Level:
Describe Factors Affecting Performance to Date:	
Going Forward:	
DO	**DON'T**

Figure 4.1: Sample report card to assess the performance of elected leaders.

Nine key leadership qualities are identified as assessment criteria. It is important to review the significance of each criterion. In this way, whether a physical report card is actually used or not, each criterion contributing to effective leadership can be used in various ways by discerning voters. This focused thinking can help frame more thorough assessment and more informed choices going forward.

Integrity

Integrity is one of the key qualities of great leaders. Integrity connotes a deep commitment to hold the moral high ground. This requires doing the right things for the right reasons, regardless of circumstances and prevailing winds. Integrity is made evident by a high correlation between words, actions, values, core principles, methodology, and outcomes. Leaders with integrity can be often seen walking the walk, after talking the talk. There is an ethical consistency and benevolence in their behaviour that evokes confidence and trust. If this behaviour inspires others to respond in kind, a culture of integrity can be fostered.

> *"The supreme quality for leadership is unquestionably integrity. Without it, no real success is possible, no matter whether it is on a section gang, a football field, in an army, or in an office."*
> —DWIGHT D. EISENHOWER

Commitment to Service

Putting service first is a key quality of leaders with enduring social impact. Servant leadership is not about opening doors and fetching coffee for others. It is leadership with others squarely in mind. A true commitment to service is made evident by a clear focus on capacity building and the promotion of social consciousness. A primary distinguishing feature is a bias towards action rather than rhetoric. This action should ultimately lead to learning and growth in others. Servant leadership entails community building, empowerment, and team work. Servant leaders are not blinded or distracted by the trappings of power. Nor are they driven by ego or self-interest. They use power to achieve their social agenda. Servant leadership is essential for addressing the complex and compounded social challenges of our post-modern age. Servant leadership gives us cause to strategically act on hope. Our challenge is to leverage the transformative potential of leadership to affect the betterment of society.

> *"There are two great forces in human nature: self-interest and caring for others."*
>
> *"As we look ahead into the next [21st] century, leaders will be those who empower others."*
> —WILLIAM H. GATES

Humility

C.S. Lewis once wrote: "True humility is not thinking less of yourself; it is thinking of yourself less." Humility is often overlooked as a quality of effective leaders. Too often, in the past, we have focused attention on strength, over-the-top self-confidence, and persuasiveness. These are useful qualities in moderation. But recent studies confirm that humility (in the business world) can contribute significantly to leader effectiveness and team productivity. The same holds true for the business of politics: where the craft of persuasion meets the art of the possible. Humility requires that ego is held in check. Narcissistic

> *"It is amazing what you can accomplish if you do not care who gets the credit."*
> —HARRY S. TRUMAN

leaders may see themselves as rock stars or Hollywood divas, but in reality, they serve at the public's pleasure. A leader's humility quotient can be assessed by checking for the following regularly occurring behaviours:

- Admitting mistakes and sharing them as teachable moments;
- Seeking input and avoiding the *know-it-all* syndrome;
- Avoiding micro-management, tight control, and constant debate;
- Quickly diverting attention to give credit to others;
- Demonstrating a gentle strength and a willingness to forgive honest mistakes;
- Demonstrating tolerance for ambiguity and uncertainty;
- Demonstrating openness to new ideas and different opinions.

In brief, humble leaders are not afraid to reveal their own humanity. They realize that they are not expected to have all the answers, but only to create opportunities for constructive dialogue to seek answers out. Humble leaders do not feel that they have to 'win' every debate or provide the 'last word' in every dialogue, to justify their position of authority.

Ability

A leader's ability can be defined as capacity to turn intellect into decisive and effective action. It is not enough to have a good idea. That idea must then be effectively executed to maximize benefits while minimizing costs. In addition, the intellectual capacity of an effective leader should allow for the conscious avoidance of bad ideas. For example, anyone promoting the

> *"Perfect execution cannot compensate for implementing the wrong solution."*
> —MARC DENNY

concept of 'seeing eye squirrels' needs to reconsider any serious leadership aspirations. This project might be achievable but, not likely at a realistic cost. Ability refers to the capacity to attend to complex matters diligently so that sound decisions are made and effectively executed. Leadership ability is not an innate gift, but rather, an acquired set of understandings, skills, and attitudes. Effective leadership is challenging and rare because it entails risk-taking. A purposeful leader knows exactly what the inherent risks are and why they are worth taking. The leader's ability to remain focused, positive, and optimistic can inspire others to assume calculated risks, in the pursuit of laudable collective goals. This 'buy in' is facilitated by the leader's demonstrated competence in leading with vision, intellect, intuition, fairness, and an even temperament. An able leader does not need to resort to fear mongering to motivate, intimidate, or persuade others.

Emotional Intelligence

Emotional intelligence refers to the sensitivity to understand and manage personal emotions, as well as the emotions of others within one's sphere of influence. For leaders, having emotional intelligence is essential for success. Effective leaders are able to quickly perceive emotional reactions to a situation, issue, or action. Emotional intelligence enables insightful sensitivity to the signals that human emotions send about relationships. Leaders with high emotional intelligence are better able to control their own emotions. This enables them to stay calm and focused in adverse situations. Such leaders are less likely to rush headlong into hasty decisions or to let anger take over their behaviour. Emotional intelligence enables leaders to quickly and accurately sense the emotions going on around them and to help resolve emerging conflict. Emotionally intelligent leaders are effectively able to put themselves in the shoes of others to provide empathy, support, and encouragement. Such leaders generate loyalty and respect. An absence of loyalty and respect can indicate a lack of emotional intelligence and humane treatment from the top.

> *"Without it [emotional intelligence], a person can have the best training in the world, an incisive, analytical mind, and an endless supply of smart ideas, but he still won't make a great leader."*
> —DANIEL GOLMAN

Flexibility

Adaptive leadership involves the ability and inclination to change plans in response to changing circumstances, without compromising core principles. Leaders with this quality embrace change, are open to new ideas, and can work with diverse people and communities. In our post-modern world, leaders need to treat uncertainty and ambiguity as the new normal and be able to function effectively in uncertain times. This flexibility can enable leaders to adapt to changing conditions and to fine-tune earlier decisions. This requires an accurate read of current conditions, a careful consideration of trends and most likely changes, and the vision to keep

> *"The measure of intelligence is the ability to change."*
> —ALBERT EINSTEIN

efforts focused on the principles at stake. Flexibility also requires adapting and revising steps to facilitate the desired progress, in light of shifting or challenging circumstances. Flexibility enables a positively minded leader to approach challenges as opportunities and to avoid the bog of negativity.

Transparency/Honesty

Transparent leadership and full disclosure reflect a commitment to honesty and open government. When transparency is not evident, public trust can be eroded. Transparency may increase vulnerability, but as Saint Mother Teresa often pointed out, it is worth doing anyway. Outside of amusement parks, people do not appreciate magical mystery tours, especially when they become standard operating procedure for cautious political leaders. Voters take com-

> *"A lack of transparency results in distrust and a deep sense of insecurity."*
> —DALAI LAMA

fort in having access to pertinent information and documentation. Freedom of Information legislation places the public's right to transparency over privacy rights. With elected officials, it is most comforting to know that what you see is what you get, and what is promised is what is delivered. Once perceived or exposed, hidden agendas generate fear, distrust, insecurity, and negativity. People support politicians that they can relate to.

In our digital age, people have the means to find out more about their leaders. In a world where there are very few secrets, full disclosure (including warts) can be the wisest long term strategy to facilitate buy in, to facilitate team building, and to build authentic relationships. The transparency provided by full disclosure can hold elected officials accountable and help fight corruption and abuse of power. The disclosure of personal business interests, contributions received, and sources of all donations received helps increase transparency, honesty, and accountability. The reluctance to disclose such information should serve as an alarm bell for discerning citizens. An honest and humble candidate should have nothing to hide. An honest politician always clearly says what is meant and always means what is said. Weasel words are counterproductive. A direct approach is most effective in building trust.

Fairness

Fairness is often linked to just and equitable treatment. The principle of fairness is often confused, under-rated and under-valued. Equity does not imply equal treatment. Equity does imply respectful treatment reflecting what is right and just. Fairness requires a spirit of benevolence to prevail. A benevolent leader seeks to serve the common good, rather than partisan interests. As such, benevolent leadership can be a catalyst for positive change. It is not enough for a leader to be fair. A benevolent leader must be seen to be fair to all stakeholders. In the corporate world, benevolent leaders and companies seek to do what is right and just, not just for shareholders, but for all concerned.

> *"It is not fair to ask of others what you are unwilling to do yourself."*
> —ELEANOR ROOSEVELT

In both business and politics, benevolent leaders acknowledge progress, reward success, and celebrate real achievement. They do not have to claw their way to the top because others gladly carry them there. When leaders are seen to consistently provide fair treatment, they nurture a culture focused on ethics, benevolence, and positivity. For true benevolent and fair leaders, being right does not excuse the unkind or disrespectful treatment of others. They avoid favouritism for cronies and contempt for those expressing diverse ideas. They surround themselves with divergent thinkers instead of parrots. Their leadership includes modelling rules and acceptable behaviour for others to see and emulate, anchored on the 'golden' imperative to treat others as you expect to be treated by others.

Growth Mindedness

At its very best, leadership positively impacts lives and futures. Leadership transcends management. Where management focuses on overseeing existing resources and schedules, leadership focuses on *envisioneering* futures. That is to say, effective leaders provide vision and direction to shape and realize improvement and growth. True leaders inspire those around them to be better and to contribute more to the common good.

Over time, great leadership enables legacy, by consistently asking the questions that help to create a better world than what presently exists. A legacy leader looks to have lasting positive impact, rather than immediate impact and notoriety. This requires a leader to carefully reflect on what is being said and done, and where these ultimately lead. Through this reflection often comes better decision making and more informed follow-up action.

> *"A leader takes people where they want to go. A great leader takes people where they don't necessarily want to go, but ought to be."*
> —ROSALYNN CARTER

The most effective leaders are governed by a *growth mindset*. They understand that perfection is not an objective reality, but they truly believe that continuous improvement is possible. They seek to continually improve and to help those around them do the same. The resulting collective growth (and progress) becomes their *leadership legacy* as a leader "who knows the way, goes the way, and shows the way," as John C. Maxwell succinctly articulates.

Growth minded leaders surround themselves with divergent thinkers and encourage "thinking outside the box." This is done to promote free and progressive thinking and not to have people to blame should something go wrong. Growth minded leaders dispense credit, not blame. They build bridges to lasting relationships. They do not focus their efforts on building walls.

These nine qualities and behaviours become key indicators for discerning citizens when choosing their political leaders. Regrettably leaders are sometimes chosen for the wrong reasons, including:

- Partisan politics;
- Fear;
- Ignorance;
- Dissatisfaction with other candidates;
- Frustration and disillusionment with the political process.

Opportunistic politicians can prey on these realities to manipulate large groups of voters in their direction. When unfortunate choices are made, regardless of the reasons, all is not lost. Discerning citizens can remain hopeful that good will ultimately prevail, once the truth is exposed.

This hope is founded on the belief that, ultimately, leadership by convenience will expose itself as leadership not directly conducive to the common good. Despite what is being preached, the actions of opportunistic leaders preying on convenience will eventually render self or partisan interests transparent.

This can trigger a boomerang effect where the outcome achieved can be the opposite of what was intended by the leader. For example, Trump's ridiculing and demeaning of his attorney general, Jeff Sessions, did not achieve the desired result. Instead of pressuring Sessions to resign, Trump's over-the-top bully tactics angered Republican party leadership and turned off many American voters.

> "A leader is best when people barely know that he exists. He is the teacher who succeeds without taking credit. And, because credit is not taken, credit is received."
>
> —LAO TZU

Furthermore, in professing noble goals and then eventually demonstrating their true colours and deep seated intentions, convenient leaders can teach voters a valuable set of lessons to be applied to future decision-making. Sometimes in life, lessons are learned from mistakes. The bigger the mistake, the greater the lessons that can be learned from it. Those who cannot learn from their mistakes are hopeless leaders. Those who refuse to admit their own mistakes and shortcomings are hopeless human beings. They have stopped growing and can realistically aspire to become nothing more.

As more citizens sharpen their understanding of real leadership, political parties will be forced to reform their recruitment practices to remain relevant to voters. This should positively affect both the quality of the candidate pool and the leadership pool available to parties. If political parties do not improve their recruitment practices and broaden their horizons, they run the risk of attracting more than their fair share of 'deplorables.' This can facilitate the disillusionment of party faithful, internal dysfunction, and a decidedly more ultra-partisan orientation. Such conditions are not politically sustainable.

Today, at first glance, Trump's leadership appears to be inspiring Americans to take giant steps backward. In the short-term, rudeness, xenophobia, and intolerance may prevail. His harsh language ("I'd like to punch him [a protester] in the face"), unfounded accusations ("Obama is the founder of ISIS") and bullying of opponents, critics, and conscientious objectors ("He [John McCain] is not a hero ... I don't like people who were captured") sets a low standard for acceptable behaviour by political leaders. Luckily, as the laws of physics teach us, every action can trigger an equal and opposite reaction.

Reflecting on the Charlottesville Riots

★ ★ ★ ★ ★ ★

The riots in Charlottesville, Virginia on August 12, 2017, were precipitated by the planned removal of a statue of Confederate general Robert E. Lee. Extremist agitators from across America flocked to Charlottesville in an attempt to "Unite the Right," a veiled attempt to promote white nationalism and to spew venom against African-Americans and Jews. Trump demonstrated an inability to quickly and strongly denounce, by name, the senseless violence of KKK, neo-Nazis and white supremacists.

> *"The violence and deaths in Charlottesville strike at the heart of American law and justice. When such actions arise from racial bigotry and hatred, they betray our core values and cannot be tolerated. Justice will prevail."*
>
> —JEFF SESSIONS

In the midst of domestic terrorism in Charlottesville, even after violent rage led to the senseless death and serious injury of counter-protesters opposed to fascist bigotry, the president chose to denounce violence "on many sides." At very least, this reflects the very *leadership by convenience* that can contribute greatly to dysfunctional democracy. At a time of such crisis, the president is expected to bring the whole country together, a nation longing for racial healing.

This brings to question the president's courage to directly condemn and confront members of his own support base. Instead, he chose to include in his generic condemnation those protesting against fascism, hatred, and xenophobic bigotry as well. Almost immediately, alt-right leaders publicly used the president's generic language as confirmation that they had a friend in the White House. With no immediate response from the president, this crisis emboldened the alt-right movement in America, including the extremist confrontational groups and individuals referred to as "a basket of deplorables" by Hillary Clinton, during the bitter presidential campaign of 2016.

The president finally condemned the hatemonger groups by name, 48 hours after the fact. This was done only after it became clear that scathing criticism about his original guarded approach would not subside. Unfortunately, the very next day he once again went off script (to the obvious dismay of staff gathered beside him) to virtually negate the previous day's condemnation of specific groups promoting racist hatred. This diatribe effectively removed the president from the moral high ground in this crisis. So, instead of confronting the real problem in America, Trump blamed dishonest media.

This presidential delay, and subsequent veiled retraction, reflected weakness and emboldened fanatical groups to defiantly march in support of "white nationalist" bigotry. Trump's harshest critics lamented that his behaviour revealed much about his own views concerning racism in America. Luckily, many communities across America chose to take the recently vacated moral high ground. They began to quietly remove Confederate statues and plaques in their own communities to avoid similar confrontations. In the absence of strong leadership from the president, this spontaneous boomerang effect helped right and justice to prevail in America. It also helped hold deplorable sentiments in check.

For the record, I am not in favour of the Taliban-like destruction of historical artefacts. I much prefer to tap and preserve the educative potential that they hold. Rather than destruction, I prefer that these statues and plaques be relocated to a museum where the appropriate education can take place. Alternatively, I would prefer to see an on-site counterbalance. For example, a statue of a civil rights leader like Martin Luther King or Rosa Parks could be erected beside a statue of Robert E. Lee. Hopefully, this could lead to honest dialogue and social progress.

A few days after the neo-fascist/white supremacist scandal exposed the president's inability to stake and stay on the moral high ground, Trump fired his chief strategist, and close friend, Steve Bannon. Bannon's ultra-right wing views were problematic for a president under fire. This reluctant firing may have adjusted the optics, but not the influence Bannon had on the president.

Republican party leadership and supporters, not confronting their morally ambiguous president, are complicit in the damage being done to America. Discerning voters, with any kind of functional memory, should hold them all accountable. Without this accountability, moral erosion is destined to continue to affect American society. Ironically, the increased political influence of the religious right and their hardline biases against abortionists and homosexuals, unashamedly expressed as God's will, has done little to stem the tide of moral erosion.

Regrettably, in a democracy, opportunistic *deplorables* can infiltrate all political parties and movements. Luckily, they do not often constitute a critical mass. So, they must keep their deplorable thoughts to themselves. They wait quietly in the background, looking for any signs of weakness that can be exploited to enable their evil to take hold. Occasionally, an individual or a small group, consumed by the extreme hate they have long harboured inside, may instigate violence to incite open confrontation.

In the long-run, the push-back from growth-minded citizens will serve to redirect, reverse, or negate the actions of *deplorables* with hate-based agendas. This push-back will also help ensure that the death of Heather Heyer, the 32-year-old civil rights activist who was deliberately run over by a neo-Nazi sympathizer, would not be in vain. Heyer was struck down along with 19 other anti-fascism protesters in Charlottesville. This push-back should ultimately result in a serious re-thinking of the *perfect storm* that brought a reality TV star to power. If *deplorables* prevail, then nothing is learned from this unfortunate experience, but at very least, Americans will get the kind of government and society they deserve.

> *"I believe that everything happens for a reason. People change so that you can learn to let go and things go wrong so that you appreciate them when they're right. You believe lies so you eventually learn to trust no one but yourself and, sometimes good things fall apart so better things can fall together."*
> —MARILYN MONROE

I do not subscribe to this notion, given the capacity for good that I have observed throughout my travels across the United States. I prefer to embrace the wisdom in Marilyn Monroe's reflection instead. She may not have been a politician herself, but I am given to understand, she was very close to major leaders and change makers in her day. Everything happens for a reason and difficult happenings are merely cleverly disguised opportunities to learn and grow. When *deplorables* do not prevail and the full extent of the law is used to hold them accountable for their hateful actions, then America will be a better place and Americans can once again hold their heads up proudly. To lead this long overdue recovery forward, America's political leaders must stake and hold the moral high ground. This will help close the current leadership gap.

An Experience Worth Noting: Educative Leadership

★ ★ ★ ★ ★ ★

As principal of Cardinal Carter Academy for the Arts, in Toronto, I had the pleasure of accompanying a group of students during a March Break trip to Italy, in 2006. I relished the opportunity to share some of the culture and historical legacy of the land of my birth, with a creative group of young Canadians. The teacher in charge of these annual excursions was an extremely capable organizer, who took great pride in providing an enjoyable learning experience. Over the years, a thorough set of rules and preparations emerged to help improve the experience for all participants.

Figure 4.2: A group photo of Cardinal Carter students and staff preparing to leave Toronto for a March Break trip to Italy, taken by the school principal in 2006.

One cardinal rule involved student consumption of alcohol during the trip. This rule clearly outlined the penalty for such irresponsible behaviour as the immediate return to Toronto, at the parents' expense. There had never been an infraction, until the first year I went along as a supervisor.

As soon as our group arrived in Rome, even with minimal free time available to them, three male students decided to pop into one of the many bars near the Trevi Fountain. On a dare, one of the students ordered an alcoholic beverage, just to see if he would be served. When he was successful, the others tried it, to see if they too looked sufficiently mature. Once they were all successful, they had to do something with the evidence. And so, it was all quickly consumed before rejoining the rest of the group. I am not sure how much alcohol was consumed, but it could be smelled on their breath as they boasted to their mates about their accomplishment. To their credit, they did not really deny it, once confronted. At first, they offered weak excuses for their actions, but none were remotely justifiable.

As school principal, this put me in a very difficult position. The rules had been made clear and accepted by all students and their parents. The rules required that these three young men be sent back to Toronto on the earliest available flight. The teacher in charge was as disappointed as I was at this turn of events. As principal, I was expected to set a strong example in this precedent setting situation. Most of the students knew what had happened and they were watching for my response. The easy thing would have been to send them all home as the rules required. This would have served as a strong deterrent.

I have always prided myself on being a servant leader. I knew these young men, and I had a sense they had been caught up in the moment. And yet, I had to be seen to be doing something serious about this glaring infraction. I thought long and hard about the best way to set an example while still maximizing the educative potential of the experience. I had each violator call their parents to explain what they had done. This was done in my presence so that I could assess the accuracy of the communication. I did not tell them, but I was also looking for evidence of contrition to help with my difficult decision.

Needless to say, all three sets of parents were very upset to receive this bad news, so early into the weeklong trip. By the time I came on the phone, parents were resigned to begin the process of securing a flight home for their son. I asked parents if they would support me in making the situation more educative than punitive, and they all agreed to leave the matter with me, pending a second phone call.

I discussed my emerging plan with the teacher in charge to build consensus and to address any concerns about the precedent my decision would set. Together, we then sat the students down and explained the final decision. According to the itinerary, on our last day in Rome, before departing for Florence, all students were given an afternoon of free time in the area of Piazza Navona, my favourite Roman piazza. Because of their behaviour, these three students forfeited all free time privileges for the rest of the trip.

Originally, I had planned to take the bus to visit an elderly uncle, who was recovering in a hospital about an hour north of Rome. Instead of enjoying the free time with their mates, my three bar patrons were now going to accompany me on my visit. I had already researched the bus fare so I could tell them how much this exped-

Figure 4.3: Piazza Navona is built on the site of the ancient Circus Agonalis. (Photo supplied by the author).

ition would cost. The alternative was to pack their bags and prepare to fly home to Toronto. The lads all jumped at the opportunity to salvage their Italian adventure, even volunteering to pay my ticket.

The next day, while visiting St. Peter's Basilica, I passed by the local taxi depot to inquire about transportation to the hospital where my uncle, Monsignor Carmelo Cristiano, was convalescing. Fortuitously, I found a cab driver who was going to be off duty on the day of our visit. He agreed to take the four of us to the hospital and back, for a set fee to be paid in cash. It worked out to everyone's benefit because, although the cost was slightly higher, the travel time was significantly less. I was able to spend more time with my uncle (zio), and we got back to Rome much sooner.

My uncle had always been a role model I greatly admired. He was a scholar and an accomplished writer. In addition to being a parish priest, zio taught at the local school, university and seminary. He proudly displayed all of his framed degrees in his bathroom. When I asked him, "Zio, why in the bathroom instead of your study?", he smiled and said, "There's already lots of paper in my study, but you never know when there might be a sudden shortage of paper in the bathroom!"

One day in 1968, zio had taken me on a memorable trip to Florence. The works of art he introduced me to were amazing, but my most vivid memory is an encounter that happened on the busy train ride from Rome to Florence. In our full compartment was a well-dressed gentleman who appeared most unhappy to share the space with a Catholic priest. This man sat directly across from my uncle. He was a hard-core communist and he continuously maligned the Catholic Church. I wanted to hit the guy, but my uncle took it all in stride, with a big smile on his face. This seemed to infuriate the comrade even more!

At one point, the comrade asked my uncle, "Reverend, can you tell me what the exact difference is between a priest and a pig?" Zio smiled, shrugged his broad shoulders and said, "Well I'm not exactly sure. But I would have to say, that at this particular moment, the difference is about two meters." The comrade abruptly left our compartment and was never seen again. With that encounter, zio taught me the virtues of patience and humour. The summer of 1968 was not a pleasant time for communists in Europe. To the escalating consternation of Moscow, communist Czechoslovakia had begun experimenting with liberal reforms that spring. A few weeks after our train trip to Florence, Soviet tanks and soldiers swarmed into Czechoslovakia to abruptly shut down the reform movement.

To many citizens, the Italian communist party was seen as an ally of the Soviet Union. The Catholic Church had a lot to do with fuelling this perception.

Greeting every exaggerated statement with smiles and laughter, zio never allowed the offender the satisfaction of taking his words seriously, effectively disarming the frustrated communist. All the while, zio waited for the right opportunity to respond. After the frustrated communist had left, zio shared the following insight with me. Many people with weak arguments tend to rationalize their position rather than attempting to justify it. An intelligent person clearly distinguishes between rationalization and justification. Some things can be rationalized but never justified. Just actions require doing the right thing for all concerned.

When I explained to my uncle what I had done with my three travelling companions, zio could not stop laughing. He said that it sounded like something he might have done in his younger years. Zio often took students on excursions to explore Etruscan tombs and other historical sites in the Sabine Hills region.

Zio also commented on how important it was for a leader (like a good shepherd) to always consider the best interests of those entrusted to his care, over his own interests. "The best measure of a leader is the growth he nurtures in others. I think these boys are going to remember this as part of their journey into manhood," zio told me with a proud smile. We got back to Rome in time to give the lads a half hour of free time in Piazza Navona. For the rest of the trip all the students were well behaved, including my three travelling companions. I like to think that how we handled the situation was a contributing factor.

The Trump experience provides discerning thinkers with a similar opportunity to reflect on the leadership qualities they can and should expect from their leaders. Trump's extremist antics reveal the political arena in its most callous, self-serving, and divisive form. His questionable behaviour will help Americans recognize suitable criteria to assess the qualities of future leaders, as well as the most cherished qualities of their fragile democracy. Trump's eagerness to hide behind the seal of his office is a convenient ploy to avoid the justification of his actions. Trump has been a proud, life-long tax avoider. Not surprisingly, after one year in office, his most significant accomplishment is "the largest tax cut in American history." As a result, Trump businesses stand to save countless millions over the next several years, while social programs face spending cuts to fund the tax cuts to America's most wealthy. Trump boldly rationalizes that this has all been done to create many new jobs for working class Americans.

If Trump were on a student trip with me, I would be sending him home right now without hesitation.

The Parable of the Imperial Vestments

★ ★ ★ ★ ★ ★

The following post-modern parable provides insight into the perils of excessive self-interest in a political world where the conviction to honestly serve the common good often takes a back seat to convenience, opportunism and self-interest.

Emperor Trump Has No Clothes

Figure 4.4: *Ann Telnaes Editorial Cartoon* used with the permission of Ann Telnaes and the Cartoonist Group. All rights reserved.

A billionaire misogynist became bored with his celebrity status and so he sought after the greatest spotlight in the free world, to become the undisputed emperor of all superstars in the nation of great dreams. He donned the mantle of **integrity** by objectifying and groping attractive young women, because as a celebrity he believed and boasted that it was his right. To don the cloak of **humility**, he exaggerated the failure of his predecessors and the wonderfulness of himself. To don the mantle of **service** he boasted about the number of non-whites he employed.

To don the cloak of **flexibility**, he reserved a sharp tongue for those who disappointed him and a thin skin for those who criticized him. To don the mantle of **transparency,** he arranged to leak to the media only one, decade old, tax return that showed him to have once paid relatively high tax rates. To don the cloak of **emotional intelligence**, he mocked a war hero, the Gold Star parents of a fallen soldier and a disabled journalist. To don the mantle of **ability**, he pointed to his great wealth and never having to apologize for anything. To don the cloak of **fairness**, he treated all politicians with equal contempt. To don the mantle of progressive **growth mindedness**, he boasted that he would single-handedly return his beleaguered nation to its former greatness, in a world long past.

After securing power, the emperor wore all his imperial vestments proudly. With the global warming caused by increased xenophobia, bigotry, fear and hatred, weather patterns became more unstable and extreme. One day an extremist wind unceremoniously knocked him on his imperial bottom. With all his imperial paraphernalia, he was left with his feet dangling in the air and his nether regions exposed for the entire nation to see.

It took him two days to regain his composure. Only to stumble and fall flat on his face, the very next day, once again exposing himself. By then, a young boy, engulfed in the innocence of youth, was heard to say what many adults refused to utter publicly, "This emperor has no balls!"

CHAPTER FIVE

THE MYTH OF POPULISM

It is often said that the first casualty of war is truth. Since politics is a form of warfare, truth can also be the first casualty of populist movements. Here is an interesting political formula to consider:

> *Tell the people what they want to hear. Find a convenient villain for their troubles. Confirm for them that it will take sweeping change to get what they want and that you are just the person to see it through. Then, ram your own agenda down their throats because sweeping change requires drastic measures and a counter to any resistance.*

Sound familiar? Well it should! This scenario has been played out many times in recent history. Quite often it begins as a populist movement seeking to empower and benefit ordinary people, through a trustworthy leader, serving as their steward.

The term *populism* is widely used today to refer to a political strategy, program, or movement that purports to champion the common people. In addition, it demonizes the villainous political and economic elite who exploit the common people.

Populism often emerges when people are disillusioned or disenchanted with current political leaders and their track record. Populism gains momentum when people are looking for a fresh face, untainted by what the establishment has done before. Populism often conveniently combines elements of the political left (such as opposing the interests of big business and big financial institutions),

> *"Populism is a stance and a rhetoric more than an ideology or a set of positions. It speaks of a battle between good and evil, demanding simple answers to difficult problems."*
>
> —GEORGE PACKER

with right-wing elements (like opposing big labour unions and big government), as appropriate to play on current concerns and hot button issues.

According to Cas Mudde, a political scientist at the University of Georgia, populism should be viewed as a "thin ideology" that merely sets up a framework: that of pure people versus a corrupt elite. This 'thinness' provides the adaptability to connect to many different "thick" ideologies, such as socialism, communism, nationalism, conservatism, fascism, or racism. Given this latitude, movements that purport to put common people first can be either democratic or authoritarian.

In its most democratic form, populism professes to maximize the power of ordinary citizens and promises to protect them from elitist exploitation. This is to be accomplished peacefully through reform rather than through revolution. The use of referenda is one example of how people can directly determine a matter (like the legalization of marijuana) without relying on elected representatives to do the right thing.

> "A politician divides mankind into two classes; tools and enemies."
> —FRIEDRICH NIETZSCHE

In recent manifestations, populism has developed an association with more authoritarian forms of politics. In this mode, populist politics revolve around a charismatic leader who claims to fully represent the will of the people. This may be a veiled attempt by an opportunistic individual to seize or consolidate power. As part of this political strategy, the charismatic leader appeals to the masses while sweeping aside institutions. In such a political environment, political parties can default their significance and role to the vision of a 'great' leader. Different ideologies lose their individual importance. The affiliation of like-minded individuals into a political party with a platform of priorities becomes redundant, if not counter-productive. Even elections can be conscripted to confirm or consolidate power rather than change it. In the end, authoritarian rule has been orchestrated under the guise of a popular or *grass roots* movement.

In spite of its vulnerability to exploitation, populism can result in progressive reform. Populists often ask the right questions and draw attention to salient issues, but rarely do they get the answers right, often because of over-simplification. The term *populist* is sometimes used pejoratively, in America today, to criticize a politician pandering to people's fear or anger.

Populism can be typically critical and leery of anything that stands between the people and their political leader or government. Institutions, like banks and courts, become targets of popular rage when they are seen to favour elites and disfavour ordinary citizens. Populism becomes more emotionally invested when a clear villain or scapegoat can be identified for the people to blame. After coming to power in 2016, Rodrigo Duterte, the populist president of the Philippines, ordered his police to execute suspected drug dealers.

Populism can be easily made to turn against the very people originally championing the movement. In addition, people can be incited to turn against each other,

> *"The human race divides politically into those who want people to be controlled and those who have no such desire."*
> —ROBERT A. HEINLEIN

further weakening the democratic union and increasing the need for law and order. How convenient for the demagogue in power!

During the first half of the 20th century, power seeking demagogues used populist movements to start or facilitate their assent to uncontested power. These campaigns led to fascist dictatorships in Italy, Germany, and Spain, and ultimately to world war in 1939. The sales pitches used by Benito Mussolini in Italy, Adolf Hitler in Germany, and Francisco Franco in Spain were remarkably similar:

> *The government is in disarray. Foreign countries have dominated us. Your political leaders have failed you. The economy is in ruins. The rich have exploited you. You have no bread to eat. The streets are unsafe. Give me a chance to govern. I am not like the others. I will look after you. What have you got to lose?*

This freedom-for-bread trade-off can be quite enticing to empty stomachs. Ruthless demagogues preyed on fear and economic, political, and social uncertainty to seize power. Once in power all opposition was immediately suppressed as being against the will and well-being of the people. Ultimately, it can be argued that the people need to be controlled, for their own good.

> *"The demagogue is one who preaches doctrines he knows to be untrue to men he knows to be idiots."*
> —H. L. MENCKEN

Later in the 20th century, the political style and programs of Latin American leaders invigorated populism. Juan Perón in Argentina, Getúlio Vargas in Brazil, and most recently Hugo Chávez in Venezuela, all offered strong government favouring centralized nationalism, industrialization, social reform, and the protection of worker rights. These strongmen were either brought to power or kept in power through military connections and support.

A Closer Look at Benny Who?

★ ★ ★ ★ ★ ★

The following narrative describes my first investigation into the populist 'great man' theory used to empower and sustain fascist dictatorship in Italy from 1922 to 1943. My father was not a fool. Like many others, he was persuaded by an intense and relentless propaganda campaign. And then, it was too late!

Benny Who?
My First Encounter with Inquiry Learning

By Angelo Bolotta

As a teacher, my belief in the power of inquiry learning can be attributed to Benito Mussolini. You may be thinking, "How does *il Duce* merit this distinction?" For my father and uncle, Mussolini was a heroic figure, a great leader. They had both served in the Italian army and were great believers in the discipline that the fascist era forced onto a nation in disarray. As a youth, I was often told that the only thing missing in Canada was two years of compulsory military service, to turn boys into men.

While studying modern history in Grade 12, my teacher Father Leo Burns ridiculed both Mussolini and fascism. After one too many wisecracks about Mussolini's only achievement being that he got Italian trains to run on time, I asked for permission to "set the record straight." To his credit, I was given an entire 40 minute class the following week to do so.

This was my first teaching assignment and I took it seriously. I had a clear mandate and mission. I had to make sure that I knew what I was talking about. I did not always have this kind of academic discipline, but this time I had no choice. Two experiences were constantly replaying themselves in my mind. I could vividly remember as a youngster, how I had to be careful around the neighbourhood park because the Hitchcock brothers had forbidden me to set foot in the park. Their uncle had been killed in Italy during the war and somehow it was my fault. This was a reminder of the raw emotion that still lingered about the war, some 23 years later.

My second consideration was that I was already on a short leash. There had recently been a history fair at the school and we were forced to participate. My friends and I had waited until the last possible moment and then on the eve of the fair, after getting into some of my father's homemade grappa in the basement, we decided to create some 'ancient' artifacts. One was a 'drinking gourd' that still had wet paint on its surface. We made a 'do not touch' sign to warn those attending the history fair.

The next day to my surprise, the guest of honour was former Prime Minister John Diefenbaker. While visiting student exhibits with our teacher, he stopped at our display and appeared genuinely interested. I politely warned him, but he picked up the gourd anyway and got a handful of wet paint for his efforts.

Figure 1: Label used to explain one piece of the infamous history fair exhibit, back in 1968. Visitors were invited to spot the real artifacts from the fake ones. The wet paint and the suspect geography confirmed this 'gourd' to be a fake. Source: Courtesy of Angelo Bolotta.

Seeing the mess on his hands, Mr. Diefenbaker noted that, "The ancient artifacts appeared to be rather fresh!" In his best teacher voice, Father Burns asked, "Bolotta, is there anything specific that you want me to mention in your eulogy?" While using a handkerchief to clean his hands, Mr. Diefenbaker laughed and replied that "he had been duly warned" and that "a eulogy would not be necessary" because he himself "was once a student." I did not agree with the man's politics, but from that encounter onward, I was always impressed by the elder statesmanship of John Diefenbaker.

Needless to say, I was in the doghouse and had to be on my best behaviour for the Italian history lesson. No grappa this time! To not make a fool of myself, after being critical of the teacher's approach, I had to do some serious research. The more I researched, the more my subject became less and less the heroic figure envisioned by my father. Despite my father's warnings that history was always written from the perspective of the victors, I could find little evidence to support his 'great man' theory.

One anecdote, confirmed by different sources during my research, helps to highlight this fundamental difference of opinion and perspective. In one demonstration of Italy's military power to his ally Adolf Hitler, Mussolini instructed the same squadron of fighter jets to follow the route of their motorcade. By the time that he and Hitler arrived at the next air field by car, the serial numbers on the jets had been changed. Thus making it look like the Italian air force was much stronger than it actually was.

My father saw this as an act of cunning. He reasoned that the stronger Italy appeared, the more it would be respected by the Germans. Other sources saw it as an act of desperation. I saw it as a strategic error because eventually, every time a fighter jet would be lost in battle, the loss would be multiplied.

As I continued to research, more questions emerged than answers. I even asked for and got an extension to do more work. This had never happened to me before. My fascination with this topic (and my research into it) continues to this day. How could a nation voluntarily give up its freedom to follow a single, powerful and uncontested leader? How can one person become synonymous with the state? At what point does the "freedom for bread" trade off become acceptable to a free-spirited but impoverished society? How powerful was the lure of a return to Roman glory for the Italian people?

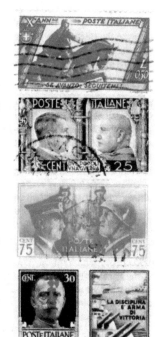

Four postage stamps from the fascist era, some rare now due to the anti-Mussolini purge after the fall of fascism, offer some insight into the propaganda machine that helped sustain the fascist agenda, by tirelessly promoting the 'great man' image of its leader. In the top stamp, in a style reminiscent of Roman imperial statues, Mussolini is shown on horseback and boldly proclaiming, "When I move forward, follow me!" In the two middle stamps he is presented as the equal (and slightly taller) of his powerful German ally. In the final two-frame stamp, the fascist insignia (another Roman symbol) is imprinted over the Italian king's face. Mussolini's declaration, "Discipline arms victory" can be found in the neighbouring frame.

Oh, the power of propaganda in desperate times and in ordinary times! Well, my father and I finally agreed on the great man theory. I just spelled it differently, g-r-a-t-e. As for my history lesson, let's just say that I went on to a rewarding career in teaching.

Figure 2: Italian postage stamps during the fascist era. Source: Courtesy of Angelo Bolotta.

Figure 5.1: Narrative from the Transformations collection of immigrant experiences.
(www.transformationscanada.com)

Populism in North America

★ ★ ★ ★ ★ ★

In the United States, populist movements have emerged, from time to time, often impacting significantly on the political landscape but never propelling an uncontested leader to the White House. The party system is one of the checks and balances intended to prevent autocratic rule by a demagogue. But waves of populism can influence election results and subsequent policy.

The term *populism* can be traced back to 1892 and the birth of the People's Party. This populist movement pitted the Democratic Party, and its primarily rural base of support at that time, against the more urban based Republican Party. The populist movement never came to power but was influential in securing a progressive taxation system and in legitimizing the use of referenda for controversial decisions. But not all that came from the populist movement was good.

In 1910, Thomas E. Watson, a populist politician from Georgia and a leader during the formative years of the People's Party, made the following pronouncement of what many other Americans were thinking:

> *The scum of creation has been dumped on us. Some of our principal cities are more foreign than American. The most dangerous and corrupting hordes of the old World have invaded us. The vice and crime that they have planted in our midst are sickening and terrifying. What brought these Goths and Vandals to our shores? The manufacturers are mainly to blame. They wanted cheap labor: and they did not care a curse how much harm to our future might be the consequence of their heartless policy.*

This xenophobic fear mongering is almost the direct opposite of the language used on the pedestal of the Statue of Liberty. The objects of Watson's bile were the large numbers of European immigrants (including Italians, Poles and Jews) pouring into America at the time. It also vilified the group recognized as most responsible. These are typical strategies for populist politicians, continuing to the present day.

This is why populist tactics can be politically volatile. Populism can ignite reform or extreme emotional reactions, like scapegoating, paranoia, and hate. In the wrong hands, populism can be a very dangerous tool. In Nazi Germany, Jewish conspiracies were ultimately blamed for all of Germany's problems. Eventually, a *Final Solution* was implemented to rid Germany of the Jewish problem. In the Holocaust that followed, six million Jews were systematically exterminated.

A 1935 semi-satirical political novel by Sinclair Lewis, entitled *It Can't Happen Here*, warned Americans about growing fascist and pro-Nazi sentiments in America. Two years later, a pro-Nazi rally in New York's Madison Square Garden attracted some 20,000 participants.

> *"When fascism comes to America, it will be wrapped in the flag and carrying a cross."*
> —SINCLAIR LEWIS

In Canada, populist movements have focused primarily on social reform. During the Great Depression, populist movements emerged in many provinces focused primarily on a more equitable distribution of wealth to the working class. It was argued that economic decline was caused by a systemic failure that left many citizens with insufficient purchasing power (or credit) to command the goods and services necessary for life.

In Alberta, evangelist William Aberhart used his Christian radio program to attract followers to his new political party. The Social Credit Party won the provincial election of 1935, capturing 56 of 63 seats in the legislature. The Party remained in power until 1971, by slowly shifting to more conservative financial and social policies under new leader Ernest Manning. His son, Preston Manning, was fundamental in the creation of the Reform Party of Canada, in 1987, and its eventual amalgamation with the original Progressive Conservative Party to create the Conservative Party of Canada.

In 1944, Tommy Douglas, a federal social democrat politician and Baptist minister, became premier of Saskatchewan as leader of the Cooperative Commonwealth Federation (CCF). This party began as a populist social welfare movement of farmers, academics, and federal politicians connected to labour unions. In 1944, the CCF formed the first socialist government in North America. The Party's 1933 *Regina Manifesto* promised unemployment and health insurance, public housing, public ownership of major industries and financial institutions, and laws to protect farmers from banks and creditors.

In 1961, the CCF became the New Democratic Party of Canada (NDP), under the leadership of Tommy Douglas. Under Douglas, the NDP never formed a national government but they often held the balance of power. Douglas became very influential in establishing Canada's "social welfare safety net" for all citizens. This safety net includes many components from the *Regina Manifesto*. In 2004,

> *"Canada is like an old cow. The West feeds it. Ontario and Quebec milk it. And you can well imagine what it's doing in the Maritimes."*
>
> *"Courage, my friends; 'tis not too late to build a better world."*
>
> —TOMMY DOUGLAS

Tommy Douglas was named "The Greatest Canadian" based on a nation-wide survey of television viewers by the Canadian Broadcasting Corporation (CBC).

The Tea Party Movement that emerged within the Republican Party, after Barack Obama came to power in 2009, was a populist-libertarian-conservative "rebellion" against increased government spending leading to escalating national debt, high taxes, and government sponsored universal health care. The *Tea Party* name came from a 1773 rebellion by Bostonians against taxation without representation. The conflict resulted in the dumping of tea imports in Boston Harbour, a catalyst for the *Declaration of Independence* three years later. The 2009 movement gained momentum within Republican circles and helped steer party ideology further to the right.

The American presidential elections of 2016, and the preceding party nomination campaigns produced two very diverse populist candidates. Bernie Sanders had a pronounced social orientation and Donald Trump had a pronounced conservative/entrepreneurial orientation. Both men have a strong bond with their followers. A comparison of the two candidates is quite revealing, especially since one was successful in acquiring the American presidency.

Although both men have a history of limited loyalty to a political party, Bernie Sanders has spent most of his political career as an 'outsider' working from

> *"Populism is ... a people's rebellion against the iron grip that big corporations have on our country— including our economy, government, media, and environment."*
>
> —JIM HIGHTOWER

inside the political arena. He sees the political arena as a battleground for opposing classes and he frames his *leftist* interests around a more equitable treatment for the working class. Sanders firmly believes in the political process and that conflicts can be effectively managed through free elections and legislation. His view of revolution is a series of socialistic reforms to fix a system that is currently rigged against the working class. Sample reforms proposed by Sanders include a tax on financial transactions, the breakup of the biggest and most powerful banks, legislation to prevent banks from making high risk investments, and a transparent system of political campaign financing to get big money out of politics.

Donald Trump, on the other hand, has chosen to present himself as the consummate anti-politics candidate. He goes out of his way to demonstrate contempt for politicians and the political process. He has gained a quasi-cult following of disenchanted and uninformed voters by promising strongman tactics to address the nation's ills. In reality, he is a television celebrity and brand ambassador for diverse business interests, pretending to be a strongman. His demonstrated hot temperament, thin skin for handling criticism, and his refusal to admit mistakes make him anything but strong. A strongman does not unravel at the slightest provocation.

> *"The man of great wealth owes a peculiar obligation to the state because he derives special advantages from the mere existence of government."*
> —THEODORE ROOSEVELT

Trump was able to grasp, and then tap to full advantage, the resentment that exists for political elites in America. He further recognized the limitations of the Republican Party's increasingly extreme right ideology evolving since the 1970s: anti-government spending, anti-taxation, pro-business, fundamentalist-Christian, and outwardly pious. Trump accurately assessed that middle-aged white working class Americans had suffered, at least as much as any other demographic group, from the ill effects of rapid globalization, low wage immigrant and foreign labour, and free trade deals. Ironically, Trump's companies exported jobs abroad to profit from cheap foreign labour. When questioned, he vilified the government that allowed him to do it, through ill-conceived trade deals and rules.

Trump accurately sensed the rage that flared from this pain and harnessed it to fuel his dangerously white-sided, ultra-right campaign. Even Richard Nixon and Ronald Reagan did not court the economic anxieties and social resentments of white Americans as much as Trump has done. Surprisingly, as a very successful entrepreneur, Trump claims to feel no obligation to the politico-economic establishment that made his rapid rise possible.

The collective North American experience confirms that populist movements can have significant positive and negative outcomes. Therefore, a critical mind is essential when assessing populism. Critical questions need to be asked to uncover the true intent, direction, and implications of populist sentiments and pronouncements. In addition, it is important for discerning citizens to debunk populist

> *"My brain has no heart. My heart has no brain. That's why when I speak my mind I seem heartless and when I do what's in my heart I seem thoughtless."*
> —CLARISSA PINKOLA ESTES

mythology before embracing any current manifestations and enabling those who champion them.

The core beliefs, motives, and past deeds of populist leaders need to be carefully examined. What is at stake is far too important to determine by a leap of faith. Considerable homework needs to be carefully done. The adjacent quote from American psychoanalyst and writer, Clarissa Pinkola Estes, presents an interesting take on the heartless/thoughtless musings and exploits of Donald Trump as a populist leader.

Debunking Populist Mythology

★ ★ ★ ★ ★ ★

1. **People instinctively know what is in their best interest.**

People may know about personal interests but they know considerably less about collective or public interests. In a pluralistic society, diverse interests are often encountered. Sometimes these interests are complimentary. Sometimes they conflict. Some populist movements conveniently favour some interests at the expense of others. Priorities set by populists are often based on popularity, rather than feasibility and practicality.

> *"Follow your heart but take your brain with you."*
> —ALFRED ADLER

One argument favouring a more homogeneous society is that it makes it easier to define the public interest. This can promote xenophobic tendencies and a low tolerance for diversity. We need to recognize that one person's wildflower can be another person's weed, and that this is perfectly normal in a shrinking world, rich in human diversity. An inclusive society stands to benefit from welcoming diverse ideas and perspectives into the social consciousness, unless that society already holds a tight monopoly on human insight and accrued wisdom.

Majority rule cannot be assumed to be automatically right and just because of its critical mass. Fairness and justice are based on where you stand relative to the moral high ground, not on the number of people standing with you. You can be with a large crowd and still be in an ethical wasteland. To make sense of populist rhetoric, both head and heart need to be engaged.

2. **Populism is a natural and justifiable reaction to perceived injustice.**

The strong emotions attached to populist movements can make responses anything but natural and just. Populism is rebellious in nature and the bile of populists is often reserved for those seen as agents of the exploitation of common folk. Sometimes, this is based on historical evidence. Sometimes, this can be based on prejudice.

> *"Prejudices are what fools use for reason."*
> —FRANÇOIS VOLTAIRE

In any battle between the forces of good and evil there have to be clear heroes and villains. The heroes are the common people. For populists, targeted villains might include Jews, Mexicans, Muslims, illegal immigrants, ruthless billionaires, or self-serving politicians.

Populism can take on a conspiratorial or apocalyptic bent propagating the belief that the country is facing imminent ruin at the hands of a particular malevolent group. The Jewish 'conspiracy' to rule the world, was used by the populist movement directed by Adolf Hitler to exterminate millions of innocent souls. The rhetoric of demonization should always be questioned.

As anti-establishment rebellions against elitism, populist movements can easily over compensate. Favouring the grieved can easily do a disservice to the aggrieving party, especially when emotions can easily shift the focus from correction and education to punishment and retribution. This behaviour can be rationalized but not justified. Resulting reforms may be equally unsustainable because they may be unfair to a different group of citizens.

3. **Populism attracts competent leadership driven by conviction.**

Populism often attracts charismatic leaders who are great orators. Unfortunately, these qualities do not always confirm the leader's true convictions. Sometimes opportunistic leaders seize the moment to acquire power. Once in power, they may turn on the very people that supported them.

> *"In these troubled times [2012] we live in, we should remain vigilant and see through populist arguments."*
> —ALBERT II OF BELGIUM

In assessing the truthfulness of populist leadership, two critical tests are needed. First, a *consistency test* is needed to carefully compare what a leader preaches to what is actually practiced. Second, an *integrity test* is needed to determine the feasibility, effectiveness, and repercussions of what is being advocated and practiced.

Leaders found lacking need to be quickly replaced to protect the movement. No righteous human movement needs to be dependent on a single leader to achieve the desired reforms. The merit of proposed reforms should be self-evident or evident, at least, to discerning minds.

Too much emphasis is placed on leadership and personality, sometimes at the expense of substance and content. All too often, populist ideals fall victim to charismatic leaders claiming that they alone represent the people and that all others are illegitimate pretenders. This kind of rhetoric should always trigger alarm bells.

4. Populism is anti-system or anti-establishment but not anti-democracy.

While populism is generally supportive of democracy, it can oppose many elements of a liberal democratic system. Representative democracy and the party system are sometimes questioned because they can create a class of political elites competing for the support of a majority of the population. This is seen as creating a buffer between a government and its people. In addition, the focus is seen to shift from serving all the people to winning over a comfortable majority. All of a sudden, it becomes prudent and feasible to leave a segment of the population behind.

> *"… in theory, theory and practice are the same but in practice they're different."*
> —YOGI BERRA

Ultimately, populists believe that politics should be based on the will of the people and that ultimate power rests with the people themselves. This may make sense in theory but it presents as a logistics nightmare.

> *"Political populism always poses a great danger because it disorients people, creates excessive expectations or … prioritises objectives that are clearly not priorities or are simply impossible to achieve."*
> —VLADIMIR PUTIN

Some populist movements have ended up as military dictatorships, fascist regimes, or socialist governments where free elections are suspended, arguably for the common good. In other cases, rigged elections are used to consolidate or confirm the leader's power. Minority rights, an anchor principle of liberal democracies, can be ignored or violated in such controlled circumstances.

The rights of those seen as abusers can easily be reduced or eliminated to protect the common good. In addition, the rights of government officials may be extended to exceed the rule of law, effectively placing them above the law. Ultimately, the critical question becomes: *How do I know that what is being advocated and done is for the benefit and well-being of all citizens?*

5. **Populism is benevolent and cannot be abused.**

If only this were real and true! In reality, things backed by large groups of people need not be benevolent. In a society with diverse interests and needs, a populist agenda can easily favour one group and disadvantage another. Populism can become reverse elitism. That is to say, the political and economic elite who once exploited the working class can become the victims of an emerging elitism, within a recently empowered working class. Both behaviours reflect class prejudice. Populist altruism can become quite selective.

One up side of populism comes from forcing elites to discuss and address issues they traditionally prefer to ignore. But the populist credo that "people are always right" can have dangerous consequences on minority rights and the rule of law. In addition, expectations can be raised beyond the political and economic system's capacity to realistically achieve them. If uncontrolled, a spirit of benevolence can raise expectations and create false hopes.

6. **Populist reform movements benefit from their honest simplicity.**

In western democracies, populist movements and parties are often the result of political dissatisfaction. Much of this dissatisfaction comes from a growing feeling that the political establishment does not want to adequately address important political issues like the fallout from increased globalization and freer trade, illegal immigration, lax border security, relatively high inner-city unemployment, etcetera.

> *"Populists often ask the right questions but give the wrong answers."*
> —CAS MUDDE

In many cases, the answers proposed by populists are flawed. Often, simple answers are based on the illusion that "one size fits all." Such strategies work about as well in the world of politics as they do in the world of shoes. Rarely can a policy decision be found to be equally good for all the people. In our material world, in any society of equals, some citizens are bound to be more equal than others.

Social problems can be significantly complicated by the intricate inter-connections, relationships, and inter-dependencies that exist in politico-economic systems. Complex social problems require diverse, concerted, and inclusive approaches. Selective, exclusive, or simple approaches rarely address these problems effectively, or in a manner that can be sustained over time.

Often, in addressing one problem you can create another. For example, a populist platform that seeks to redistribute more of a nation's wealth to the working class poor (like increasing the minimum wage or minimum annual income) can result in increased public debt, price inflation, and unemployment. Each of these outcomes can trigger serious problems in their own right.

In the final analysis, discerning consumers should expect limited honesty from a political world, focused on the craft of persuasion, where next to nothing is ever simple or straight forward.

Critical Questions for Discerning Minds: Dealing with Populist Rhetoric

★ ★ ★ ★ ★ ★

1. How can I tell when something is too good to be true?
2. What do I already know and what do I need to find out to make a responsible decision?
3. What is being advocated? What benefits are promised? What costs or re-percussions can be realistically expected?
4. What costs or repercussions are recognized by leadership? What costs are currently ignored or down played? What do critics and opponents have to say?
5. What is at stake? Who stands to gain? Who will benefit most? Who stands to lose? Who will be most harmed? Where do I fit in?
6. Is this ultimately a choice between good and not so good, good and bad, or bad and worse? What evidence can I use to support my judgement?
7. In this matter, how can I sort facts from opinions, substance from myth, and perspective from emotional reaction?
8. How do I know that what is being advocated is not an over-simplification of complex realities?
9. How is this idea and/or leader empowering, growth oriented, or constructive?
10. How is this idea and/or leader demeaning or negative?
11. What am I being sold? What am I not being told?

12. What makes this idea an improvement that can be sustained or built upon over time?

13. Is there consistency between what this leadership advocates and what it actually practices?

14. How feasible, realistic, and workable are proposed actions and goals? What evidence can I use to support my judgement?

15. How do I know that proposed programs and goals are not dependent on a single leader or group?

16. How do I know that proposed programs will not trample on existing democratic and civil rights?

17. How do I know that what is advocated and done is for the benefit and well-being of all citizens?

18. How do I know that what is being advocated and done will not fix one thing while wrecking another?

19. What other options are available and what are their benefits and costs?

> *"Pundits talk about 'populist rage' as a way to trivialize the anger and fear coursing through the middle class."*
> —ELIZABETH WARREN

20. Overall, which available option is the best and right thing to do?

21. Will this decision reflect well on me as my legacy? Is this how I want to be remembered?

An Experience Worth Noting: Revisiting Benny Who?

★ ★ ★ ★ ★ ★

My father, Mario Bolotta, spent most of the Second World War serving in the *Carabinieri*, Italy's royal military police force. On April 29, 1945, he was in Milan when the bodies of Benito Mussolini, his mistress, Clara Petacci, along with 14 other fascist leaders, were dumped in Milan's Piazzale Loreto. Mussolini and his mistress were captured attempting to escape into neutral Switzerland and executed by partisan freedom fighters. Although officially off-duty, my father was one of many police officers in the area on that day. This dumping spot was highly symbolic because, eight months earlier, fascists and Nazis publicly displayed the bodies of 15 executed partisans in the same square.

What my father saw that day was a very dark side of humanity. The angry crowd of citizens turned violently on their dead leader. They spit on, threw refuse at, urinated on, kicked, and beat the fascist cadavers with wooden clubs. Mussolini's face was so badly beaten, it was virtually unrecognizable. Some of these angry citizens were former supporters of the fascist regime, now donning the self-preserving mask of plausible deniability. Some were communists, who also favoured dictatorship, but were ideologically the arch enemies of fascism. Many were Italians who had lost loved ones during the war. They felt betrayed by all the fascist propaganda and lies. The bodies were eventually strung up on meat hooks and hung upside-down on the metal girders of a gasoline station under construction.

My father had been a supporter of fascism. His cousin, Francesco Bolotta, had been the *podestà:* (principal fascist authority) in our village. Known affectionately by his nickname, *Ciccio di Manghetta*, he was one of the few fascists who was

not arrested and punished after the fall of fascism. This was largely due to the fact that he treated the villagers firmly but fairly. He believed in discipline and strong government, but not in the excessive abuses of the absolute power enjoyed by fascists in Italy. One abusive practice involved the forced feeding of castor oil to dissidents, to make them soil themselves as public humiliation. According to villagers, my uncle never resorted to such abuses.

My grandmother, Maria Manfredi, often told a story about this remarkable uncle. During the mid 1930s, civilians were asked to help fortify the

Figure 5.2: Francesco and Maria Bolotta, celebrating their 50th wedding anniversary, in 1977. (Courtesy of the Bolotta family).

Italian state, by donating their gold jewellery. The state used these donations on armaments. Her younger sister, Rosina, had donated her gold and received a metal ring, from the *podestà*, as a token of appreciation from the Italian state. This engraved ring proclaimed, "Oro Alla Patria" (Gold to the Fatherland).

My grandmother was a widow with four young children. When she reluctantly went to turn in her gold wedding ring, the *podestà* gave it back to her. He told her, "This is the only thing you have left from your husband. Go put this away some place safe. Your family has already done enough for the fatherland." She never forgot this gesture and they remained life-long friends. As fate would have it, in 1950, her daughter married into the Bolotta family.

When I visited this uncle in 1976, and 1980, he was still a staunch fascist, although he admitted that many, many mistakes had been made. He would patiently cut up pamphlets from rival political parties to use as toilet paper. The preferred pamphlets were those circulated by the communist party. Uncle Francesco confirmed my grandmother's account as "the only right thing to do, politics be damned!"

This experience taught me that any politics distracting people from the human imperative to do the right thing is a perpetrated evil. Entrusting power to the few, to effectively address the interests of the many, can be problematic at the best of times. Since people are incapable of governing themselves, without recurring conflicts, the political system must be recognized as a necessary evil.

Given this reality, political leaders must be watched carefully. Their claims must be fact checked, and their actions must be held accountable. A free press is vitally important to help hold elected officials accountable. Any politician attacking freedom of the press has ulterior motives, and quite often, something serious to conceal. Once the public trust has been betrayed, politicians must be removed from office, and made to pay for their misdeeds. Not that I am advocating what was ultimately done to Italy's fascist leader!

Many 'popular' things seem like good ideas at the time, but in retrospect, they are awkward and flawed. In this

Figure 5.3: Making a popular fashion statement, in 1973. (Courtesy of the Bolotta family).

regard, politics is no different than fashion. Popularity comes and goes! The issues raised by populist movements are often genuine, but their solutions are usually unworkable, as highly emotional, simplistic, and reactive constructs. It is important for humans to be driven by the heart. But they must always take their head along for a more fruitful outcome. An old proverb states, "A mob has many heads but no brain."

The Trump experience provides discerning thinkers with a similar opportunity to reflect on the many dangers of populist rhetoric. To his credit, Trump tapped into growing voter dissatisfaction with seasoned and self-serving politicians. Like Mussolini in Italy, he then milked this disillusionment to acquire the minimum support base necessary to assume power. Like Mussolini, Trump ran on the promise of making his broken nation great again.

Like Mussolini, Trump exploited the worst fears of his supporters. He then relentlessly used dirty tactics to demonize his enemies. Like Mussolini, Trump told his people what they wanted to hear. Once in power, there were plenty of scapegoats to blame for not delivering on those unrealistic promises.

Like Mussolini, Trump enjoyed the company of young female companions. Early in 2018, the *Wall Street Journal* broke the news of Trump's alleged affair with an adult film star, said to have happened in 2006, one year after his marriage to Melania. According to the paper, just before the 2016 election, a Trump lawyer used a shell company to funnel $130,000 in hush money to the porn star. But she had already spilled the beans in a detailed interview with *InTouch* magazine, in 2011. Apparently, Trump is about as effective and endearing in the bedroom, as he is as POTUS. When reflecting on populist movements and their 'great' leaders, it is important to remember the words of British historian John Dalberg-Acton. Lord Acton said, "Power tends to corrupt, and absolute power corrupts absolutely. Great men are almost always bad men." A person's moral sense can be easily compromised in the pursuit of greater power.

Trump has demonstrated a marked propensity to occasionally embrace fascist sentiments. He has tweeted Mussolini quotes because he found them "interesting." He has openly admired the strong governments of dictators like China's Xi Jinping, Russia's Vladimir Putin, and even North Korea's paranoid Kim Jong-un. Yet he has been harshly critical of government decisions made by democratic allies like Canada, France, Britain and Germany. In my experience, courting fascism is always a dangerous proposition. Fascism has ultimately manifested as state sponsored capitalism with state sanctioned murder. Regretfully, around the globe, current waves of populism seem to be turning against liberal democracy. Trump's proto-fascist inclinations need to be held in check to protect American democracy.

Critical Thinking Checkpoint Two

★ ★ ★ ★ ★ ★

Reflect on the following probing question to apply your critical thinking skills.

Will Trump's flirtations with proto-fascist ideas, leaders, and styles of government harm or help American democracy in the long run?

JUDGEMENT CRITERIA On what would a reasonable and objective person base this decision?	MY DECISION
☐	
☐	
☐	
☐	
☐	
SUPPORTING EVIDENCE What evidence can be used to confirm this decision as sound?	**RELIABILITY** How do I know my sources are objective, accurate and trustworthy? Can I find other sources to independently corroborate the facts?

The Parable of the Unpopular Populist

★ ★ ★ ★ ★ ★

The following post-modern parable depicts how populist movements can be hijacked to promote an anti-elitist agenda of negativity and a divisive climate of anger and fear.

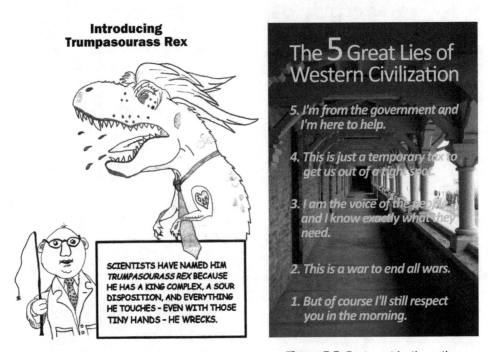

Introducing Trumpasourass Rex

SCIENTISTS HAVE NAMED HIM TRUMPASOURASS REX BECAUSE HE HAS A KING COMPLEX, A SOUR DISPOSITION, AND EVERYTHING HE TOUCHES - EVEN WITH THOSE TINY HANDS - HE WRECKS.

The **5** Great Lies of Western Civilization

5. I'm from the government and I'm here to help.

4. This is just a temporary tax to get us out of a tight spot.

3. I am the voice of the people and I know exactly what they need.

2. This is a war to end all wars.

1. But of course I'll still respect you in the morning.

Figure 5.4: Pencil sketch by the author.   **Figure 5.5:** Poster art by the author.

A billionaire misogynist spent his charmed life trying to be popular with beautiful women and powerful people. In time, he became bitter towards the many "elitists" who dared to shun him. First, he was not accepted by the wealthy elite because he came from new money and did not have a truly upper class pedigree. Next, he was shunned by the casino and gaming elite because he was arrogant and brash. He was also shunned by the celebrity elite. As a reality TV star, he was seen as a "flash in the pan" with terminal appeal.

He was shunned by the political elite because he was seen as a proto-fascist with no impulse control. At first, he resorted to throwing stones at the elites, from his tower of glass and steel in the middle of a great metropolis. When this proved boring, he started courting bitter people to make him their leader. He milked their bitterness, fear, and disillusionment all the way to the highest office in the land. "Now," he thought, "I will fix all the elites who ever shunned me!" But the shunning continued.

One by one, his key advisors and senior staff had to be fired because they either refused to do his bidding, or they were a bit too zealous in doing it. He was shunned by political elites from his own party who refused to pass his ill prepared reforms. The elitist "fake news" media shunned him by refusing to admit that everything he lied about was absolutely true. They preferred to report only what could be verified with facts.

In the end, he got very little work done because of all the controversy being stirred up and all the government shutdowns being threatened. "This serves them right," he fumed angrily, "Because my subjects refuse to think and do exactly what I tell them to. I am an expert on their pain."

He fully expected that the bile of the bitterly disposed would protect him from small, petty matters like the truth, the rule of law, minority rights, racist sentiments, having to talk things carefully through with diverse stakeholders before taking action, and anything else that questioned his ability or authority. In the end, he resorted to distraction to obscure the way forward, and hatemongering to keep his subjects fighting among themselves. This made it less likely that they would rise up against him.

CHAPTER SIX

WHEN MEAN SPIRIT TRUMPS FAIR PLAY

FOR MOST OF his adult life, Donald John Trump has been a man on a mission. As a young entrepreneur and real estate developer, he carefully cultivated his public image as *"The Donald."* He presented as a cool, young, bright, cocky, and successfully wealthy tycoon with diverse interests. *The Donald* used exaggeration, hyperbole, and braggadocio to cement the impression that everything he touched turned into gold. The truth is quite different from this golden boy mythology.

When he was 13 years old, his parents shipped him off to the New York Military Academy (a private boarding school), in the hope that the discipline of the academy would help to positively redirect his energy. Donald's attraction to the bright lights of Manhattan was one of their concerns. He was able to complete his formal education and assumed the reins of the family's real estate business in 1971. He changed the company name to the Trump Organization and focused on building and renovating office towers, hotels, casinos, and golf courses.

> *"A wise therapist taught me that anger is the emotion we snatch up to avoid less comfortable feelings— confusion, fear, sadness."*
> —JILL HERZIG

In 1985, Trump finally acquired the historic *Mar-a-Lago* estate. He had offered a generous $28 million for the property but was turned down. Frustrated, he claimed anti-Semitism as one of the reasons for this rejection. When challenged about this wild claim, he revealed that he was planning to bring many Jewish friends to the property. The original estate had been built in 1920 by heiress and socialite Marjorie Merriweather Post. Ironically, she envisioned her home as a future winter retreat for American presidents. Trump eventually got the furnished property for $8 million by purchasing neighbouring beachfront property and threatening construction that would block *Mar-a-Lago's* pristine ocean view. Eventually, Trump used the estate as a second home and an expensive private club, for those who could afford the $100,000 initiation fee plus annual dues.

This anecdote provides insight into the Trump psyche as well as the 'old money' elitist mentality trying to keep the brash upstart away from their affluent enclave. Trump had experienced this condescending exclusionist/elitist behaviour before, when he first tried to break into the major league of real estate development in Manhattan, against his own father's advice. He was put off by being shunned. Over time, pent-up anger can create a mean spirit in people.

By 2016, Trump and his businesses had been involved in over 3,500 state and federal legal actions. In slightly more than half the cases he was actively suing another party. In the rest, he was defending himself and his business practices. Trump has demonstrated a tendency to use lawsuits to annoy and intimidate business rivals. Sometimes, the threat of legal action persuaded opponents to acquiesce or move on. On other occasions, some opponents decided the nuisance and expense of legal action was not in their long-term interests. When being sued, Trump demonstrated a tendency to draw out proceedings as long as possible, in the hope of securing a favourable out-of-court settlement, where a formal admission of liability was avoided.

> *"Holding on to anger is like grasping a hot coal with the intent of throwing it at someone else; you are the one who gets burned."*
> —BUDDHA

One classic example of this strategy at work is the *Trump University* fiasco. This limited liability company (LLC) was founded by Trump and two associates, in 2004, to operate a profitable real estate training program. The cost of the individual courses offered to clients ranged from $1,500 to $35,000.

In 2005, Trump was formally notified by State of New York authorities that using the word "university" was misleading and violated state law. After a second notification in 2010, the business name was finally changed to *Trump Entrepreneurial Institute*. In addition, Trump was found liable for failing to obtain a business licence for the operation. The State of New York filed a $40 million civil suit in 2013, alleging that Trump University made false statements and defrauded consumers. In addition, two class-action law suits were filed in federal court, against Trump University, Trump personally, and his companies. Judge Gonzalo P. Curiel was assigned to oversee the two class-action lawsuits.

During the presidential election campaign, Trump publicly criticized this judge alleging unavoidable bias in any of his rulings because of his Mexican heritage. After all, Trump was advocating the immediate building of a *Great*

Border Wall for which Mexico would be paying. This feeble attempt at intimidation fell flat on its face. Shortly after Trump won the election, the parties involved in all three pending court cases agreed to an out-of-court settlement. Trump paid $25 million but denied any wrongdoing.

Although Trump has never filed for personal bankruptcy, his hotel and casino businesses have been declared bankrupt six times. This strategy was used between 1991 and 2009 to re-negotiate debt with banks,

> *"I do play with the bankruptcy laws—they are good for me."*
>
> *"I've used the laws of this country to pare debt ... We'll have a company. We'll throw it in a chapter. We'll negotiate with the banks. We'll make a fantastic deal. You know, it's like on The Apprentice. It's not personal. It's just business."*
>
> —DONALD TRUMP

investors, and creditors. In each case, Trump was able to use Chapter 11 bankruptcy to continue to operate over-leveraged hotel and casino businesses in Atlantic City and New York. Ultimately, this allowed him to legally pay much less than the amount actually owed to banks, investors, and creditors. His money troubles began with the dramatic failure of the lavish *Trump Taj Mahal* in Atlantic City. When it opened in 1990, it was the most expensive casino complex ever built, but its gambling machines were calibrated to pay-out less than normal winnings to patrons.

Critics have often remarked that Trump manages to come out of bad and over-extended investments relatively unscathed. But his bankers, creditors, and shareholders must often settle for a fraction of what they were entitled to from the enterprise. In some investment projects, Trump put up little more than the Trump name, in return for a large up-front fee and exclusive rights to manage the property. This left other investors and creditors to assume all the risks.

Toronto's infamous *Trump International Hotel and Tower* project is one classic example of this strategy being played out. In the end, the new owners had to pay the Trump Organization close to $6 million, in 2017, to remove the Trump name from the project, even though the Trump Organization had no ownership stake in the property. The project was plagued with insufficient funding, sluggish condo and retail space sales, construction delays, and lawsuits almost from its inception.

In a 2016 analysis of Trump's entrepreneurial career, *The Economist* concluded his "... performance [from 1985 to 2016] has been mediocre compared with stock market and property in New York." The golden boy clearly laid his share of rotten eggs. In the aggressive New York business environment, Trump learned to be as aggressive as needed to get ahead. It appears that over time he liked playing hardball because he could see others being intimidated by his tough guy routine. With the pent-up anger from being shunned by many of the 'elite' circles he wanted to join, Trump's contempt for them slowly and constantly intensified. He resented being treated as a second-rate outsider. He never forgot and he never forgave. In time, they became convenient target groups for his bile.

Trump's contempt for the political world, and the political elite that infested it, came naturally. He used every law available to him to minimize tax payments and to take full advantage of opportunities to get away with paying less than his fair share

> "*I fight very hard to pay as little tax as possible.*"
> —DONALD TRUMP

of debts and obligations. In his mind, the villains were the incompetent political elites who passed the laws he was using to full advantage. He would have been foolish not to exploit every available opportunity.

In time, *The Donald* began to show contempt for and anger towards all groups he saw as pretentious and elitist—socialites, academics, scientists, politicians, journalists, business moguls, celebrity performers, etcetera. Contempt for so many 'entitled' groups can sour one's disposition and demeanour over time. In the end, mean spirit can easily prevail. Even groups that accepted Trump into the fold were often viewed with contempt.

The time invested in creating a 'strongman' persona or a personal brand can be fruitful for an entrepreneur, especially when one's notion of leadership involves constantly shining the spotlight squarely on the great leader. In the 1970s and 1980s very few leadership models focused on servant leadership. There was still considerable cachet connected to the 'great man with all the answers' model of leadership. And so, *The Donald* did his best to become one.

Unfortunately, somewhere along the way, he started to believe his own hype and propaganda. Trump started to believe he was better and smarter than most. He believed he could do no wrong. He started to believe that he should never be expected to apologize for anything. In time, Trump became a caricature of his narcissistic self.

But deep down inside, his sheltered life and combatively hungry spirit always left him longing for something else to prove. His public persona demonstrates toughness, success, and "the art of the deal." But Trump's recent behaviour also confirms an innate insecurity, a propensity to exaggerate and embellish, a tendency to use the truth only when convenient, a hyper-sensitivity to criticism, and a demand for unquestioned loyalty from others. This exposes a remarkable double

> *"Always remember this fundamental truth about Trump: He has always felt like the guy on the outside looking in, the guy people wouldn't accept in their social circles and wouldn't let into their club. Stuffing it in their faces is the primal motivation for everything in his life."*
> —CHRIS CILLIZZA

standard. Trump is scathing in his criticism of others with effectively little impulse control. This is especially the case for those he considers "bad people" or disappointments. At the same time, he cannot deal constructively with any criticism directed at him.

Regrettably, these qualities help render him unfit as a head of state, especially for the United States of America. Trump often comes across as an irreverent insult comic, schoolyard bully, and curmudgeon. Given that his every act and message has repercussions around the world, Trump should hold himself to a much higher standard. His behaviour should reflect the diplomacy, integrity, and tact required of his prestigious leadership role in America and throughout the free world. Instead, Trump often comports himself as an aggressive radio 'shock jockey' or a seedy 'ambush TV' host.

One example of his failing to meet the standard of a dignified head of state arises from his public bullying and mockery of his chosen attorney general, Jeff Sessions. Those who fail to show undivided loyalty to *The Donald* (even when they conscientiously object on a point of principle) instantly become targets for attack and ridicule. Trump vindictively turned on his attorney general a few months after hiring Sessions. The attorney general's offence was to recuse himself, due to a possible conflict of interest, instead of continuing to do the president's bidding in formal investigations into Russia's confirmed pro-Trump meddling in the election that brought him to power.

For his conscientious decision, the attorney general was publicly ridiculed by the president, in the hope of forcing a resignation or reversal. Clearly, Trump was very concerned about the FBI investigation into connections between Trump

> *"Sessions should have never recused himself, and if he was going to recuse himself, he should have told me before he took the job and I would have picked somebody else."*
> —DONALD TRUMP

campaign leadership and Russian agents trying to discredit Hillary Clinton, to improve the chances of getting a more favourable president into the White House. Trump appears terrified that the FBI investigation he has long called "a witch hunt" may uncover something serious, implicating him or those close to him. First, he fired FBI director James Comey when he did not like how Comey was conducting the investigation. Trump was hoping for a far more superficial approach.

Trump reluctantly approved the appointment of Robert Mueller, a former FBI director, as special counsel to lead the ongoing investigation into possible collusion and Russian interference. He became annoyed when Mueller impanelled a grand jury in Washington. This made it easier to subpoena records, get sworn witness testimony, and potentially issue indictments. Trump became furious when Mueller expressed an interest in looking closely into Trump's records. He strongly hinted at a willingness to fire Mueller if he were to look too closely into Trump's personal finances.

> *"The president plays with fire when he attacks his military, law enforcement, and Justice people. They are the bulwark of our safety. Demeaning them harms all of us."*
> —ROBERT RABIN

The backlash from this brash statement came from all sides of the bitterly partisan Capitol. This forced Trump's hand and thwarted his effort to control the investigation he feared. Instead, he began a series of calculated distractions to take news media and public attention away from the investigation, including picking fights with the homicidal dictator of North Korea and the "dishonest" media.

> *"I said, 'Please don't be too nice.' Like when you guys put somebody in the car and you're protecting the head. You know? The way you put the hand over [the head], like 'Don't hit their head' and they've just killed somebody.... I said, 'You can take the hand away, OK?'"*
> —DONALD TRUMP

A second example of Trump's failure to meet the standard of a dignified head of state is reflected in his propensity to court violent rhetoric, in a nation too often victimized by excessive violence. In July of 2017, during a speech on immigration, *The Donald* openly instructed a gathering of law enforcement officials in Long Island, New York, "don't be too nice" with the suspects and thugs being arrested. This may have been a fitting adlib and pep talk for a police state, but not for a constitutional democracy.

Condoning police brutality (even in jest) is unconscionable. In light of police shootings and beatings of civilians across America, now under scrutiny for excessive use of force, such commentary brings the office of the President of the United States into disrepute. The fact that a disproportionate number of these victims are African-Americans makes the matter racially charged.

No sensitivity is evident for innocent victims and their families. No respect is shown for the rule of law in a civil society, preventing law enforcement officers from becoming a law unto themselves. No importance is attached to the principle of fundamental justice that assumes a person to be innocent until proven guilty, beyond reasonable doubt, by a jury of peers. No understanding of or appreciation for community based policing is demonstrated. The respectful treatment of all civilians is clearly not a priority. Trump appears quite comfortable incorporating qualities of a proto-fascist police state into the American model.

A third major strike against Trump's presidential fitness is evident in his guarded response to the Charlottesville riots leading to the death of three Americans. His original equal denouncement of violence "on all sides" lumped neo-Nazis, KKK white supremacists, and fascists with those conscientious Americans protesting against fascism, bigotry, and racism. This glaring error was corrected only after two days of relentless criticism across the nation.

The very next day, this correction was negated by *The Donald's* rambling ad-libbed commentary blaming the media for twisting his words, while conveniently using only selected portions of his original condemnation, deliberately leaving out all the damaging words. When radical extremist groups like anti-black, anti-Jewish, and white fascists are made to feel they may have a sympathetic ear in the White House, this does not bode well for civility and tolerance in America. Responsibility for any subsequent escalation of hate crimes in America must be blamed squarely on this proto-fascist president.

> *"Our movement is a movement based on love.... We all share the same home, the same dreams and the same hope for a better future. A wound inflicted on one member of our community is a wound inflicted upon us all."*
> —DONALD TRUMP

Not that a fourth strike should be necessary, but a clear fourth strike against presidential integrity occurred during Trump's August 22 rally in Phoenix, Arizona. Trump enjoys considerable support in Arizona, where many people see his border wall as improving national security. This was a clearly orchestrated event to rally his base of support, manipulate uninformed Americans, and take nasty shots at Trump's designated villains. While thousands protested outside, Trump ridiculed protesters from inside the convention centre and told his supporters that very few actually showed up to protest. Eventually, the police used tear gas to disperse protesters.

This rally was supposed to focus on national unity. Instead, it turned into a 75-minute attack on all those opposed to Trump's agenda, including (without being named) Arizona senator John McCain, who was recovering from brain cancer surgery. McCain was blamed for casting the decisive vote against Trump's failed attempt to "repeal and replace *Obamacare*." Most of his rambling speech was spent attempting to unpeel and displace what Trump had said about the Charlottesville rioters and to vilify the dishonest media for twisting his excellent words.

The use of campaign style rallies to attempt to cover up past mistakes and reverse declining polls can be dangerous in the charge of a thin-skinned narcissist with limited impulse control. Rallies may be a great vehicle for basking in the spotlight and performing safely before an adorning throng. But rallies drawing a hyper-partisan crowd can be counterproductive when trying to build bridges, to engage diverse groups, and to heal divisions. A scathing attack on the integrity of a free press runs counter to democratic principles. If discerning citizens read between the lines of Trump's demagogic language, racial and ethnic undertones, and hints of villainous treason are not hard to detect.

> *"And yes, by the way, they [media] are trying to take away our history and our heritage. You see that ... I really think they don't like our country. I really believe that."*
> —DONALD TRUMP

Immediately after the Phoenix rally, South African comedian Trevor Noah had an interesting insight into the increased polarization being caused by Trump's leadership. Juxtaposing images of Americans in denial and protesters being injured in delicate places, Noah concluded, "Yup, that's Trump's America people. One side doesn't see anything wrong. The other side feels like it's being shot in the dick." American comedian Steven Colbert was even more blunt, referring to Trump as "America's first 'racist grandpa' president" after the Charlottesville riots.

In the absence of a clear, firm, and direct moral compass from their president, Americans have to look to one another to define the moral high ground. Regrettably, close to 33% of the population drank the Kool-Aid® and have settled firmly on Trump's side, allegedly against the political elite. This seems to be the core base of his support. While politics is usually a game of addition by persuasion, the anti-politician Trump shows no interest in catering to anyone other than the people he can count on.

Even more regrettably, the *Racist Deplorables of America* also have an opportunity to white-wash this search for the moral high ground, with their fear mongering and hate. In the end, the American people will have to determine the kind of society they wish to live in. Hopefully, this division will not lead to a second civil war. But some positive action is needed to address the injustices being perpetrated under the guise of returning America to greatness.

I agree wholeheartedly with Canadian activist Craig Kielburger. When we care to, we can change the world for the better, one small step at a time. But to make it so, to paraphrase Mahatma Gandhi, we must be the change we wish to see in the world.

> *"Collectively we have what it takes to create a just and peaceful world, but we must work together and share our talents. We all need one another to find happiness within ourselves and within the world."*
>
> —CRAIG KIELBURGER

The American psyche has long supported the principles of rugged individualism and fair play. In addition, Americans have long demonstrated a soft spot for the underdog. Trump may be an underdog taking on the political establishment, and he may be right about the need to deal with the entitled and self-serving political elite. But this does not grant him permission to behave in an uncivil manner toward them or any other Americans. Bullies are ultimately cowards preying on weakness. The silence

> *"Every person must live their life as a model for others."*
>
> —ROSA PARKS

of bystanders enables them. Confrontation disarms them. This confrontation cannot be violent without further injuring a fragile democracy. It is important to confront the harmful ideas expressed and the person responsible, but not the presidency itself.

Seven months into his mandate, Americans started to publicly confront Trump's leadership. Corporate executives resigned *en masse* from his business advisory council. Green companies approved carbon emission reducing initiatives in response to his climate change denial, disbanding of the federal climate change advisory panel, and abrupt withdrawal from the Paris Climate Accord. The mother of the civil rights activist murdered in Charlottesville publicly refused to take the president's phone call. Growing groups of protesters appear everywhere he is speaking.

With increasing confrontations, Trump is visibly not enjoying his presidential workload as much as he expected. He enjoys the attention, but not the criticism.

> *"Donald Trump isn't a president—he's just playing one on TV."*
> —TREVOR NOAH

Some critics observed that after eight months in office, he appeared tired, confused, and disinterested. Luckily, he has had to face very few crises not of his own making. After his first year in office, only the devastating hurricanes in Texas, Florida, and Puerto Rico were crises beyond Trump's control. Yet, he still found a way to aggravate the situation in Puerto Rico by using condescending language when responding to the devastated island's pleas for immediate help.

Some observers suggest that his time in the White House is winding down. In one scenario, he is not expected to run for a second term and the vice-president is quietly building a transition team. Based on the current rate of deterioration, and the ongoing advancement of the Mueller investigation towards impeachment territory, I am not sure that he will complete a full first term, unless this rapid descent is reversed. The business model he practiced so diligently provides a plausible face-saving exit strategy:

> *When the going gets tough, cut your losses, negotiate a favourable settlement and get out. Find a scapegoat to blame. Spin an argument that confirms your departure as a success story. Repeat it often. Assure people that they will be left in good hands. No apologies. No regrets.*

Trump had this strategy well in place during the election campaign. His unsubstantiated declaration, "This election is rigged," was repeated often to provide a plausible explanation for the eventuality of a defeat at the polls. When he won, the claim was quickly dropped. A similar articulation can be easily fabricated to explain his premature exit:

Dishonest media and other enemies of America will not let me provide you with the kind of government you deserve. They are making everything about me. You deserve better. For the good of the nation, I will turn the reins over to my hand-picked successor. He is a very good man. I will continue to support and advise him. Together, we will make America great again.

Unfortunately, this rhetoric and exit strategy would not change the sad reality that Trump is leaving a more polarized, divided, and dysfunctional America than he inherited from his predecessor. Without a corrective strategy, the longer he stays in the White House, the greater the slide downward. There is no denying that Trump enjoys being in the spotlight much more than he enjoys the frustrations and workload required of the President of the United States. If Trump ever comes to enjoy basking in the spotlight enough to seek a second term in office, he may require a bloody conflict to help galvanize his tenure.

> *"I think it [the presidency] should be a very powerful office, and I think the president should be a very strong man who uses without hesitation every power that the position yields; but because of this fact I believe that he should be closely watched by the people [and] held to a strict accountability by them."*
> —THEODORE ROOSEVELT

With a base of hardcore supporters hovering below 40 percent, any re-election bid would prove quite challenging without a galvanizing conflict.

As the re-election of George W. Bush painfully reinforced in 2004, American voters are reluctant to dump, even a weak president, during a war or time of serious conflict. In a very close election after the horrors of 9/11, Bush strategists used the *war on terrorism* to help defeat John Kerry and stay in power. Historically, there are numerous other examples of American voters favouring incumbents during times of serious conflict. Trump can easily instigate a bloody conflict with Iran or North Korea to improve his chances of re-election and to extend his 'emergency' powers even further. Regrettably, his advisors know this sad reality all too well. Discerning voters must be vigilant to hold the entire Trump team accountable for all their choices, including all failures to act as responsible and faithful servants of the people.

Needless to say, Trump will have a long list of villains to blame for every one of his failures to serve the greater good of the American people. More blatantly,

> *"He [Trump] played to his base and he treated his other listeners, the rest of the people who have been disturbed about him or oppose him, he treated them basically as 'I don't care, I don't give a damn what you think, because you're frankly like the enemy."*
>
> —DAVID GERGEN

Trump will have a convoluted rationale explaining why his choices all represented clever triumphs for America. Much discernment will be needed to sort through the hype and misinformation with which the American people will be bombarded. Sadly, when America most needed a warm spirited statesman, to foster the process of healing and redirection, they got a shameless self-promoter with a mean spirit and sour disposition. During his tumultuous first year in office, Trump went out of his way to:

- Give patriotism lessons to professional football players (after personally using several deferments to avoid military service, during the Vietnam War, and then publicly criticizing war hero John McCain for being captured by the enemy);

- Console the grieving widow of fallen soldier LaDavid Johnson with the words: "He knew what he signed up for but I guess it still hurts";

- Cut funding for social programs (health care, education, the arts, and environmental protection) to allow a substantial tax cut for the wealthy;

- Criticize devastated Puerto Ricans for not doing enough to help themselves and "wanting everything done for them," after a hurricane he called *not* "a real catastrophe like Katrina."

Today's America is clearly a nation divided, and has been for quite some time. The Trump experience has only exacerbated and accentuated this reality. Clearly, this divisiveness can be exploited by mean spirited politicians with self-serving agendas. Discernment is needed to learn from past experience and build upon it, rather than foolishly allowing others to continue perverting the requisite healing.

Together is Better

★ ★ ★ ★ ★ ★

Americans need to come together to heal their divided nation. The public confrontation of proto-fascist inclinations must continue, but it must not be allowed to escalate into violent clashes with police or extremist groups looking for an excuse to attack. Freedom of speech is an important component of American democracy. But this expression must be violence-free, destruction-free, and hate-free. Freedom of speech is forfeited by such uncivil and illegal actions. In addition, such actions play into the proto-fascist addenda by fuelling the argument that a crackdown against violent protesters is needed to control an unruly mob and preserve law and order.

> *"Darkness cannot drive out darkness; only light can do that. Hate cannot drive out hate; only love can do that."*
>
> *"Non-violence means avoiding not only external physical violence but also internal violence of spirit. You not only refuse to shoot a man but you refuse to hate him."*
> —MARTIN LUTHER KING JR.

The non-violence advocated by civil rights leader Martin Luther King Jr. during the 1960s is equally appropriate today. Powerful news images of people peacefully marching arm-in-arm to overcome injustice, being needlessly violated by law officers and police dogs, helped turn the tide across America. Graphic images confirmed that this was not right or just treatment of one human being by another. Eventually the discrimination and hate rhetoric was exposed and disarmed with minimal violent confrontation.

Fighting hate with more hate will only encourage the ultimate triumph of brute force. Radicalized hate mongers, claiming to take back their country from those who would bastardize it, need to be confronted and stopped. When the government does not act to stop it, citizens are compelled to become engaged, but not to fight fire with fire. That would only succeed in bring the 'morally right' down to the level of the 'deplorables.'

Watching quietly from the sidelines empowers the oppressor not the victim. Therefore, it is important to stand together to show support for what is right and decent. But this public manifestation is only a first step. The problem is that often it becomes the only step. To succeed, any public demonstration requires follow-up to sustain any positive inertia. The realization of lasting change requires a process not an event. Positive social change is most often evolutionary not revolutionary.

A show of personal conviction and solidarity is an important first step that must

> *"If you are neutral in situations of injustice, you have chosen the side of the oppressor."*
> —DESMOND TUTU

then be followed by honest dialogue. Until Americans talk openly and honestly with each other, about their differences, real progress will be limited. Until white Americans feel comfortable talking to non-white Americans about social issues, rights, and dreams for the future, real progress will be fleeting. Such dialogue must look past obvious physical differences to recognize and reinforce the inner and spiritual qualities of goodness transcending humanity.

It is important in such dialogue to not let the lowest common denominator within a group be used to define the entire group. Such negativity would only reduce all groups to charter membership in the *United Deplorables of America*. In any honest and constructive dialogue, it is important to avoid playing the blame game. This practice only causes resentment on all sides. Blame helps neither the transgressor nor the victim to grow. In fact, it can be used by skilled manipulators to thwart or highjack the conversation. The most important game to be played is the 'moving forward together' game.

> *"Please accept my resignation. I do not want to belong to any club that will accept people like me as a member."*
> —GROUCHO MARX

Human beings need to stand together, talk together, and break bread together to be better able to walk in each other's shoes. This will help rebuild and revitalize not only the American Dream but the entire human journey. Key constructive dialogue points include:

> *How do you really feel?*
> *Why do you feel this way?*
> *What are your hopes and dreams for the future?*
> *How can I help?*

This process of 'civil' dialogue requires the following steps, from discerning citizens, to break through and systematically undo the current impasse and to promote the growth of goodness in America.

1. Become personally invested—peacefully confront or challenge questionable behaviour and recognize the problems created (use your head and your voice, not your fists);

2. Use honest dialogue to carefully analyze causes and consequences to determine the full extent of the problem (from the perspective of diverse stakeholders);

3. Use honest dialogue to carefully assess all viable alternatives and their benefits and repercussions;

4. Force elected politicians to take a principled stand and then hold them to it (talk is cheap);

5. Replace the negativity of problem makers (wall builders) with the positive energy of solution finders (bridge builders);

6. Remain personally invested—do your personal part and remain vigilant that elected politicians do the right things in the right way;

7. Assess outcomes, celebrate progress and define a next growth step that can be taken together.

Confronting the current impasse will require a concerted, peaceful, principled, inclusive, and relentless approach. Justice and fair treatment do not happen spontaneously. It is naïve to think that any human made democracy has sufficient systemic safeguards in place to always ensure justice and fairness. Often, justice and fair treatment need to be made to happen through mindful effort.

Ultimately, discerning citizens need to develop both emotional intelligence and functional crap detection skills. Too often our crap detectors are not adequately calibrated. The gullible believe almost anything that supports their world view. The cynical, sometimes appearing to be locked in perpetual adolescence, reject most ideas coming their way as human, and therefore, flawed. Discerning citizens need carefully calibrated crap detectors, to avoid falling victim to deception or disillusionment. See if you can find the logical flaws and excessive *crappage* in the following Trump-like statements:

All politicians are bad. I am not a politician. Therefore, I am good.

The first statement is a sweeping generalization. The second is conjecture rather than fact. One is defined more by what one does, than what one claims to be. The third reflects the fallacy of single causation. Innate goodness cannot be confirmed because of a single act, association, or trait.

Critical Questions for Discerning Minds: Assessing Spirit and Fairness

1. What does Trump say when he sticks to his prepared speech?

2. What does Trump say when he departs from the prepared speech?

3. Is the message consistent? If not, which is the real Trump and more honest message? What proof do I have to support my judgement?

4. Is there consistency between what Trump advocates and what he actually practices?

5. What is being advocated? What benefits are promised? What costs or repercussions can be realistically expected?

6. What costs does Trump recognize? What costs are being ignored or down played? What am I not being told that I need to know?

7. What do knowledgeable supporters and opponents have to say? Which camp is most believable? What proof do I have to support my judgement?

8. What is at stake? Who stands to gain? Who will benefit most? Who stands to lose? Who will be most harmed? Where do I fit in?

9. In this matter, how can I sort facts from opinions, substance from myth, and reasoned perspective from emotional reaction?

10. How do I know that what is being advocated is not an over-simplification of complex realities? What proof is there that the matter has been carefully studied and diverse stakeholders have been consulted?

11. How feasible, realistic, and workable are proposed actions and goals? What evidence can I use to support my judgement?

12. How is this particular idea or message inclusive, growth oriented, or constructive in nature?

13. How is this particular idea or message mean spirited, demeaning, or negative?

14. What makes this idea an improvement that can be sustained or built on over time?

15. How do I know that what is being advocated and done will not fix one thing while wrecking another?

16. How do I know that proposed programs will not trample on existing democratic and civil rights?

17. How do I know that what is advocated and done is for the benefit and well-being of all citizens?

18. What other options are available and what are their benefits and costs?

19. Overall, which available option is the best and right thing to do?

20. Will supporting this idea or message make me proud? Is this how I want to be remembered?

> *"I am not the product of my circumstances. I am the product of my decisions."*
> —STEVEN R. COVEY

An Experience Worth Noting: Winning and Losing

★ ★ ★ ★ ★ ★

Sport has always been a useful release for me, an opportunity to take out my frustrations and play out my competitive instincts. By fulfilling these needs, athletics helped keep me calm, cool, and collected, the rest of the time. During my teaching career at Madonna High School, my competitive drive attracted me to coaching. For years, I coached the school's senior basketball team. Shortly after the birth of my daughter in 1982, I was coaching my homeroom team in an intramural floor hockey league organized by the Girl's Athletic Association. My Grade 12 homeroom had won the senior school championship three years in a row. With each championship came greater pressure to repeat. This pressure came primarily from within me, and this desire was reflected in everything we did as a team.

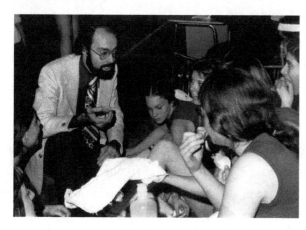

Figure 6.1: Coaching the senior basketball team, in 1976. (Courtesy of the Madonna High School Photography Club).

In retrospect, this focus on winning did my girls a disservice, since it set them up as "the team to beat." This often resulted in very hard fought contests. I rationalized that this additional adversity would help build character and bond the team closer together. This strong team bond was essential, in my system oriented approach to winning, where every player had a defined role to play.

While most other teams were just out there to have fun, I saw it as an opportunity to have the most fun possible by winning.

During a scoreless playoff game, in which we could not get ourselves untracked, I noticed that Patricia, one of our most reliable wingers, was just not her usual self. In fact, during the last few games, her effectiveness in going into the corners and coming out with the puck had been dropping. On the next line change, I asked Pat if everything was okay and she replied that it was. I asked her if she felt that she was fighting the puck and she emphatically said, "No!" We talked about a tactical adjustment and she agreed to try it.

On her next shift, she seemed even more tight, so I called her off in mid-shift to better explain the adjustment I wanted her to make with my reasons. She agreed that it made sense and that it was an easy adjustment to make. However, when she returned to the game, there was no sign of improvement. If anything, there had been a giant step backwards. Pat gave up the puck in the neutral zone and the other team got lucky and scored a goal, on a weird deflection off one of our defenders.

This time I shouted out to her from the bench, "Come on Patricia. Try it my way. Obviously, your way is not working, is it?" I happened to raise my voice just as the noise level in the gym dropped right down. Everyone in the gym heard my comments. Pat reacted by slamming her stick to the floor and shouting back, in tears, "It's not easy playing this game with cancer, let alone with you on my back! I'm doing the best I can." With that she disappeared into the dressing room.

I was left totally speechless. Her teammates were looking at each other in shock. None of us knew! Patricia had been keeping her leukemia a secret and the burden was taking its toll. My harsh contribution certainly did not help. I asked for a timeout and instructed the captain to take over the team. I followed Patricia into the dressing room. Pat and I had a long talk.

I told her that I had to go in for a series of tests because of a lump forming on my left knee, and that I too was keeping it a secret from everyone. I confided that I too was worried. She told me about her situation and how it was quite serious. Her doctor had told her not to play anymore contact sports. As we talked, players kept popping in with reports on the changing score. A couple of students stood guard at the entrance to the dressing room, so that we would not be disturbed.

We won that game 3-1 and proceeded to win the championship, but it really did not matter as much to me anymore. It meant a lot to Patricia though! She just had to go out a winner. She told me that she had been waiting to be on my team since Grade 9.

After graduating from Madonna, Patricia went on to York University before settling on a career in family law. She came back several times to visit with me, and we became good friends. Her cancer was effectively treated by her doctors, and eventually she was given a clean bill of health. I too have had to give up contact sports because of my knee problems, but my problems ended up being far less serious.

I learned something very important about winning through this experience. Life is not primarily designed to learn from winning. Most any fool can do that! Life challenges us to learn from losing. To take a loss and turn it into a learning experience, and therefore, a growth opportunity and 'moral' victory —that is the real challenge of life. Subsequent teams seemed a bit disappointed by my changed attitude towards winning. To be honest, for the rest of my stay at Madonna High School, my teams did not win another championship, although they always put in a valiant effort. On the other hand, each loss was no longer a total devastation.

The Trump experience provides discerning thinkers with ample opportunity to reflect on winning and losing. Trump's meticulously crafted public persona is that of the consummate winner. According to the fabricated myth, most everything he touches turns into gold. Trump goes well out of his way to deny any losses and to distance himself from 'losers,' or anything that smells remotely like defeat. He is cold and calculating in his demeanour. Trump often behaved like a shark in his business dealings, yet according to a former lover, he has *selachophobia*. In addition to his fear of germs, immigrants from "shithole countries," functional democracy, and low-fat snack foods, Trump is afraid of sharks. How ironic!

Trump relishes in ridiculing rivals and dismissing those who disappoint him. This is done to flaunt the power he wields over others. Trump demands absolute loyalty from others, yet he fires disappointing 'losers' without providing them any opportunity to learn from their mistakes. Under his watch, America has become a much more divided house, where mean spirit prevails. With Trump as POTUS, America has begun to more callously distinguish between winners and losers, and in Trump's America losers only have themselves to blame. All Democrats are sad losers unable to resign themselves to the fact that they lost a crucial election. Inner-city Blacks are losers for having trusted Democrats to help them. Wealthy Americans are winners as recipients of unprecedented tax cuts. Working class Americans are losers qualifying for only modest and temporary tax cuts. And so, divisions are perpetuated!

The Parable of the Big Chip on the Fragile Shoulder

★ ★ ★ ★ ★ ★

The following post-modern parable helps reveal the infectious negativity and polarizing climate of anger and condescending judgement emanating from and leading to mean spirited bully tactics.

Judging Colours

Figure 6.2: Courtesy of editorial cartoonist Clay Jones.

A billionaire misogynist spent his charmed life wrapped up in himself. He loved himself so much that he hated everyone who stood in his way. He learned to be pushy to get ahead in the exclusive circles he liked to frequent. He learned to be aggressive in the competitive business he inherited from his parents. He learned to be tough to hide his insecurity and vulnerability.

He assumed a 'tough guy' persona to avoid being pushed around. In time, he developed an actual chip on his shoulder. To improve his self-worth, he devoted his life to making more and more money to own more and more things and buy more and more people. At the same time, the chip on his shoulder kept growing larger and larger.

At first, he dared people to remove it by taking legal action. Then he hired un-documented immigrants to steal it. But the chip just kept getting bigger and strong-er each time. As he became more wealthy, arrogant, and bold, the chip on his shoulder kept growing, eventually needing its own zip code. He dared elitists and rivals to knock it off. Their failure made him feel better. But this was still not enough. To further improve his self-esteem, he continued making more money, owning more things, and buying more people. The people he bought all told him how beautiful the chip looked on his shoulder.

He paid beautiful young women to seduce it off. He brought in religious leaders to exorcize it. He even consulted Russian 'acquaintances' to see if the chip could be laundered away. When all this failed, he hired branding experts to make the shoulder chip look cool. This proved so successful that he acquired a cult following. But still this was just not enough to break his melancholy. He used his great wealth to develop a potion to infect others, so they too could have a chip on their shoulder —just not as HUGE as his. Many unhappy people drank the potion. They all looked to him as a powerful leader and role model. They made him their undisputed king, but this was still not remotely enough.

The chip on his shoulder continued to grow exponentially. It eventually became its own planet, totally immune to global warming. His contempt for those who refused to drink his potion also grew exponentially. Ultimately, the shoulder chip turned on itself, totally devouring him in the process. This left him claiming "a HUGE moral victory against very bad people" but, of course, it was still far from enough to satisfy the anger and hate that consumed him from within.

CHAPTER SEVEN

WHEN EXTREMISM AND POLARIZATION TRUMP MODERATION AND DIALOGUE

DONALD TRUMP DID not create the dysfunctional polarization currently plaguing American politics. It was clearly well in place before he arrived, but he used it to full advantage. He exacerbated the political landscape by intensifying the extremism, polarization, and paralysis. Under the guise of populist rebellion, he brought in more extreme elements to fight what he saw as the established political elites.

Trump's White House team was dysfunctional from the start. It included a forced aggregation of political opposites with radically different world views and diametrically opposed ideologies, goals, and priorities. A first

> *"Political extremism involves two prime ingredients: an excessively simple diagnosis of the world's ills, and a conviction that there are identifiable villains back of it all."*
>
> —JOHN W. GARDNER

group consisted of anti-establishment political outsiders with an ultra-conservative populist orientation. They were bent on reversing what they saw as the blunders of incompetent and self-serving politicians. Chief strategist Steve Bannon and deputy assistant Sebastian Gorka were two examples of far-right influence inside Trump's original team.

Bannon and Gorka were both fired in August of 2017, in response to Trump's sagging popularity. Trump's ill-advised comments regarding the Charlottesville riots proved explosive. As close friends, Trump and Bannon assessed the situation and came to the conclusion that Bannon would be more helpful to the cause as a free-speaking outsider, rather than as a heavily muffled White House insider. Bannon immediately returned to his leadership position with the far-right *Breitbart News Network*, but he was forced to resign five months later, as a political liability for the news service.

Chief of staff Reince Priebus and attorney general Jeff Sessions represented the Republican Party establishment on Trump's original White House team. Son-in-law Jered Kushner and daughter Ivanka Trump provided a more progressive liberal perspective. Retired general Michael Flynn was named national security advisor to provide a hawkish military perspective, in stark contrast to the approach taken by the previous Obama administration. Flynn was forced to resign in less than a month, after he failed to declare payments received from Russian sources and after he lied to the vice-president.

> "We are tired of Obama's empty speeches and his misguided rhetoric. This, this has caused the world to have no respect for America's word, nor does it fear our might."
> —MICHAEL FLYNN

These extremely different frames of reference created an opportunity to bring diverse perspectives to the same table. Instead, the result was a White House team prone to in-fighting, back-stabbing, and strategic leaks of damaging information. In the end, Trump was not capable of the leadership required to bring these vastly different people effectively together. This kind of polarized thinking had begun rendering the American political landscape dysfunctional long before Trump's arrival on the political scene. Polarization refers to the increasing number of cases where an elected politician's position on a particular issue, policy, or person is strictly defined and almost pre-determined by party affiliation or ideology (liberal or conservative).

Often, polarized positions become non-negotiable, killing any opportunity for meaningful dialogue. This loss of dialogue can be a double-edged sword. First, little learning and personal growth happens when a person is closed to diverse perspectives and ways of thinking. Second, little mutual respect can be garnered when honest dialogue between opposing views is deemed pointless. Moderate voices often lose power and influence in a polarized two-party system, like America's current reality. Extremist voices can feed off each other to develop even more exaggerated perspectives over time.

Political scientists often distinguish between 'elite' and 'popular' polarization, depending on whether polarization emanates from party organizers and elected officials (as the party elite) or from the electorate or general public. In either case, the end result is strict adherence to party lines and the opportunity for dialogue, negotiation, and compromise is severely curtailed. Often one type of polarization can influence more extremism, and less moderation, in the other. For example, when political parties sense radical shifts in voter sentiments, they carefully recruit appropriate candidates and adjust party platforms to cater to shifting public moods.

Political observers note several consequences of increasing political polarization in America:

- Polarization reduces the number of moderate voices in Congress and increases gridlock and inefficiency, ultimately limiting the volume and quality of the legislation being passed;
- Polarization incentivizes members of Congress to use stall tactics (like filibuster) to block, hamper, and frustrate unfavourable business;
- Polarization reduces the quality of the legislation that is finally passed by limiting debate and amendments and by excluding minority party members from committee deliberations.

The severely partisan tactics promoted by polarization can decrease transparency, increase oversight, and lead to inferior legislation. Filibustering tactics allow an elected representative to use up the maximum allotted time, even when they have nothing constructive to add to the discourse. Sometimes they go off on time consuming tangents.

> *"We've seen filibusters to block judicial nominations, jobs bills, political transparency, ending Big Oil subsidies— you name it, there's been a filibuster."*
> —ELIZABETH WARREN

This can effectively delay any vote on a proposed bill. For this reason, the paralyzing practice of filibuster is sometimes referred to as "talking a bill to death."

Another way of preventing a vote on an unfavourable bill is strategic departure to remove quorum. Elected officials plan to walk out prior to a contentious vote. Without sufficient numbers, any vote must be deferred. When the political landscape is tightly partisan and closely divided, a single vote can make a significant difference. Big money and interest groups can take advantage of political gridlock to lobby and influence the individual politicians judged to be the most malleable.

In a polarized political environment, long-term issues and needs can be sidelined when the myopic preoccupation becomes placing the party in a position to prevail in the next election. Any long-term vision or thinking outside-the-box is effectively discouraged, when elected representatives are instructed to strictly tow the party line. In addition, instead of focusing on serving all Americans, each

> *"We shouldn't deny the right of the minority to filibuster, but we need to do a much better job of making them own it. That way, the American people could figure out who is being obstructionist and who is willing to compromise."*
> —CLAIRE MCCASKILL

party can safely focus on carefully crafting the political platform that will provide majority support. Often, this can mean as little as 51 percent of those who actually voted.

Within the general population or electorate, polarization attracts political candidates and platforms void of any moderate influences and catering only to the targeted audience that is expected to provide a victory on election day. This makes politics more a game of calculation and less a game of persuasive dialogue. In a highly polarized political environment, candidates tend to safely preach primarily to the choir of the already converted (the 'target' audience).

Big money and special interest groups further exacerbate the situation by spending large amounts in an attempt to sway popular opinion in their direction. By using attack ads to incite fear and resentment towards politicians representing the opposite side, lobby groups effectively intensify polarization. In time, very little common ground and civility remains for an honest dialogue focused on the best interests of all Americans.

In the current polarized logjam, the programs of a Democrat president can be effectively obstructed by a Republican Senate or House of Representatives. A Republican president can be obstructed by a Democrat majority in Congress. In both cases, the American people fail to receive the functional democracy they need to objectively make difficult decisions. Regrettably, voter perspective may not be objective enough and voter memory may not be long enough to hold partisan obstructionists accountable for hijacking the law-making process. The paralysis brought about by partisan polarization needs to be addressed. Since no political party created to date can be seen to hold a monopoly on good ideas and appropriate legislation, the value and benefit of dialogue, negotiation, and compromise cannot be over stated.

Some of America's political polarization is racially motivated. In his 2015 publication, American writer and social justice activist, James E. Wallis refers to racism and white privilege as "America's original sin." America's racial divide will not be reconciled until whites feel comfortable speaking openly with African-Americans and Latino-Americans. Honest dialogue about race relations is long overdue, but expanding polarization makes this conversation less likely. This impasse needs to be broken. Hopefully, it will be broken by illumination, rather than by violent confrontation.

When African-Americans refer to Barak Obama as "our president" and white-Americans refer to Obama as "not my president," the paralysis caused by racially motivated polarization is self-evident. Pompous, old

> *"Hope unbelieved is always considered nonsense. But hope believed is history in the process of being changed."*
>
> *"Trump's election provides both a great danger and a real opportunity to finally deal with race in America."*
> —JAMES E. WALLIS

guard Republicans claim that they did not give president Obama as hard a time as he deserved because of his race. This is further proof of the racial tensions white Republicans fallaciously give themselves credit for having overcome. Reading between the lines of this logic, it becomes clear that they wanted to confront and obstruct even more than they did, but they did not want to be seen as racist. In reality, proportionately fewer African-Americans are card carrying Republicans today, even though the Democrats were originally strongly linked to legalized slavery. Today, large numbers of African-American voters have just not felt comfortable in Republican circles. This discomfort speaks volumes.

Trump seized the opportunity presented by this dysfunctional polarization in America to take control of a Republican party eager, at all costs, to find a candidate who would be successful in the coming presidential elections. Tea Party reformers within the Republican Party had moved Republican thinking further to the right and stifled the voices of party moderates.

In the end, the fractured, right-justified party had many presidential candidates, but all carried significant baggage and quickly exposed critical flaws. Performing as the quintessential outsider and 'anti-politician,' Trump was able to nastily eliminate competitors without tarnishing his own brand or shrinking his partisan populist base of support. In the process, he got candidate Marco Rubio

> *"You ask him [Trump] about the economy and all he does is launch into an attack about this 'little guy' thing."*
>
> *"I'll admit he's taller than me. He's like 6'2", which is why I don't understand why his hands are the size of someone who is 5'2" ... And you know what they say about men with small hands? [long pause] You can't trust them."*
> —MARCO RUBIO

to take the bait and get into a childish scrum about height, hand size, and male genitalia. By mocking the wife of Ted Cruz, he managed to anger and throw another contender off balance. In the end, he secured the party's nomination.

During the bitter presidential elections that followed, Trump continued his outlandish and irreverent ways. He mounted a mean spirited and vicious attack-based campaign against a veteran, experienced candidate running a conventional campaign. He often suggested that Hillary Clinton should be locked up in jail rather than running against him. Tactics and rhetoric that would have ended the career of other politicians left him immune as the consummate 'anti-politician.'

Near the end of the campaign against "crooked Hillary" Clinton, when he had fallen some 6 percentage points behind in the polls, all of a sudden, numerous e-mails surfaced allegedly containing evidence of illegal actions and subsequent cover-ups by the Clinton camp. After the FBI investigated and found nothing wrong, Clinton's lead in the national polls had been cut to 3 percent. This small lead was now what statisticians and pollsters often refer to as "well within the margin of error." By the time FBI director Comey announced his findings, it was too late for Clinton to recover from the damage done by the misinformation being circulated.

During the campaign, Trump continually claimed to have damaging evidence that would be used at the appropriate time to expose Clinton. This effectively planted the seed of wrongdoing. Even though the promised evidence contained nothing of consequence, some pundits argue this episode cost Clinton the election. I see it as a contributing factor, along with her decision to run a conventional campaign, insensitive to the signs of growing and widespread voter disillusionment with conventional politicians. Decisions to spend less time in traditionally Democrat friendly 'rust belt' states proved costly when Clinton lost many of those states on election night. In retrospect, perhaps more attention should have been paid to the fears and future prospects of 'rust belt' voters and less time looking for a suitable venue in which to smash a symbolic glass ceiling on election night.

In the end, Trump and his strategists were accurately able to gauge the amount of voter dissatisfaction and resentment with conventional candidates. His over-the-top, 'bad boy', anti-establishment persona attracted enough support to take him to the White House. He scored a decisive Electoral College victory, despite losing the popular vote by almost 2.9 million—votes that Trump boldly claimed were illegal.

In office, Trump's polarizing rhetoric and tactics appear to be making matters worse. He openly criticized Obama for what he saw as a lack of transparency about his actual birthplace. Yet, once in power Trump showed far less transparency and openness than his predecessor about personal holdings and tax returns. Trump foolishly insisted that there were some "good people" on the fascist/white supremacist side of the Charlottesville riots. Talk about fanning the flames of polarization and division.

During his infamous 75-minute speech at an August 22 rally in Phoenix, Arizona, the president hinted at shutting down the government if it got in his way. This reveals two realities: paralyzing polarization and total disinterest in taking the time to fix it. Trump preferred to use paralysis to his own advantage.

Three days later, while Hurricane Harvey was devastating the Texas coastline, Trump boldly pardoned former Arizona sheriff Joe Arpaio. This proved to be another polarizing decision, severely criticized by civil rights groups, some Republican senators, as well as house leader Paul Ryan. From 1993 to 2016, Arpaio served six controversial terms as sheriff of Maricopa County. He styled himself as "America's Toughest Sheriff." Arpaio was convicted of criminal contempt for ignoring a court order in a racial profiling case.

Arpaio has been accused for years of violating basic human rights in his prisons, police misconduct, abuse of powers, failure to investigate sex crimes, unlawful enforcement of immigration laws, and ongoing racial profiling. Over the years, his office has paid more than $146 million in fees, settlements, and court awards to victims. Arpaio is also famous for having investigated president Obama's birth certificate. As late as 2016, he continued to claim that the birth certificate was forged.

> "Sheriff Joe is a patriot. Sheriff Joe protected our borders. And Sheriff Joe was unfairly treated by the Obama administration."
>
> "He's done a great job for the people of Arizona, He's very strong on borders, very strong on illegal immigration."
> — DONALD TRUMP

Presidents have the power to pardon. Often this is reserved for the end of an administration and rarely are pardons granted without consultation of legal experts and authorities. Trump defiantly issued this polarizing pardon without consultation and early in his mandate. Controversy notwithstanding, it appears he might have wanted to get a head start on the traditional pardon of his very first Thanksgiving turkey.

Donald Trump has long been a vocal critic of global warming. He has long insisted the ultimate intent of the "hoax" is to tax American industry, making it unable to compete with Chinese industry, where no restrictions are in place. He

> "The concept of global warming was created by and for the Chinese in order to make U.S. manufacturing non-competitive."
> — DONALD TRUMP

mocked scientists and ridiculed their research. As satellite images confirmed polar ice caps continuing to disappear at alarming rates, Trump tweeted that ice caps were actually growing along with the polar bear population.

Once POTUS, as a show of support for his 'clean coal' industry supporters, Trump disbanded the federal climate change advisory committee and pulled the United States out of the Paris Accord. This was done without engaging in any consultation to better understand the growing scientific evidence. Sadly, his comportment did not become more objective, conciliatory, or less 'in your face' partisan as president.

Critical reflection on current partisan political impasses reveals ten significant problems:

1. **Pontification trumps active listening.**

   When people refuse to listen to different points of view personal growth and learning can be stifled. Refusing to consult or engage others reveals arrogant tunnel vision. There is no need to listen when one person or group already has a monopoly on all the right answers. Without listening there is limited hope of understanding others and how their ideas and concerns are shaped.

2. **Uniformity trumps diversity.**

   A polarized environment can easily generate an "us versus them" mentality. Tolerance for differences can be effectively diminished. Paranoid citizens can see diversity as a challenge to national unity. Different people and ideas can be more easily dismissed as 'un-American' by bigoted minds. Those with different ideas can be bullied into keeping their ideas to themselves. This muffling of free speech undermines democracy.

3. **Braggadocio trumps honest self-reflection.**

   Honest self-assessment is compromised along with the ability to recognize personal bias, community bias, and institutional bias. The blame game is effectively used to undermine and sometimes demonize opposing viewpoints. But often, insufficient scrutiny is applied to the assessment of favoured viewpoints. These viewpoints and messages are accepted at face value. This double standard can distort perceptions of reality and what can best serve the common good. In addition, errors in judgement and past mistakes become more difficult to recognize and admit.

4. **Ignorance trumps informed decision making.**

    In a politically polarized environment, an uninformed electorate presents a greater danger to the democratic process. Uninformed voters can be more easily manipulated by crafty, self-serving politicians. Accountability for the decisions of elected politicians can be effectively diminished by voter ignorance. Repeated buzz words, media bites, and catchy slogans can have undue influence on uninformed voters. Regrettably, in a polarized political environment, sweeping and complex decisions are sometimes made with high levels of emotion (often driven by fear) and limited facts.

5. **Vindication trumps reconciliation.**

    Polarization invites demonization and blame. A rationale and rhetoric often emerges in polarized partisan environments where opponents are blamed for all that is bad and wrong and allies are given credit for all that is good and right. Trump is a master at vindictive rhetoric. He declared Obama "the founder of ISIS." Once in power, Trump took credit for an immediate improvement in stock market performance completely ignoring the reality that he had not made a single economic change. This effectively denied the effects of his predecessor's attempts to stimulate economic recovery after the serious recession Obama inherited. Trump also appeared to completely ignore the transition time needed for change to work its way through an economy. All of this "wall building" and isolationism is often done at the expense of building bridges of reconciliation.

6. **Favouritism trumps objectivity.**

    Favouritism can become as prevalent in the polarized political world as it has always been in the passionate world of sports. Fans cheer for their favourite sports teams and boo their rivals. In the political world, subjective citizens cheer ideas, leaders, and programs from the favoured ideological orientation and mercilessly reject those coming from the other camp. Often this rejection comes without objective analysis and assessment. At the heart of this categorical rejection is the premise that the information comes from unacceptable sources. Regrettably, the ideas of friendly voices are not held to the same scrutiny as the ideas of rivals. Polarized political environments tend to kill objectivity.

7. **A rush to judgement trumps empathy.**

    As polarization intensifies, one of the first casualties can be empathy. Any empathy left is reserved for like-minded people. In place of empathy, a rush to judgement is reserved for people with different ideas and priorities. Not only is this judgement rushed, it is often also harsh. Judgementally, the proponents of ideas determined to be bad are fallaciously seen as equally bad people. In such an environment, a healthy respect for differences is difficult to achieve. Putting yourself in another's shoes, to better understand where their differences come from, is less likely to happen under such circumstances. In the final analysis, the honest dialogue needed to break through prejudice and discrimination is stifled, instead of being promoted.

8. **Short-sightedness trumps vision.**

    In a polarized and tight political environment, survival instincts often kick in. Focus can be unduly shifted to an immediate crisis or coming election. There is little incentive to look much beyond these most proximate critical points. Long-term vision and future building is sacrificed to more pragmatic pursuits. The errors of rivals must never be forgotten. Personal errors must never be admitted. A rationalization is often developed to show errors and omissions in a more favourable light. Sometimes people cling to indefensible positions. Rather than enable learning and personal growth, this short-sighted thinking can help perpetuate mistakes. In addition, short-sighted thinking can stifle the outside-the-box thinking needed to approach problem solving in a more creative manner. The noble arts of dreaming and big picture formation can also be curtailed as dangerous or wasteful.

9. **Confrontation trumps critical thinking.**

    In a polarized political environment people can easily default to thinking with their fists or their feet. The fight or flight instinct can lead to confrontation, where the taking of sides is based on allegiance or convenience, rather than merit. The alternative is to acquiesce to avoid attention and conflict. Critical thinking is needed to accurately assess situations and options to make a reasoned judgement, based on appropriate criteria. Without this critical analysis, it becomes difficult to separate objective fact from hype, opinion, bias, and innuendo. The absence of critical thinking renders people incapable of appropriate discernment and renders them prone to misinformation and manipulation.

10. **Alternative facts trump objective facts.**

   In a polarized political environment with a fair number of uniformed voters, and an outcome too close to call, unscrupulous politicians can lie or misrepresent facts to increase their persuasiveness. Ultimately, this becomes a matter of integrity and ethics.

Any of these problems can adversely affect the dialogue, compromise, and consensus building needed to sustain a healthy and functional democracy. When several of these problems are seen to co-exist, the negative effects are compounded. When good will triumphs over partisan interests, the resilience of the human spirit can help overcome even compounded negativity. But a concerted and collective effort is needed. Dismantling years of pent-up polarization will require the same intensive therapy that medical patients must endure if they hope to overcome paralysis. The political healing process begins with honest and constructive dialogue. Ethics and integrity must be seen to lead the way.

One powerful example of goodwill triumphing over division was made clearly evident by the Hurricane Harvey disaster in Texas. When this giant devastating storm pummelled the Texas coast three separate times, the people of Texas set aside personal differences related to class, race, sexual orientation, and politics to focus squarely on saving human lives. It is an interesting paradox that it sometimes takes the worst of Mother Nature to bring out the best in human nature. While a handful of parasites looted abandoned properties, thousands of civilians joined first responders to rescue both neighbours and strangers from the raging flood waters and devastation. News images of human nature at its very best brought tears of solidarity to the eyes.

The political landscape needed a good power wash much more than the people of southern Texas ever did. Regrettably, some comparable political crisis may be needed to bring out similar humane spirit. Ironically, a sizable block of Republican politicians from Texas voted vehemently against federal relief funding after Hurricane Sandy devastated the Eastern Seaboard in 2012. It will be interesting to see how these same people react this time around.

> *"The problem with that particular bill is it became a $50 billion bill that was filled with unrelated pork. Two-thirds of that bill had nothing to do with Sandy."*
> —TED CRUZ

> *"Let's remember what Senator Cruz was trying to do at the time. He was trying to be the most conservative, the most fiscally conservative, person in the world. And what I said at the time ... is that someday ... a disaster is going to come to you. And when it does, I'm going to promise him that New Jersey congress people will stand up and do the right thing."*
> — CHRIS CHRISTIE

Ted Cruz led the charge against the *Sandy Relief Fund* claiming the bill was "unclean" and the majority of the money would not go to relief victims and reparations. This second accusation was eventually proven false. Staunchly conservative in his political ideology, Cruz consistently demonstrated a tendency to favour smaller government and lower taxes. The giant relief fund was seen as a huge cash grab where much of the money would be mismanaged in public hands or diverted to "pet projects." This is an example of partisan politics overriding common decency. It remains to be seen how Cruz will handle the Texas disaster relief funding issue and the inevitable criticism of his earlier cold-hearted decision. How he handles this situation and how he explains the polarized partisan behaviours of the past will speak volumes about the quality of his character. So far, his silence is deafening.

Bitter polarization can lead to "pork barrel" politics, where friends are rewarded and political enemies are punished. Fat contracts (often referred to as "lard" by political rivals and "justified" by allies) are awarded to cronies, key supporters, and supporting districts. Instead of basing appointments and contracts on merit, these highly politicized decisions are based on political affiliation.

In addition to the strategic *patronage* or favouring of allies, the pork barrel model of politics involves the punishment or rejection of those considered to be rivals or critics. When strict sides are taken, boundary lines cannot be crossed without political fallout. For example, New Jersey governor Chris Christie was severely criticised by many Republican allies for having publicly shaken president Obama's hand as relief funding was finally activated to address the disaster caused by Hurricane Sandy. It appears that, for many diehard Republicans, even in the midst of a devastating natural disaster, political partisanship must prevail.

Interestingly, governor Christie himself is not immune to the pettiness of severely partisan politics. His ambition to secure the Republican party's presidential nomination, in the 2016 campaign (and later the vice-presidential nomination) were both cut short by the Washington Bridge lane closure scandal of 2013. In September of 2013, a staff member and political appointees of governor Christie colluded to create traffic jams in Fort Lee, New Jersey by closing lanes at the main toll plaza for the upper level of the Washington Bridge for five days.

This caused traffic chaos during rush hour and endangered lives. It was alleged that the closures were orchestrated to cause a massive traffic problem for the Democrat mayor of Fort Lee, who did not support Christie in the gubernatorial election earlier that year. A massive federal investigation resulted in the conviction of three Christie appointees, including his deputy chief of staff. Although Christie was never connected directly to the "Bridgegate scandal," it badly damaged his political standing. He was once considered a leading contender for the American presidency.

Patronage appointments can lead to inefficiency and incompetence. Retribution and payback can inflict further harm on government operations. Another indicator of partisan politics at work is the deliberate starving of funds for projects and programs initiated by opponents. Again, merit takes a back seat to cold politics. President Trump used funding cuts to fiscally bankrupt the *Obamacare* he vehemently opposed.

In the final analysis, regardless of who is in power (and who is screaming from the outside), one net result of polarization is

> "We need to get away from labels. That's the way people talk in Washington D.C. — through labels, through ideological frames, through partisan frames."
> — WENDY DAVIS

that, often, the public dollar is made to not go as far as a private dollar. This adds fuel to the argument to downsize government and reduce taxes. Regrettably, private interests are not always keen or equipped to tackle public/collective issues. The need for balance is clearly evident.

Because human nature is human, by nature, sometimes political action plans achieve unintended results. Human behaviour is not always predictable. People can surprise or disappoint. In a polarized political environment reactions to highly partisan decisions can sometimes trigger unexpected counter-reactions. Sometimes these reactions help to challenge and negate what is seen as prejudiciously partisan. These reactions can help reason prevail over sentiment and ideology.

For example, when president Trump unilaterally took the United States out of the Paris Accord to address climate change, former New York mayor Michael Bloomberg saw this denial of global warming and climate change as "embarrassing." He said, "It just makes us look foolish." As one of the wealthiest Americans, he immediately pledged to personally donate the $15 million the United Nations would have lost, due to America's withdrawal from the international accord.

> *"I hate politics. It's slimy. Any job where the people pander for votes, I don't like. The country has gotten so partisan that if you're not on my side, you're the enemy. The only thing I ever try to support is a third party ... We need more parties and more choice."*
> — MARK CUBAN

Although bitterly partisan polarization can sometimes trigger reactions that are positive and constructive in nature, it is important for any functional democracy to keep levels of partisanship at a productive level. It is incumbent on the electorate to hold their elected representatives accountable for the paralysis and dysfunction inflicted on the democratic process. It is incumbent on the electorate to insist on politics that maximize integrity, dialogue, compromise, and consensus building. The electorate deserves more quality choices.

A Polarizing and Paralyzing POTUS

★ ★ ★ ★ ★ ★

As president of the United States (POTUS), Trump has taken full advantage of the bitterly partisan political landscape and a frustrated electorate. He has effectively used this dysfunctional environment to full personal advantage. Missteps and indiscretions that might have ruined the careers of other politicians have not cost him any political support to date. Even in a toxic environment where much of what he touches soon dies, Trump still professes to have the Midas touch. Supported by the jaded journalists from Fox News and the 'talking parrot' newscasters of the Sinclair Broadcasting Group and its more than 170 influential television stations in 80 markets across the United States, Trump continues to do no wrong in the eyes of diehard supporters. He can fix problems fifty years in the making in one act.

Paraphrasing Winston Churchill in describing how difficult Russia's moves were to anticipate, Trump also presents as a riddle, wrapped up in a mystery, inside an enigma, shrouded in paradox and contradiction. America's bitterly partisan political landscape allows Trump to escape his numerous contradictions virtually unscathed. He presents as a family man, yet he stands accused of extra-marital affairs. Trump is said to be germ-phobic, yet he is said to have preferred unprotected sex with a porn star and a former playmate. He is a senior citizen who devours junk food like a teenager. Trump presents as a hard and crusty tycoon, yet he is clearly thin-skinned and unable to tolerate criticism. He claims to believe in a free press but prefers to define it as a press that can be freely manipulated to unequivocally support his every action. Trump demands absolute loyalty, yet he is quick to throw those around him under the bus. He is a self-confessed genius, yet Trump hates reading briefs and becomes easily disinterested or confused by too much detail, preferring instead to get the bulk of his information from Fox News.

While keeping his adversaries distracted by all these contradictions, Trump engages in political deal making shrouded in tactics akin to hostage taking, blackmail, and spiteful retaliation. For example:

- Unless Congress provides the funds needed for the Great Border Wall, "the military" (later corrected to the National Guard) will be deployed to patrol the Mexican border.
- Unless Democrats grant the concessions demanded, Republicans will let the DACA provisions run out (a ticking time bomb that Trump created), leaving hundreds of thousands of 'dreamers' exposed to deportation. These deportations will all be the fault of the uncooperative Democrats.
- Desperate parents caught trying to illegally enter the United States will have their children taken away from them.
- Unless Congress supports the president's agenda, a government shutdown will be orchestrated.
- After several allegations of child molestation, Republican candidate Roy Moore was still endorsed.
- Unless Canada and Mexico agree to more favourable trade terms, America will kill the North American Free Trade Agreement (NAFTA).

- Unless China agrees to America's trade demands, stiff tariffs will be imposed on Chinese exports into the United States (like the 25% tariff on steel and aluminum).
- Unless allies do what America wants, they can no longer count on America's help to fight off foreign aggression.

These tactics reveal the politics of brute force, where might makes right and previous agreements are all void because they were made by incompetent predecessors. In Trump's bitterly partisan world, where thinking is pushed to polarized extremes, negotiation and compromise are seen as signs of weakness.

Critical Questions for Discerning Minds: Dealing Constructively with Polarization

1. Am I part of the polarization problem or part of the solution? How do I know for sure?
2. Is this candidate or elected official part of the problem or part of the solution? How do I know?
3. Is this idea, proposal or initiative part of the problem or part of the solution? How do I know?
4. What factors guide my thinking to a more extreme, one-sided, and un-negotiable point of view? How can my thinking be made more moderate, balanced, and objective?
5. Does this ___ reflect a bias towards active listening? What evidence supports my judgement?
6. Does this ___ reflect a bias towards diversity? What evidence supports my judgement?
7. Does this ___ reflect a bias towards honest self-reflection? What evidence supports my judgement?
8. Does this ___ reflect a bias towards informed decision making? What evidence supports my judgement?
9. Does this ___ reflect a bias towards reconciliation? What evidence supports my judgement?
10. Does this ___ reflect a bias towards objectivity? What evidence supports my judgement?
11. Does this ___ reflect a bias towards empathy? What evidence supports my judgement?

12. Does this ___ reflect a bias towards vision? What evidence supports my judgement?

13. Does this ___ reflect a bias towards critical thinking? What evidence supports my judgement?

14. Does this ___ reflect a bias towards honesty? What evidence supports my judgement?

15. Does this ___ reflect a triumph of ethical considerations and integrity over cold partisan politics? What evidence supports my judgement?

Something to Think About:

Don't be so concerned about what your polar opposite is thinking to completely ignore the enemy within. When your thinking is significantly flawed, insular, or superficial, you can easily become your own worst enemy.

> *"My best friend is the one who brings out the best in me."*
> — HENRY FORD

An Experience Worth Noting: Party Politics

★ ★ ★ ★ ★ ★

Since I was a young man, I have always been interested in serving the community. Growing up alongside many immigrant families, in southern Etobicoke, my Canada was always a multicultural mosaic. During my university years, I became involved with the local community centre and the planning of an annual Italian Festival. Ourland Community Centre is in a working class area of the borough, originally known as the town of Mimico. There was a significant concentration of Italian families in the neighbourhoods within a ten-minute drive from the community centre. Eventually, I was elected chair of the community centre's advisory board and president of the festival committee. Our festival was designed to appeal to all ages with live music, dancing, bike races, bocce tournaments, art exhibits, greased pole climbing, garden competitions, watermelon eating contests, and piñata breaking. One of the biggest attractions was the annual tug of war contest between our local fire and police departments.

In time, we grew the festival into the largest annual gathering of Italian Canadians in Etobicoke. We attracted interest from many federal, provincial, and municipal politicians. Even the Premier of Ontario, William Davis, joined in the

Figure 7.1: Ontario Premier, Bill Davis (third from the right), presiding over and presenting the trophy to the winners of the tug of war contest, in 1974. (Courtesy of the Ourland Community Centre Italian Festival Committee).

celebrations. The Prime Minister of Canada, Pierre Trudeau, was never able to attend in person, but a delegation of ministers and members of parliament was sent each year.

Everything progressed nicely until party politics started to rear its ugly head. Community members began to fight amongst themselves over opportunities to showcase their favoured political party (and candidates), while neutralizing the opportunities for rivals. Infighting and back stabbing resulted in a marked decline in the effectiveness of the planning committee, and ultimately, in the quality of the festival.

During my university years, I had joined the Young Liberals and attended provincial and federal conventions as a delegate. This afforded me an insider's view. Like many other Italian immigrants, I associated the opportunity to come to Canada with the Liberal government that opened the doors for us. Over time, some of the more successful members of our community adopted a more protectionist perspective and switched their support to the Conservative Party. Some Italians who belonged to labour unions joined the New Democratic Party, as the champion of the working class. Community leaders were solicited by each major party to help recruit new party members. This aggressive recruiting resulted in numerous conflicts of interest and public confrontations. Eventually, at the insistence of the mayor, the festival was scaled back to become a neighbourhood gathering with a reduced budget.

I resigned from the advisory board, and festival committee, but not without one final salvo against those committee members who contributed to the festival's demise, by pursuing self-serving politics, instead of looking after the best interests of their community. I had always kept my politics personal and private. In my final address, I scolded bickering committee members by saying: *"We have done* this to ourselves. There is no one else to blame. Throughout history, petty Italians have done more harm to each other, than the rest of the world has collectively inflicted upon us! Congratulations for continuing the foolish tradition. I trust that your new political friends will treat you well. But never forget the words of the philosopher Nietzsche. A politician divides people into two groups; tools and enemies. You, my friends, have proven yourselves to be a bunch of tools."

Over time, I was approached by representatives from all three major parties to test out my interest in joining their ranks as a potential candidate. First, the New Democrats approached me because they allegedly were impressed by my public speaking skills and my

PRIME MINISTER · PREMIER MINISTRE

It gives me great pleasure to be able to send my greetings to all those involved with the annual Italian Festival in Etobicoke.

Canada's strength lies in its diversity. We are enriched by the cultures of many lands, and very prominent among these is that of Italy. The hard work, skill, imagination and initiative of Canadians of Italian descent is an inspiring example to us all.

As well, this year's theme for the Festival, "The Way We Were", is a valuable one. Homage to the past invites hope for the future. It is my wish that your future will be a bright and fulfilling one.

Pierre Elliott Trudeau

Ottawa,
1 9 7 5.

Figure 7.2: Letter from the Prime Minister of Canada, in 1975. (Courtesy of the Ourland Italian Festival Planning Committee).

social conscience. Liberals encouraged me to stay on as a community activist and candidate-in-training. Finally, representatives from the local riding's Conservative executive approached me to gauge my interest in running as their candidate. Although flattering, I found these probing visits quite peculiar. How could one person be seen as leadership worthy for such diametrically opposed political ideologies? How can one size possibly fit all in the nasty world of politics?

I discussed each opportunity with my wife and she finally convinced me that this political world was not a safe or principled place to invest my energy. I found other opportunities to give back to my many different communities. This proved to be the right decision, as one by one former colleagues who did accept the political overtures found out how very quickly and easily they could be bypassed, or relegated to the scrap heap, whenever a better option happened along. In addition, once branded as the "damaged goods" of one party, it was very difficult to switch to an opposing party, after a bad fit was recognized. Those who were successful demonstrated to me how much the quest for power can compromise a person's integrity. I know that mine was the right decision for me and my family.

The Trump experience provides discerning thinkers with ample opportunity to reflect on the paralysis caused by bitterly partisan politics. As POTUS, Trump demands the supreme respect of all Americans, yet he actively antagonizes those who do not share his interests or agree unequivocally with his exaggerated claims. At every opportunity, he confronts and ridicules political opponents. Even the parents and wife of two fallen soldiers were disrespected because of their political affiliations. A real POTUS rises above petty politics to do the right thing. But then (to paraphrase Abraham Maslow), when all you have in your tool box is a hammer, in time, you start "to treat everything as if it were a nail."

Trump's administration has gone out of its way to hammer the innocent children of illegal immigrants. Despite the protests of alarmed citizens and law makers, from both sides of the political divide, these children have been forcibly removed from their parents and kept in fenced in quarters resembling chain-link animal cages. This torture tactic was used to punish desperate parents for illegally entering the United States, and to deter others from attempting illegal entry.

In its callous defence, the Trump administration boldly claimed to be following a law that Obama had made, and doing its best to protect the nation until the desperately needed border wall is built to keep dangerous criminals from sneaking into America. By far the most callous of Trump surrogates dared to describe this incarceration as something resembling a summer camp. The families of victims killed by illegal immigrants were put on public display to further defend the indefensible. Cries of "Shame, shame!" could be heard across America and around the free world. Clearly, the Trump mandate has descended into a bitterly partisan battle for the soul of America.

Critical Thinking Checkpoint Three

★ ★ ★ ★ ★

Reflect on the following probing question to apply your critical thinking skills.

Has the Trump mandate descended into a battle for America's soul?

JUDGEMENT CRITERIA On what would a reasonable and objective person base this decision?	MY DECISION
☐	
☐	
☐	
☐	
☐	
SUPPORTING EVIDENCE What evidence can be used to confirm this decision as sound?	**RELIABILITY** How do I know my sources are objective, accurate and trustworthy? Can I find other sources to independently corroborate the facts?

The Parable of the Falling Sky

★ ★ ★ ★ ★

The following post-modern parable depicts the dangers of truth denying, fear mongering, and polarizing politics and the bitterly partisan negativity that can result from this extremism.

The Polarizing POTUS   **A Polarized Tug of War**

Figure 7.3: Cartoon by the author.   **Figure 7.4:** Pencil sketch by the author.

A billionaire misogynist spent his charmed life wrapped up in himself. He loved himself so much that he wanted to share himself with the entire world. Because he was too smart to be a follower, he became a leader. He ridiculed all the other leaders until he maneuvered himself to the front of the class. To make his 'clean coal' buddies happy, he ridiculed all the scientists who warned about silly hoaxes like global warming and the dangers of more extreme weather. He ridiculed those with different ideas as "extremist hacks with small minds." He declared all who disagreed with him "enemies of the state."

One day a rouge pigeon pooped on the top of his head. The poop splattered into a hundred pieces. This was so humiliating that he vowed he would never let it happen again. He ordered all his loyal subjects to constantly look up to the sky to protect him. When some people refused, he did what he thought all honourable leaders would do. He lied. He told people that the sky was falling and they needed to constantly look up to save their own lives. His fear mongering worked because, in time, all of his gullible subjects refused to look away from the falling sky. They lived their lives constantly looking skyward.

This made it easy for the leader to pick their pockets and to control where they walked. But he was a good leader, so he only did this whenever he felt like it. A bright person eventually figured out what the leader was up to. When she criticized the leader, he called her a "polarizing witch and only a 4+." Insulted, she told the leader that a flurry of meteorites was headed his way. The leader had a deep bunker built, to protect him from the meteorites that never came. Embarrassed, he finally came out of his bunker, to a chorus of snickers from his detractors. He quietly asked his cronies to find rocks that looked like meteorites. These were displayed, as evidence of falling sky, in a special museum he had built.

One day a bolt of lightning suddenly came, from out of nowhere, and struck the leader on his ample posterior. In the end, the extremely violent weather resulting from global warming zapped him squarely in the rear end. His last painful words as leader were: "This proves that I was right to warn you all about the dangerous sky. You should all build a monument dedicated to me." So, the people made a HUGE hot air balloon in his likeness.

On Turkey Day, they released the balloon. It soared skyward, briefly eclipsing the sun, before exploding into a million pieces. And the people cheered as the pieces fell from the sky.

CHAPTER EIGHT

GLOBALIZATION IN THE GOLDEN AGE OF THE TRANSNATIONAL CORPORATION

NORTH AMERICAN DREAMS have long been laced with hopes of progress and economic security, and American dreamers have often led the way forward. In the process, Americans have created one of the most productive economic systems, driven by free enterprise capitalism. In theory, in this system the consumer is supposed to be sovereign. Competition between several manufactures and vendors is supposed to keep everyone honest and unable to manipulate the marketplace.

Through the judicious exercise of consumer choice, the sovereign consumer rewards some in the free marketplace and not others. The government, elected by consumers, is there to protect the rights of consumers and to punish businesses or private interests colluding against the public interest. Over time, this consumer sovereignty has been compromised. Today, it still exists on paper, but seldom in practice.

In today's world of big business and constant media bombardment, the consumer is no longer king. With the advent of business consolidation through mergers and acquisitions, corporate giants like IBM, Microsoft, General Electric, Wal-Mart, Monsanto, Exxon Mobile, Home Depot, General Motors, Koch Industries, and Proctor & Gamble have emerged in America. Since each of these corporate giants conducts significant business in at least two countries, outside of their national home base, they are considered multinational corporations.

As successful enterprises either force weaker competitors out of business or acquire them, in many industries today the marketplace has been left to a few corporate giants. This concentration of power can effectively limit the level of competition. In these less competitive markets, often called oligopolies, dominant companies are more able to influence prices, even by sheer suggestion. Consumer wants can be further manipulated to corporate advantage through massive advertising campaigns. The establishment of brand preferences, where consumers favour one brand over another, is one way to further manipulate pricing and market share.

To further consolidate the corporate agenda, all of the major media networks in America (ABC, CBS, NBC) were purchased by corporate giants during the 1990s. Small independent television stations continue to be bought up by large media companies, like the Sinclair Broadcasting Group, owning and controlling content in many localities across America. This provides big business further control over the airwaves, and ultimately, how people see and think about their world.

> *"The unrestricted competition so commonly advocated does not leave us the survival of the fittest. The unscrupulous succeed best in accumulating wealth."*
>
> *"It is a government of the people, by the people, for the people no longer. It is a government of corporations, by corporations, for corporations."*
>
> —RUTHERFORD B. HAYES

This *"corporations are your best friend"* movement did not happen as one giant conspiracy against consumer sovereignty. It resulted from a series of shrewd (and sometimes unscrupulous) individual moves, over an extended period of time. Each of these moves was calculated to acquire or maintain a competitive edge over rivals and to maximize corporate profit and influence.

Ironically, the reflections of president Hayes apply even more today than when he first voiced his concerns about America's future, back in the 1880s. In a nation still rebuilding after a devastating civil war, Hayes was a one-term compromise choice for president in 1877. In his lifetime, he observed the early stages of the industrialization of America, and the great accumulation of capital wealth and power that followed.

Big business has grown even more powerful in today's world. Some corporate profits have been invested in politics. Donations to political parties and individual candidates have steadily increased. In the United States, these transparent donations are furthered by less transparent political action committees (PACs). These newer organizations pool donations and use them to fund campaigns for or against candidates or proposed legislation. An organization becomes a PAC when it receives or spends more than $1,000 for the purpose of influencing a federal election, and registers with the Federal Election Commission. Rules for state elections vary by state.

Super PACs (officially known as *independent expenditure only committees*) are not allowed to make direct contributions to political parties or individual candidates, but they are allowed unlimited spending independent of campaigns. They can raise funds from individuals, corporations, labour unions, and other groups without legal limits on donation size. By creating new shell corporations, individual donors can effectively conceal their identity. Super PACs can then independently promote or attack individual candidates or proposed legislation via massive advertising cam-

> *"To all the worrywarts out there who said super PACs were going to lead to a cabal of billionaires secretly buying democracy. WRONG! They are publicly buying democracy."*
> —STEPHEN COLBERT

paigns. Even though these campaigns are officially unaffiliated with individual candidates, the constant message bombardment they can afford to sustain, across all media, is bound to influence some voters. Most of the monies received by these PACs come from extremely wealthy Americans.

According to a New York Times/CBS News poll published on June 2, 2015, the vast majority (84%) of Americans, regardless of party preference or affiliation, believe money has too much influence in political campaigns. However, getting big money out of politics is not an issue Americans prioritize. The same poll found the economy and jobs are top priorities, followed by healthcare and immigration. Less than 1% identified campaign funding as the most important issue faced by Americans. This reality provides Big Business ample incentive to keep American voters worried about incomes, job security, and healthcare.

> *"Something is out of balance in Washington. Corporations now [2015] spend about $2.6 billion a year on reported lobbying expenditures— more than the $2 billion we spend to fund the House ($1.18 billion) and the Senate ($860 million). It's a gap that has been widening since ... the early 2000s."*
> —LEE DRUTMAN

America seems to be constantly in election mode; either preparing for, engaging in, or winding down from hotly contested political campaigns for various levels of government. Not only can campaigns be influenced, but elected officials can be further influenced once in office. Lobbyists are professional 'persuaders' who earn a comfortable living attempting to influence government decisions. Typically, they operate behind closed doors, through quiet discussion with elected officials. Washington, D.C. is overflowing with paid lobbyists promoting special interests.

Over time, successful lobbyists have found the following tactics most effective in the strategic influence of elected politicians.

1. **Conversation Control**

   Lobbyists are most successful when they manage to steer the terms of conversation or public debate away from those they cannot win and on to those they can. For example, if a public discussion on a corporation's environmental impact is unfavourable, lobbyists manoeuvre the focus to hypothetical economic benefits, like the potential for job creation. Once they succeed in making this narrowly framed conversation prevail, dissenting voices can be made to appear marginal, irrelevant, or un-American.

2. **Media Spin**

   Effective lobbyists know when and how to use the press and when to avoid communication. Media messaging is carefully crafted to maximize and accentuate public benefit. For example, if the corporate goal is profit maximization, messaging will be dressed up to appear synonymous with national interests, such as economic growth and jobs.

3. **Engineering Critical Mass and Credibility**

   When a giant corporation is the only voice pitching its message to government, the voice can easily be written off as self-serving and highly specialized. Lobbyists can engineer and mobilize a critical mass of voices singing the company's tune. Lobbyists also recruit credible and seemingly independent sources to help carry and authenticate the corporate message. Sometimes, think tanks are sponsored and co-opted to voice important messages.

4. **Opposition Neutralization**

   Lobbyists use focus groups, public meetings, and feedback sessions to flush out voices of criticism. In doing this, key opponents and their arguments can be identified and ultimately neutralized. Lobbyists often see their battles with opposition forces as a kind of guerrilla warfare. They act to gain the ear of government and to block or neutralize counter arguments from opposing groups such as environmental activists and social justice advocates. When giant corporations feel threatened, lobbyists have also undertaken to infiltrate key opposition groups, with paid spies, to report activities or to stir up internal dissention.

5. Internet Control

Lobbyists monitor the web to detect early warnings of building protest or resistance. They seek to identify the leaders and most influential members of the voices of opposition. They can then distinguish militant from more friendly voices and use divide-and-conquer strategies to get moderates to argue with hardline advocates within the opposition ranks. When used effectively, this tactic can drive a wedge between opposing camps and expose the public to opposing forces and viewpoints at their worst. One key strategy to control online information is to flood the web with positive content that is not as benign or objective as it appears. Lobbyists hire experts to create fake blogs and other carefully worded positive content that fools search engines into placing this content ahead of others. This effectively drives opposing voices down Google rankings and off the most often viewed first page of search results.

6. Networking Politicians

Lobbyists need access to politicians to exercise any influence. Access, over time, creates working relationships. This access can be bought. Examples of paid access include buying corporate tables at expensive fund raising dinners and paying politicians for speaking appearances. If not through a cash transaction, amounting to an access fee, an investment in relationship building is made over time to build trust, offer help, and provide favours. Sometimes, jobs are found for close friends of politicians. Sometimes, lucrative consulting opportunities are made available to politicians, for after they leave public office.

Over time, the lobbying of corporate interests has increased exponentially. If this activity was not seen to yield positive results, corporations would not have been willing to invest as much into it. Corporate lobbying has now grown

> *"Does the Senate work for Big Pharma that hires lobbyists and people who make giant contributions, or does it work for the American people who actually sent us here?"*
> —Elizabeth Warren

in influence to effectively overwhelm countervailing forces. Lobbying has changed how Big Business interacts with government. Instead of trying to keep government out of business matters, corporations are now increasingly trying to bring government in as a partner — looking to what the country can do to better reward their enterprise.

As American corporations became more politically active during the 1990s, their lobbyists became more ambitious and forward thinking. For example, Big Pharma has long opposed the inclusion of a drug plan into the Medicare program because it would effectively give government more bargaining power through bulk purchasing. Bulk purchasing discounts would inevitably lead to reduced profits in the pharmaceutical industry.

Early in the new millennium, Big Pharma lobbyists proposed and supported what became Medicare Part D in the *Medicare Modernization Act of 2003*. This resulted in a prescription drug benefit, effective January 1, 2006, which explicitly banned bulk purchasing. In doing so, an estimated $20 billion in annual profits for Big Pharma was effectively preserved. This 'modernization' also confirmed Big Pharma's right to charge what the market will bear for their prescription drugs.

In 2015, upstart Turing Pharmaceuticals acquired the American rights to the drug *Daraprim®*. This drug had been approved for use by the FDA since 1953.

> "The United States is the only advanced country that permits the pharmaceutical industry to charge exactly what the market will bear, whatever it wants."
> —MARCIA ANGELL

It is used as an anti-malaria and anti-parasitic drug and as a treatment for some AIDS related complications. Overnight, the price of the drug increased from $13.50 per dose to $750. Company founder and CEO Martin Shkreli publicly defended the price hike by saying, "If there was a company that was selling an Aston Martin at the price of a bicycle, and we buy that company and we ask to charge Toyota prices, I don't think that that should be a crime."

In the public outrage that followed, Shkreli was vilified as "the most hated man in America." He promised to change the price but then reneged. In his nationally syndicated column, political commentator Robert Reich wrote that what Shkreli did wrong was to be more audacious, otherwise he was playing "the same game many others are playing on Wall Street and in corporate suites." With the law firmly on his side, Shkreli saw himself as untouchable. In 2016, Shkreli was called before a congressional committee investigating the *Daraprim®* price in-

crease. He refused to answer any questions. On the same day, Shkreli posted a Twitter message arrogantly saying, "Hard to accept that these imbeciles represent the people in our government." He later accused the politicians of being motivated purely by "self-interest." Ultimately, in August of 2017, Shkreli was convicted on two counts of securities fraud and one count of conspiracy to commit securities fraud, during his time as an investment fund manager.

> *"The bigger issue is whether it is perfectly fine to treat pharmaceuticals as ordinary market commodities or whether they should rather be recognized as essential public goods. Should governments allow the private sector alone to determine the dynamics and, therefore, the access issues that confront health systems around the world?"*
> —JILLIAN CLARKE KOHLER

In 2017, Marathon Pharmaceuticals of Deerfield, Illinois, raised the price of a steroid called *Deflazacort®* to $89,000 annually for a generic drug to treat Duchenne muscular dystrophy. Many American patients were previously getting this drug from Europe or Canada at an annual price between $1,000 and $2,000. This represented a staggering 6,000% price increase. The company argued that extensive and expensive mandatory testing was required by the FDA to approve the drug for use in America. Existing laws permit this kind of pricing to encourage companies to develop new drugs for rare diseases.

Clearly, tighter government oversight is needed to hold Big Pharma, and by extension all large and powerful corporations, accountable for their actions. Laws need to be reviewed to ensure that they do not allow corporations to abuse their power in the quest for greater profit. Unethical practices and practices seen as a disservice to the public good, need to be exposed and prosecuted. Then, punishments need to be substantial enough to serve as an effective deterrent.

Ultimately, free range capitalism needs to be replaced by capitalism with a social conscience. Human nature has not advanced sufficiently to make laissez-faire capitalism any more workable, for the advancement of humankind, than its socialist counterpart. The power shift that has allowed the pendulum to swing too much in favour of large corporations needs to be reversed, to address many of the harmful consequences of the new world order being created. A more balanced reality is required.

When bigness is allowed to gain power and influence, because of volume rather than merit or good corporate citizenship, individual and collective rights can easily be marginalized, in favour of corporate privilege and profitability. Consequences (sometimes referred to as *diseconomies*) include:

- the depletion of natural resources;
- environmental contamination;
- a reduction in workers' rights and the countervailing power of unions;
- tax avoidance by large corporations;
- a decline in public funds available for social services;
- a rapidly shrinking middle class;
- a badly skewed distribution of national wealth;
- a reduced quality of life for marginalized groups of people.

> *"There is something profoundly wrong in America when one out of five profitable corporations pay nothing in federal income tax."*
> —BERNIE SANDERS

One of the biggest and most power lobby groups in America is the *National Rifle Association* (NRA). This group has successfully lobbied politicians to ensure that Second Amendment rights are never diluted. Under the NRA's watch, the right to bear arms has not only been protected in America, it has been effectively expanded to include the latest weapons and assault technology. Why civilians need military grade assault weaponry has never been adequately justified, only rationalized by eager gun makers.

After the Sandy Hook school massacre of 2012, I expected something was finally going to be done about the proliferation of guns in America. I believed the murder of 20 innocent school children and six adults was going to finally force common sense to prevail over gun culture. The final outcome was most disappointing. At first, the NRA took down its Facebook page amid an angry backlash, blaming it for an escalation of gun violence in America. The NRA then launched a massive lobbying effort to protect the constitutional right to bear arms. NRA spokesperson Wayne LaPierre went as far as to state that gun-free school zones attract killers. His proposed remedy was for the government to hire armed security guards for every school in America. Clearly, the right to bear arms is sacred for many Americans.

On October 1, 2017, a gunman opened fire on 22,000 people attending a country music concert in Las Vegas, Nevada. From his hotel window, 32 floors above, he was able to murder 58 people and wound several others before killing himself, with the police at his door. He was found with 23 guns in his hotel room, including semi-automatic rifles that had been converted to fully automatic assault weapons. These conversion kits were legalized after a massive lobby effort by the NRA. An additional 19 weapons were found at his Nevada home. It is not clear why a retired accountant needed all this weaponry and bomb making materials. In the end, 548 people were injured either by gun fire or from the stampede that followed.

This carefully planned attack became the deadliest mass murder/

> *"And uh, Second Amendment, I guess, our forefathers wanted us to have AK-47s, uh, is the argument, I assume."*
>
> *"Senate majority leader Mitch McConnell and speaker of the house Paul Ryan and a number of other lawmakers who won't do anything about this because the NRA has their balls in a money clip, also sent their thoughts and their prayers today, which is good. They should be praying, they should be praying for God to forgive them for letting the gun lobby run this country because it is, so crazy."*
>
> *"What I'm talking about tonight isn't about gun control, it's about common sense. Common sense says that no good will ever come out of allowing a person to have weapons that can take down 527 Americans at a concert. Common sense says you don't let those who suffer from mental illness buy guns."*
>
> —JIMMY KIMMEL

shooting in American history. Ironically, the following week, the House of Representatives was scheduled to debate and pass an NRA backed bill to legalize the sale of silencers for guns. Comedian Jimmy Kimmel, who grew up in Las Vegas, delivered a raw, emotional monologue the night after the massacre, appealing for common sense relative to gun proliferation in America. Needless to say, he was harshly criticized by the gun lobby and their mouthpieces. Until America comes to terms with this escalating, and mostly self-inflicted, gun violence and does something to restore common sense to the long-contested gun debate, the dream of peaceful existence will remain elusive. Americans have much more to fear than foreign terrorists. They must also fear the well-armed evil within, capable of instantly transforming any dream into a recurring nightmare.

Productivity, Globalization, and Transnationalism

★ ★ ★ ★ ★ ★

> "The diseconomies of capitalism are treated as the public's responsibility. Corporate America skims the cream and leaves the bill for us to pay, then boasts about how productive and efficient it is and complains about our wasteful government."
> —MICHAEL PARENTI

Once considered beneficial for all participants, the movement toward economic globalization has actually made matters worse.

Productivity advances have long been considered the principal catalyst driving economic growth for nations and profit maximization for corporations. In theory, productivity allows the efficient use of productive resources, allowing the maximization of goods and services available to consumers, while reducing prices. In practice, successful corporations are able to ruthlessly pare down their operating costs to maximize profits. Reduced consumer prices are not an automatic eventuality, given the corporate propensity to charge the highest price the market will bear. In addition, corporations tend to avoid responsibility for the side-effects or external costs of economic activity. They systematically pass all those responsibilities on to government, further complicating the social fabric of free-enterprise capitalism.

In its most basic sense, productivity means improved efficiency. The push to improve the productivity of capital has led to automated mass production technology and the advent of worker displacing robotics. The push to improve labour productivity has resulted in fewer costly workers producing more goods and providing more services. The push to improve resource productivity has led to large scale extraction and processing enterprises. As the Alberta tar sands initiatives have painfully demonstrated, conservation and environmental protection have often taken a back seat to the most efficient exploitation of natural resources.

The quest for productivity can create natural conflicts among different economic stakeholders. If you consider yourself lucky to have a job, then you might be reluctant to bite the corporate hand that feeds you. Asking for a pay raise to keep up with rising food prices may be out of the question. If you consider your labour to contribute significantly to company profits, then you should expect a fair share of those profits. People downstream from polluting industries have as much right to safe drinking water as those living upstream. Low interest rates help make small business loans more affordable and help young families buying their first home. Low interest rates punish people with bank savings, like pensioners living on their life savings.

> *"Productivity growth, however it occurs, has a disruptive side to it. In the short term, most things that contribute to productivity growth are very painful."*
> —Janet Yellen

In each of these cases, there are clear winners and losers. The problem, according to social critics, is that the winner camp appears to be shrinking as the loser camp grows significantly over time. Corporate interests have strategically manoeuvred themselves into the winner's circle by using productivity growth to maximize profits. Social concerns, often very expensive and complicated, have been effectively passed on to government.

The promise of globalization was to promote prosperity both nationally and internationally. In recent years, many countries have agreed to reduce trade tariffs to promote freer international trade. Regrettably, the corporate focus was on free trade to remove profit shrinking barriers like import taxes (tariffs) and restrictive quotas. New markets were opened up for corporations to enter. The notion of fair trade was not sufficiently addressed in the unregulated globalization that followed. In many ways, the globalization experienced to date has mirrored the frontier injustice experienced as America first expanded westward.

Increased global trade has made the world more interconnected and interdependent. By removing trade barriers, corporations have been able to increase productivity by conducting large scale operations employing available natural resources, labour, and capital most efficiently, wherever they can be brought together in a productive enterprise. They can then sell the goods and services they specialize in both domestic and international markets. Specialization and trade can increase the quantity of goods and services available to consumers. Opening markets to foreign imports can provide consumers more choice and lower prices. Developing nations can use specialization and trade to expand their economies and increase incomes for their workers. Given the promised benefits, this was to be a classic win-win scenario. The reality proved quite different. The benefits of specialization and global trade were not shared equally among all participants. Regrettably, the emphasis was placed on free trade rather than fair trade.

Profit motivated globalization led to the exploitation of cheap labour and resources to maximize corporate profits. Jobs were exported to developing nations where labour costs and environmental regulations were minimal. Corporate profits increased significantly but consumer prices did not improve as significantly. If they had, this would have triggered a sharp downward drag on corporate profits. Product quality has declined in some cases, causing consumers to replace products more often. This results in the wasteful over-consumption of the world's limited natural resources.

Many giant corporations became multinationals, conducting significant business in different nations. This allows corporations to play off one host nation against another to secure the most profitable deals possible. In order to improve profitability, sometimes multinationals prefer to do business in countries where environmental regulations are lax.

In order to meet corporate demands for cost cutting, sometimes unsafe working conditions and child labour are used by small foreign companies supplying goods to multinationals. In many cases, the lion's share of the benefits of freer international trade and globalization remain with the multinational corporations. Developing nations, and their exploited labour force and environment, seldom receive appropriate compensation.

> *"Globalization has gone wrong, as it has no rules. Multinationals are almost above the law. They are so huge they are bigger than governments."*
>
> —DICK SMITH

In time, some multinationals like Nestlé, General Electric, General Motors, McDonalds, Exxon Mobil, Nike Inc., Pfizer Inc., and Apple became larger, more wealthy and powerful than many of their host countries. These powerful corporations can effectively bypass government regulation and avoid taxation by shifting activities from one nation to another. They have, in effect, become '*transnational*' corporations accountable only to themselves. When profits are on the line, *transnationals* may have limited loyalty to any one country, way of life, or political system.

The following two perspectives clearly distinguish between the promise and potential of globalization and the exploitative reality that emerged.

The American Dream

"But what does our American Dream mean today? ... Today, it also means a better life now, as well as tomorrow. And to achieve our better life we want a better job, a better income, more opportunity, and more options. We want to continuously move up life's ladder, and we want that ladder to keep reaching so our children have a chance to go even further tomorrow than we do today. In short, we want the stuff that dreams are made of.

It is these dreams of opportunity that are so inexplicably tied to our growth in trade. The days of selling to each other to support America's economy are over. America may produce 28% of the world market in GDP—but we're just 5% of the world's population. In our global economy, we must increase our trade if we are to improve our well-being. Trade makes the American dream real."
— C. MICHAEL ARMSTRONG
(SPEECH TO THE *DETROIT ECONOMIC CLUB*, JAN. 15, 1997)

One of America's Hottest New Businesses Candidly Explains its Success

"We have a factory in China where we have 250 people. We own them; it's our factory. We pay them $40 a month and they work 28 days a month. They work from 7 am to 11 pm, with two breaks for lunch and dinner. They eat all together, 16 people to a room, stacked on four bunks to a corner. Generally, they're young girls that come from the hills."
— IRWIN GORDON
(PRESIDENT OF AVA-LINE COMPANY OF WHIPPANY, NEW JERSEY SPEAKING TO *BUSINESS WEEK MAGAZINE* IN 1996, AFTER HIS LAPEL PIN COMPANY WAS NAMED ONE OF THE "HOTTEST NEW SMALL BUSINESSES IN AMERICA" BY *ENTREPRENEUR MAGAZINE*)

American business executive, and former CEO of telecommunications giant AT&T, Michael Armstrong, makes a compelling case for why America could not afford to ignore the movement toward economic globalization. However, his life ladder of perpetual growth is quite ambitious and unrealistic for a world with finite resources. Millennials will be the first generation of Americans needing to scale down their expectations relative to their parents' generation. The negative impacts of globalization on American workers were clearly not anticipated. Despite high productivity levels, American labour has not always been able to compete favourably with foreign workers earning as little as $1 per hour.

To date, American workers have had to curtail their wage demands for fear of losing more jobs to foreign workers, willing to work for much less. Unfortunately, wages in developing countries have not moved significantly closer to American averages. Clearly, Armstrong did not foresee that the benefits of globalization would be so skewed in favour of corporations and the corporate elite. He also did not foresee the devastating impact globalization, corporate primacy, and the neutering of labour unions would have on America's rapidly shrinking middle class.

The amazingly candid comments of Irwin Gordon, in 1996, provide insight into the business plan of a rapidly growing enterprise. This company unashamedly based its growth on the exploitation of young girls, working for all intents and purposes, as indentured servants of a corporation. Gordon needs to be commended for his honesty. Most corporate executives would have put a much more positive spin on this sad reality. One possible spin might highlight the provision of steady work, for desperate people previously unable to support themselves. Defaulting to such explanations, over time, the corporate face of globalization has learned to become rather two-faced.

In industrially developed countries like Canada and the United States, globalization has benefitted consumers more than workers. Many jobs have been outsourced to developing nations where labour costs can be one-tenth of the average domestic wage. With stubbornly high unemployment rates, remaining workers have had to settle for modest wages to remain competitive with foreign labour costs. This, workers are often told, is the only way to avoid further outsourcing. In communities where many factories are closed down, like America's badly affected 'rust belt', the mood has swung drastically away from globalization.

Anti-trade sentiment and isolationism have become more popular in the hardest hit communities. The problem is that communities and nations cannot cocoon themselves from globalization and expect to successfully return to a world, as it was, circa 1970. Globalization's potential for good needs to be harnessed and corrections need to be implemented to ensure that a fairer version of globalization prevails over the current one-sided, two-faced model.

The push towards productivity in America has contributed to the dominance and subsequent decline of the big box store. Many small independent merchants, operating businesses like local hardware, book, home electronics, and variety stores, have been effectively forced out of business by big box warehouses like Home Depot, Barnes & Noble, Best Buy, Wal-Mart, and Costco. These big box stores operate efficiently through economies of scale.

Big box stores tend to carry a diverse product line, in large quantities. They systematically phase out low demand products that are proven to be less profitable. They then persuade their customers to switch to more profitable alternatives. Big box retailers are now experiencing challenging times because of the consumer switch to online shopping through mega corporations like Amazon and eBay. Big box stores and other major retailers may become the dinosaurs of our post-modern age.

Current one-sided, two-faced practices connected to globalizing the world economy are not sustainable. In time, discerning citizens and exploited workers will revolt against injustice. The corporate elite will have to use strong arm tactics to control growing dissent. Governments will have to make a clear moral choice regarding whose interests they are elected to serve. Citizens must play a key role in this transition to a more balanced and just form of globalization. It would be naïve to expect corporations and governments to get this transformation right, if left to their own devices.

To make this badly overdue transition possible, several key problems need to be overcome. First, citizens need a more functional understanding of how the economic world works and how their choices can contribute either to the problem or to the solution. Second, citizens need to know how to become effective change agents, both politically and economically. They need to know how to mobilize the power they still hold to affect desired changes. Civic and economic education must both be improved.

> *"Greed has been severely underestimated and denigrated —unfairly so, in my opinion. There is nothing wrong with avarice as a motive, as long as it does not lead to anti-social behaviour."*
> —CONRAD BLACK

Another problem is that conscientious corporations, with a demonstrated social conscience, may not be recognized for their good corporate citizenship. These corporations may be painted with the same brush as their greedy counterparts. Citizens need to be able to distinguish clearly between these two types of corporate citizenship. Self-interest powers the business world. Without rewards, individuals and groups would be reluctant to assume risks. The key question is: When does greed become excessive and harmful to the common good? Business tycoon Conrad Black's quote about the need for greed is quite revealing. Even more revealing was his attempt to raid his Canadian workers' pension fund surplus, when his corporate empire was facing a monetary shortfall. Similar unauthorized seizures of money, from his American companies, landed him in prison for three

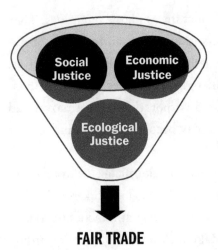

FAIR TRADE

Figure 8.1: Fair trade requires economic, social and ecological justice.

years. It would appear that he did not follow his own advice. Alternatively, he got caught up in his own web of greed, unable to discern when the critical line was being crossed.

A further problem requiring immediate attention is the important distinction between **free** trade and **fair** trade. Freer trade without social justice serves the corporate agenda much more than it serves the human development agenda. Fair trade enables economic, social, and ecological justice. Under fair trade, all parties involved share significantly (rather than nominally) in the benefits of trade. Under fair trade only sustainable development is promoted. No person or environment is exploited. Under fair trade, the wealthy and the powerful do not take advantage of small producers and vulnerable workers.

When consumers buy products from companies that exploit workers and the environment they become part of the problem, not part of the solution. Some products produced in Asian sweatshops are sold as luxury items in North America.

When a nation enters into a trade agreement with a nation that violates human rights, they are condoning this abuse. Major trade deals with China clearly fall into this category, yet many nations import large amounts of relatively inexpensive Chinese products. The peaceful relations dividend alone cannot justify this choice of economics over social justice.

A number of organizations are working to address unfair trade. For example, *Fairtrade International* is a partnership of workers, producers, farmers, traders, businesses and consumers making trade fairer for everyone. *Fairtrade International* supports sustainable development and seeks to ensure that producers, workers, and buyers get a fair price through the certification of *Fairtrade* products. The *Fairtrade* label on products confirms that:

- a fair price has been paid to workers all along the production/distribution chain;
- no child or forced labour has been used;
- working conditions are safe and clean;
- the environment has been respected;

- a commitment has been made to non-discrimination and gender equity;
- disadvantaged workers, farmers and producers have been empowered.

This *Fairtrade* initiative has been very effective in achieving fairer trade practices for several commodities. Consumers have responded positively to the initiative and this consumer power has motivated supermarkets

> "*It's frustrating to witness how popular fair trade bananas, coffee, and tea have become with shoppers and supermarkets while plenty of unfair trade goes on, largely unnoticed, in our own backyard.*"
> —ROSE PRINCE

to stock more *Fairtrade* products. The initiative now needs to be expanded to include more products and trade partners each year. In addition, a mechanism needs to be put in place to identify products and companies fraudulently using a *Fairtrade* logo or knockoff.

A similar strategy needs to be implemented for the identification of good corporate citizenship. In this golden age of the multinational corporation, good corporate citizenship needs to be more tightly defined and celebrated. The following example is adapted from the work of renowned economist Robert Reich and is appropriate for corporations with headquarters and a main base of operations in the USA.

SAMPLE PLEDGE OF SOCIALLY CONSCIOUS CORPORATE CITIZENSHIP

The [name] company pledges allegiance to the people of the United States of America. To that end, we further pledge to:

1. Create more jobs in the United States than we create outside the United States, either directly or in our foreign subsidies and subcontractors;
2. Provide a severance package to laid off American workers consisting of one week of normal wages for every two months they have worked for the company (including contract workers);
3. Ensure that no more than 25 percent of our total labour costs will be outsourced abroad;
4. Require subsidiaries, suppliers and contractors to bring wages, working conditions and environmental emissions closer to American standards

each year (rather than dragging American standards closer to foreign conditions);

5. Hold payments to executives to no more than 50 times the median pay of American workers (defining 'pay' to include salary, bonuses, health benefits, pension benefits, deferred salary, stock options and every other form of compensation);

6. Pay at least 30 percent of the money earned in the United States in taxes to the American government, without shifting money to offshore tax havens and without using accounting tricks to conceal true earnings;

7. Not use our money to influence elections or to lobby politicians.

Source: Adapted from Robert Reich at RobertReich.org

> *"Every time you spend money, you're casting a vote for the kind of world you want."*
> —ANNA LAPPÉ

> *"Let's face it. You have to make money to stay in business. Otherwise you have a charity, not a business. At the same time, when you build a thriving business in a community, it is important to give something back to that community. People never forget kindness, value, and service. And you have to have a sense of humour too. If you are too serious you should be in the funeral business or a banker. If you share one good laugh every day, you will enjoy a fuller life."*
> —HONEST ED MIRVISH

Companies that make this pledge, and are seen to be working diligently at delivering the individual undertakings made to the nation, can proudly display their seal of honour and serial number in promotional materials and communications. American consumers should be encouraged to look for and to support these socially conscious corporations in their business dealings.

A mechanism would have to be put in place to allow corporations to demonstrate and report achievement and progress relative to individual undertakings before an impartial adjudicating body. There should be an appeal process for unfavourable rulings.

This strategy, along with other forms of informed consumer activism will make the transition to a fairer economic reality possible, both domestically and globally. Good corporate citizens can in turn pressure associated companies and partners to join the transformation movement.

The adjacent quote, from an American-Canadian business magnate, theatre impresario, and philanthropist succinctly expresses a socially conscious view of the business world. I encountered Ed Mirvish, in front of his flagship discount house *Honest Ed's*, while on a photography excursion with some high school students, circa 1980. The students recognized him and got all excited. He stopped to briefly chat with them. When one of my students asked about his business model, this is what he shared with them. I have used this message regularly in my economics classes.

This vision has been reinforced by several extremely successful entrepreneurs and business magnates that I have met. More important than the words, their altruistic actions spoke volumes. Bill Gates is one universally known example of this enlightened leadership. Gates was a visionary leader, fiercely aggressive competitor and a ruthlessly shrewd executive while at the helm of Microsoft Corporation. In 2006, he became a leading philanthropist through the Bill and Melinda Gates Foundation. Gates credits the generous philanthropy of David Rockefeller as a major influence.

So, there is hope that a concerted effort can redirect both globalization and corporate citizenship to more socially and environmentally responsible practices. This effort will require the collaboration of government, labour unions, business leaders, corporate executives, and discerning citizen/consumers. But dreaming will not make it so. A concerted and sustained effort is required from all stakeholders. Growth strategies, professing suspect economics, need to be exposed and dismissed before they create further harm. Trickle-down economics, where the poor are helped vicariously by first helping the rich to become richer (through massive tax cuts and social program cuts) is one such strategy. In this Trump favoured plan, the rich will then pass some of their tax savings on to others, in the form of new jobs.

Critical Questions for Discerning Minds: Dealing Constructively with Globalization, Trade, and Corporate Power

★ ★ ★ ★ ★ ★

In light of the politico-economic dilemma facing Americans today, discerning citizens need to ask themselves the following critical questions.

1. Where are this politician's campaign funds coming from? What does this reveal about commitments and priorities?

2. What are this politician's views on globalization?

3. What benefits are recognized?

4. What realistic improvements, adjustments, or corrections are being advocated?

5. How realistic are economic promises? How detailed are economic strategies and action plans?

> *"When buying and selling is controlled by legislation, the first things to be bought and sold are legislators."*
> —P. J. O'ROURKE

6. How workable is what is being proposed to improve the economy? What evidence do I have to support my judgement?

7. How does this candidate or leader propose to make trade fairer for people? Is this workable?

8. How does this candidate or leader define good corporate citizenship? Is this workable?

9. How does this candidate or leader propose to support corporate America? Is this workable?

10. Can present leadership be trusted to right a listing ship in the direction of the common welfare of citizens rather than continuing the preferential treatment of the corporate elite? What evidence can I use to support my judgement?

11. Can the trickle-down approach to economics that did not work during the Reagan administration, during the 1980s, be expected to work better in today's golden age of the corporation? What evidence can I use to support my judgement?

> *"Trickle-down economics is a fraud. Giving tax breaks to the rich and large corporations does not create jobs. It simply makes the rich richer, enlarges the deficit and increases income and wealth inequality. We need economic policies which benefit working families, not the billionaire class."*
> —BERNIE SANDERS

12. Which economic strategies should be prioritized? What evidence do I have to support my judgement?

An Experience Worth Noting: Socially Responsible Corporate Citizenship

★ ★ ★ ★ ★ ★

Since 2013, I have been proudly working on a project, funded by the Government of Canada, to create an online educational resource documenting the immigrant experiences of Italian Canadians. The resulting interactive website features interesting personal, family, and community narratives along with classroom ready learning activities for teachers. Since narratives clearly outline how living in Canada has helped transform Italian immigrants, as well as how these immigrants have, in turn, helped to transform Canadian society, this labour of love has been called the *Transformations Project*.

HOME   ABOUT US   NARRATIVES   LEARNING ACTIVITIES   ADDITIONAL RESOURCES   CONTRIBUTE   CONTACT US

TRANSFORMATIONS
The Italian Canadian Experience

Transformations: The Italian Experience documents the challenges and changes experienced by new Canadians. In their own words, it recounts how these immigrants adapted to cope with the challenges of culture shock, the nostalgia for the traditions they left behind and the new life and identity they built for themselves through hard work and perseverance.

It celebrates the accomplishments of Italian Canadians and the contributions they have made to Canada and Canadian society. It documents what first generation Canadians valued and internalized most from their immigrant parents.

NATIONAL CONGRESS OF ITALIAN-CANADIANS

The project was funded by a government of Canada grant, through *Citizenship and Immigration Canada's Inter-Action Program*, to the *National Congress of Italian Canadians – Toronto District*, in the fall of 2012. This website is only one portal to Canada's reality as a "land of immigrants." The narratives and learning activities included in this growing collection serve as a 'living tribute' to the resourcefulness and uniqueness of the Italian Canadian spirit.

FIND NARRATIVES THROUGH:

🕐 ARRIVAL   ⬡ EMIGRATION FROM   ⬡ IMMIGRATION TO   ✏ THEME   ▦ KEYWORDS

Figure 8.2: Home page screen for the Transformations Canada website. (Courtesy of the National Congress of Italian-Canadians and the Toronto Catholic District School Board). [www.transformationscanada.com]

As project leader, I was required to ensure that the collection of narratives reflected a representative cross-section of experiences, including the achievements and contributions of successful entrepreneurs. For some thirty years, my father operated a successful barbershop business. One particular experience, during my days as a senior high school student, had left a bitter taste in my mouth regarding certain business practices. At the time, my father would buy heating oil to heat the building that included his shop and our living quarters.

An up-and-coming Italian businessman was operating a heating oil company. Being a fellow Italian, my father decided to give him his business. My father was in the habit of paying all his bills promptly. When he noticed that he was being double billed for an oil delivery, he confronted his supplier in the barbershop one day. From my study, directly behind the barbershop, I heard the entire exchange. At first, the bill was claimed to represent a different delivery. When that position proved untenable, a billing error was finally claimed. While laughing, the supplier then asked: "What have you got against a fellow Italian trying to get ahead in this country?" This puzzled me because my father had switched his provider to favour the same Italian who was now accusing him. My father's quick response was: "I have absolutely nothing against an Italian getting ahead—as long as he does it honestly!"

After the next double billing, my father switched suppliers. I wondered how many others might get caught paying the second bill. Through diverse business interests, this fellow went on to become quite wealthy. But the experience left me with a cautious sensitivity regarding the entrepreneurial spirit.

Years later, while researching appropriate subjects for the *Transformations Project*, I found many successful business leaders, from across Canada, with a powerful recurring theme in their stories. Whether it was Johnny Lombardi and Nunzio Tumino in Toronto, Bruno and Silvio Di Gregorio in Thunder Bay, Ontario, Frank and Teresa Spinelli in Edmonton, Alberta, Joe Bova in Winnipeg, Manitoba, Josephine and Ennio Corsini in Hamilton, Ontario, Santo Montemurro in Rouyn, Quebec, or Joe Mancini in St. Peter's, Nova Scotia, each narrative recounted the successful entrepreneur's role in building community. All of these success stories underscored the need to give back to the community that sustained a successful enterprise. It was most encouraging to note the respectful treatment of customers and clients to establish long-term relationships based on mutual benefit and trust. This prevailing social consciousness was refreshing to encounter in the often hard and cold world of business.

The Trump experience provides discerning thinkers with ample opportunity to reflect on the tenements of *socially responsible corporate citizenship*. Trump's business dealings reflect a clear focus on profit taking, over community building. As a businessman, Trump used available infrastructure to generate sizable profits, but he proudly avoided paying taxes to contribute to infrastructure maintenance and expansion. By using foreign suppliers, he increased company profits while exporting American jobs to countries where workers were drastically under paid. He expressed no remorse in regard to his winner take all, losers be damned approach to business. All the while, Trump considered himself to be a patriotic American, simply because he cited the Pledge of Allegiance with his right hand over his heart.

In an America where top CEOs earn almost 300 times more than the average wage paid to their workers, no claim that the nation's wealth is equitably distributed can be even remotely justified. Trump has been a voluntary contributor to this harsh discrepancy. As president, he has furthered this divide by ensuring record high tax cuts for America's most wealthy and relatively modest tax cuts for working class families. Sustainable business practices re-

> *"What we've seen is a kind of backlash to liberal democracy. Masses of people feel they have not been properly represented in liberal democracy."*
> —AMANDINE CRESPY

quire economic justice, social justice, and ecological justice to prevail. This requires a social contract between citizens, government, labour unions, business executives, and corporate enterprises to be responsible stewards of the democratic society they claim to hold so dear. Given human nature, *socially responsible corporate citizenship* is not an automatic by-product of capitalism. It is something that must be worked on constantly, openly, and honestly.

This experience is by no means exclusive to Trump's America. Liberal democracies are currently under attack throughout the free world. For some 70 years since the end of World War II, the shared tenements of free and uncompromised elections, collective peacekeeping through international military alliances, and prosperity through international trade agreements, all helped to maintain peace and promote economic development. Aggressive nationalist sentiments were also held in check. But by 2015, the cooperative model emerging from the bloody rubble of World War II had become increasingly more fragile as nationalist sentiments gained political momentum and nationalist interests reacquired primacy. The spirit of multilateral cooperation has been dealt a powerful blow by frustrated, angry, and quasi-tribal voices screaming for autonomy to address escalating social, political and economic problems closer to home — thus pitting "nationalists" against "globalists."

For growing numbers of citizens, the cooperative/global approach has been far too costly. The working class have lost jobs and have seen their living standards decline. They feel betrayed by their political leaders and policies consistently enriching the wealthy elite. Clearly, very few of the gains of globalization have trickled down to the masses. Great Britain's highly politicized decision to exit from the European Union (EU), as well as the growing ultra-right movements in Germany and France to reclaim lost autonomy from the EU, thus assuming greater control over national borders, immigration, crime rates, economic decision-making, and job creation are clear examples of this changing tide — a dangerous backlash to the maldistribution of wealth and power.

If this backlash is left unchallenged, we may be returning to power politics where might makes right. China has not become any more democratic or compromising since joining the World Trade Organization in 2001. Since joining in 2012, Russia has promoted increasingly more confrontational policies in world affairs. As a possible state supported breach of international protocols against meddling in the sovereign affairs of other nations, the suspected collusion of Russian cyber hacks to help sway British sentiments away from remaining in the EU, so as to weaken a rival power block, requires careful investigation and appropriate punitive sanctions in response.

> *"Many people in Europe and the United States have not benefitted much from overall economic growth over the past few decades, and they are naturally skeptical of the leaders and policies in place. But the solution is not to throw out the liberal order. It is to complement it with government policies that allow people to share in the benefits."*
> —DOUGLAS W. ELMENDORF

Returning to the American scene, voices of moderation and globalism have continually lost influence in Trump's White House, as nationalists clearly gained the upper hand. Trump has antagonized traditional allies with stiff tariffs on steel and aluminum and threatened to reverse trade practices long favouring or being abused by China. Over the years, Communist China has violated trade rules, stolen innovations from foreign competitors, and subsidized state-owned companies to reduce prices. China has never been seen as a stabilizing force in the world community, but America has. Regrettably, under Trump, America is now seen as a destabilizing force, like Russia and China. This must change for liberal democracy and social consciousness to prevail.

By using tariffs to force trading partners to acquiesce to new trade deals, more favourable to America, Trump has initiated a highly-publicized trade war where retaliatory tariffs are only the first step down a slippery 'protectionist' slope. This kind of pig headed strategy helped prolong the Great Depression of the 1930s.

Canadians, and their political leaders, have been singled out as "weak" and "dishonest" schemers and cheaters, much to the consternation of the governors of the many states that share the long border with Canada. Most of these governors have spoken out publicly to recognize the mutually beneficial trade relations with their Canadian neighbours.

Dating back to the 1980s, most trade disputes between Canada and the United States that have ended before the World Trade Organization (WTO), like the bitter and ongoing softwood lumber and dairy product supply management disputes, have been ultimately decided in Canada's favour. It is not in the collective Canadian psyche to cheat, browbeat and exploit. But it is equally not in our nature to back down when being pushed around, even when being pushed around by the suddenly belligerent giant next door.

This climate of escalating hostility (and punitive tariffs) must change to preserve the mutually beneficial relationship between the two trading partners, military allies, and liberal democracies, without further harm to both political economies. Trump's aggressive, heavy handed notion of 'winner take all' must be replaced by the collaborative spirit of 'give and take' which has served both nations well for many years.

The Parable of the Infallible Dealmaker

★ ★ ★ ★ ★ ★

The following post-modern parable depicts the flawed and one-sided assumptions of trickle-down economics, in a global reality currently favouring the rich and powerful while exploiting the poor and vulnerable.

Trickle-Down Economics

Figure 8.3: This political cartoon presents a scathing indictment of trickle-down economics, where tax breaks are afforded to the rich to create new jobs and income streams for the working class. Regrettably, most of the jobs created in this manner constitute low-end employment where wages are generally not enough for people to live on. In reality, money is magnetically drawn upward in most economies. When you have money, it is easy to attract and accumulate more. When you don't have much, money is hard to acquire. (Courtesy of editorial cartoonist Ed Hall, halltoons.com).

The Transnational Corporate Pledge

Figure 8.4: When profit comes first, environmental and human rights issues can be pushed to the periphery. (Courtesy of cartoonist Roy Tuck. © Roy Tuck, 2018).

A billionaire misogynist spent his charmed life in the company of beautiful women. He discovered that money was a magnet attracting beautiful women. Luckily, he inherited a fortune from his parents so he always had lots of money to play with. Next to himself, the thing he loved best was to use money to make even more money. In time, he learned that the best deals are those where you make big profits while other investors assume all the risks. He was so proud of himself that he wrote a book about how to make money by wheeling and dealing. As gullible and curious people bought the book, he laughed all the way to the bank thinking, "As if I would ever reveal my real secrets to the rest of the world!"

One secret strategy he liked to use was to always have a designated fall guy to take the blame when a deal went badly. That way, his deal making record always remained perfect. Another strategy was to avoid paying taxes because governments waste tax dollars on the poor. A third strategy was to create his own charity. That way, he could give himself fancy toys and lavish gifts while earning huge tax breaks.

In time, he wheeled and dealed his way to the highest office in the land. He became dealmaker-in-chief for the entire nation. The very next day he took credit for an increase in stock market prices, claiming that the economy was already better with him in charge. A year later, faced with a sluggish economy, he blamed the incompetence of his predecessor and his current political foes.

After all, his economic plan was flawless. To deal with poverty and unemployment, instead of providing handouts to the needy (which is what stupid people would do), the dealmaker drastically lowered taxes for the rich. "As the rich become richer," he reasoned, "they will hire more poor people to work for them, just like I always did."

By keeping domestic wages competitively low, even more workers would eventually be hired. There would be no need to ship work contracts to China (like he had often done himself) to profit from cheap labour. That way, more jobs would stay at home. For the dealmaker, this created the perfect win-win situation.

First the rich win, and then, the rich win again!

CHAPTER NINE

THE SPECTRE OF SUSTAINABILITY

SPACESHIP EARTH HAS a limited amount of fuel to sustain life. Therefore, the sustainability of all human activity is of paramount concern. The Earth's resources must be used frugally today to enable future generations to sustain themselves on our planet. Responsible stewardship becomes a moral imperative.

Regrettably, responsible stewardship is not often congruent with profit maximization. Where 'green' initiatives have proven to be profitable, such as electric automobiles, wind turbines and solar panels, great strides forward have been made. These positive results often required massive investments in research and product development. The new 'green' technologies that emerged, such as wind turbine and solar panel technology,

> *"We are living on this planet as if we had another one to go to."*
> —TERRI SWEARINGEN

have resulted in the creation of new 'green' industries. These industries have created new jobs for skilled workers and considerable returns on the risky corporate investments undertaken. It is estimated that by 2010, renewable energy industries alone had created 2.5 million new jobs globally. Sadly, where environmental protection has resulted in a significant drain on corporate profits, quite often the responsibility has been defaulted to government, to clean up the mess at public expense.

The recipe for sustainability is not complex, but it is quite challenging to achieve

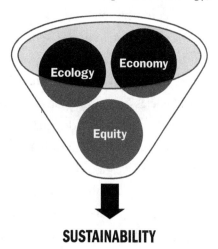

SUSTAINABILITY

Figure 9.1: Sustainability is rooted in economy, ecology and equity.

none the less. True sustainability must be rooted in the three essential elements of economy, ecology, and equity. This means that waste and inefficiency, environmental damage, and unfairness and exploitation must be kept to an absolute minimum.

With so many diverse stakeholder interests and needs, the recipe for sustainability is not always easy to achieve. For example, in the forestry industry, allowing forests to be clear cut faster than they can be replaced is not a sustainable practice. It may be very economical and profitable for company shareholders today, but it cannot be sustained for a long period of time without creating environmental and ethical issues for society.

Governments can choose to direct activity towards sustainable practices like conservation, reforestation, and recycling, or they can choose to prioritize corporate profits and job creation. Either political choice will have significant consequences. It is important to recognize the priorities expressed by political choices and to identify all consequences involved. Consequences must be considered as the price we pay for the alternatives we choose and the trade-offs we make to get what we want or prefer. Rarely do people

> *"Our personal consumer choices have ecological, social, and spiritual consequences. It is time to re-examine some of our deeply held notions that underlie our lifestyles."*
> —DAVID SUZUKI

(political leaders included) carefully calculate all applicable consequences before making difficult choices. To complicate matters, consequences can be positive or negative; foreseeable or unexpected; intentional or accidental; short term or long lasting; direct or indirect; localized or widespread; instant or delayed. The net result of not carefully considering consequences is a series of decisions with limited sustainability and maximum harmful side effects.

One classic example of this sad reality is the mass production of consumer electronics deliberately designed for a short lifespan. Planned obsolescence is certainly one way to keep the wheels of consumerism rolling, but there is a significant downside. Some global consequences include:

- Many Asian manufacturers of electronics and parts use lax environmental protection regulations and low wages to make production worthwhile;
- Congolese warlords use child labour to mine the tantalum used in the manufacturing of cell phones and other consumer electronics;
- Consumers in developed nations frequently discard and replace prod-

ucts like cell phones. Ads and promotions are used to further entice consumers to buy "newer and better" electronics;

- Toxic minerals and chemicals used in consumer electronics create mountains of e-waste that need to be disposed of safely;
- Toxic e-waste is being imported by China and India where workers, including women and children, sort through the waste to recover reusable components and recyclable materials.

The economic, ecological, and equity issues involved render current practices far from sustainable and safe for our fragile spaceship. Since many consumers are eager to acquire the latest 'lifestyle' gadgets, current practices are definitely profitable for many companies in the consumer electronics industry. But profits alone do not satisfy the economic consideration required. The waste of natural resources, driven by runaway consumerism, does not represent the efficient or responsible use of finite resources.

> *"To become a true global citizen, one must abandon all notions of "otherness" and instead embrace "togetherness."*
> —SUZY KASSEM

In addition, *external costs* of production (including environmental damage and worker exploitation) are effectively avoided by venders and consumers. These *external costs* (passed on to others) help render current practices economically, ecologically, and ethically unsustainable. In our increasingly interdependent and shrinking planet, it should not matter that the exploited are all in distant lands. When one group is abused, when one local environment is contaminated, we all suffer in the end —as one human family.

Perspective taking is so important in analyzing decisions and assessing their inherent sustainability. Applying diverse perspectives helps provide a more informed and objective point of view. Each perspective provides a valuable lens from which to understand the nature and probe the complexity of the practices and related issues being examined. Sometimes different perspectives share common concerns. Sometimes different perspectives lead to conflicting choices, priority setting, and trade-offs.

Some of the main perspectives are summarized in the table on the following page. Note that economy, ecology, and equity are featured prominently in this table. Economic perspective is expanded to capture business, consumer, financial, labour, and political/government frames of reference. Perspectives are presented in alphabetical order rather than in rank order or logical sequence.

PERSPECTIVES ILLUMINATING ISSUES AND CHOICES

PERSPECTIVE	PRIMARY INTEREST	IDENTIFYING CONCERNS
Business	Profitable return on any investment	Profit; interest rates; budgets; lower taxes; cost reduction; competition; confidence; investment
Consumer	Value and choice (high quality at low price)	Employment; income; goods and services; price inflation; confidence; spending; savings; lifestyle
Economic	Efficient use of scarce resources to meet needs	Efficiency; productivity; production growth; resource management; demand and supply
Environmental	Protection of environment and ecological balance	Clean air and water; soil and habitat conservation; pollution control/reduction; healthy food
Ethical	Doing what is fair, right and just for all	Equity; social justice; fair treatment of all concerned; humanitarianism; values; morality
Financial	Banking services and the circulation of money	Interest rates; investments; loans; mortgages; savings; financial services; profit
Labour	Fair and safe treatment of workers	Wages; working conditions; benefits; job security; job action/strike
Legal	Administration of justice	Justice system; law enforcement; legal rights; personal freedoms; penalties for violations
Medical	Individual and collective health and welfare	Medicine; health care; treatment; prevention; research; insurance
Political	Collective decision-making via elected government	Policies; regulations; social programs; taxation; budgets; elections; common/greater good; deficit
Scientific	Research to explain patterns in the natural world	Theories; models; experiments; observations; predictions/forecasts; research grants
Sociological	People living together in community	Safety; progress; lifestyle; health; family; community; common good
Spiritual/Religious	Meaning of life and the human journey	Faith based beliefs; worship; soul searching; inter-faith connections; respect for life
Technological	Applied science, making things work better	Design; invention; effective prototypes; problem solving; applying scientific knowledge

Current practices in the consumer electronics industry are politically viable because numerous local business and consumer interests are being served. Many jobs are created and taxes are paid to government. This comes at the expense of the environment and desperate workers, in distant parts of the world. Toxic e-waste creates an environmental hazard that cannot be ignored. When discarded as garbage the toxins in electronics slowly break down and leach into the soil and ground water.

Poor workers (often women and children) processing e-waste in Asia are exposed to health risks without sufficient protection. Most often, medical treatment and safety equipment/technology is not affordable. Looking at the bottom line politically, local voters are being favoured. Distant non-voters are being ignored. This unethical reality again renders the outcome unsustainable. In our rapidly shrinking world, any "us versus them" mentality is problematic. When

> *"Consumerism diverts us from thinking about women's rights, it stops us from thinking about Iraq, it stops us from thinking about what's going on in Africa—it stops us from thinking in general."*
> —PINK

one group or environment is abused, we all suffer in the end. When we do business with abusers, we are condoning and enabling their abuse. Consumers today need to be more aware that their choices have serious consequences.

The morality of such behaviour is questionable at best. Even when it is done in ignorance, the damage done is significant and lasting. In the final analysis, current practices relative to the global consumer electronics industry fail the sustainability test on all three counts. Current practices are not economically, ecologically, or ethically sustainable. But there are more sustainable alternatives, if humanity makes a concerted effort to invest in them. The required transformation must start with consumer awareness and action. Otherwise, the profitable status quo will continue to prevail, until it is rendered unprofitable. This 'greener' approach should include:

- Public education to highlight the dangers of existing practice and the availability of 'greener' alternatives;
- Scientific research to find safer alternatives to toxic components and materials;
- Technological innovation to design consumer electronics that last longer;
- Holding profit takers (retailers and service providers) accountable to collect and safely dispose of discarded electronics;

- Promoting certified fair trade electronics, where child labour, unsafe working conditions and environmental contamination are eliminated.

> *"Consumerism is at once the engine of America and simultaneously one of the most revealing indicators of our collective shallowness."*
> —HENRY ROLLINS

The consumer electronics industry is certainly not the only industry currently engaged in unsustainable practices. However, by reflecting on this one very large and important industry in our digital age, much can be extended to other industries in making their practices equally more sustainable. Overall, the push towards consumerism needs more careful consideration. Our economic world is far too dependent on constantly increasing consumption levels to fuel growth and prosperity. Regrettably, this short-sighted growth and prosperity often creates unsustainable consequences.

The present societal focus, clearly skewed on behalf of the business agenda, needs closer examination, monitoring, and overhaul. The propaganda enticing people to consume must be mindfully dealt with and overcome. This is not to say that business becomes the enemy. Business must remain an equal partner in the pursuit of sustainable prosperity, just not the commanding or dominant partner.

Consumerism, and its shallow focus on material things, leaves increasing numbers of citizens unsatisfied and longing for more substance in their lives. In

> *"The only true and sustainable prosperity is shared prosperity."*
> —JOSEPH E. STIGLITZ

the final analysis, the most important things in life are never things. To significantly improve human satisfaction, material things need to be de-prioritized in favour of relationships and service to others. Service industries should flourish in this new environment. Each of the perspectives on the previous table needs to reflect more closely on the following critical question:

Fully recognizing the importance of living in the now, what do I/we want my/our ultimate legacy to be? What am I/we prepared to do about it?

This needs to be asked personally, collectively, and continually to begin the long overdue process of transformation.

From Trumpeting Environmental Consequences to Trumping Them

★ ★ ★ ★ ★ ★

After leaving politics, former vice president Al Gore has done much to focus attention on the "inconvenient truth" of global warming and climate change. Around the world, the burning of large quantities of carbon rich fossil fuels has increased the levels of carbon dioxide in our atmosphere. Sufficient scientific evidence exists to confirm this reality. One need only look at the rapid shrinking of the polar ice sheets, on satellite images of Earth, to see the effects of global warming.

Around the world, great advances have been made in the development of alternative technologies using renewable forms of energy like hydroelectric, geothermal, biomass, wind, and solar power. By 2010, this environmentally friendly or 'green' renewable energy movement had resulted in some 2.5 million new jobs worldwide. This amount is expected

> *"You see that pale, blue dot? That's us. Everything that has ever happened in all of human history, has happened on that pixel. All the triumphs and all the tragedies, all the wars and all the famines, all the major advances ... it's our only home. And that is what is at stake, our ability to live on planet Earth, to have a future as a civilization. I believe this [global warming] is a moral issue, it is our time to seize this issue, it is our time to rise again to secure our future."*
> —AL GORE

to double by 2030, with further advances in solar and wind power. Investments in renewable forms of energy will improve technology and bring generating costs down. In addition, more people can assume responsibility for the production of energy to provide for their own power needs. Surplus power can be sold to existing power grids.

With the election of president Trump, much of the progress made in greening America has been effectively scuttled or given lower priority. While his opponent could only promise retraining programs, Trump's solemn election promise, to get unemployed coal miners quickly back to work, has caused a series of post-election dominos to fall.

First, all coal in the United States has automatically become "clean" coal. How lucky is that? Most other parts of the world only have dirty coal to burn. Second, miner retraining, to find suitable employment elsewhere, has been de-prioritized. Third, the myth of global warming has been exposed as a giant hoax perpetrated by Chinese interests to keep America down. Al Gore, passionate about the need to address global warming, must be secretly working for the Chinese. This third domino is most dangerous.

To begin, the entire scientific community has been attacked and federal advisory councils have been shut down. Somehow, it has become un-American to accept that global warming is a serious problem resulting from human activity. Americans are now expected to believe what is happening is nothing more than a natural cyclical occurrence on our planet. After all, ice ages come and ice ages go, as do periods of global warming. Human activity, it is claimed, can never change this natural occurrence.

In addition, the promised return to 'clean coal' power generation in America is simply not Earth friendly. This was an excellent election ploy but even the coal mine canaries have figured out, by now, that this will never fly as sustainable and environmentally responsible practice. Yes, it can be rationalized to gullible and desperate people. But it can never be justified given environmental issues in a world faced with carbon-fuel induced climate change due to increased levels of carbon dioxide in the atmosphere.

Of course, by dismissing the massive scientific evidence, by ridiculing scientists, and by cutting government funding for scientific research, climate change deniers feel vindicated. These deniers can rest assured that unlike the ostrich, a flightless bird incorrectly known for sticking its frightened head in the cold ground, they have their heads fully inserted in a much warmer hole, conveniently located "where the sun don't shine."

It is important to recognize the misguided and false assumptions in Trump's approach to global warming, climate change and "clean" coal.

1. **How can there be global warming while blizzards and cold temperatures set new winter records?**
   Any cold spell in the weather does not refute the ongoing heating of the planet. The difference between momentary weather patterns and long term climate patterns needs to be recognized. In addition, the growing extremes in weather patterns need to be associated with changing atmospheric conditions, and not just treated as freak natural occurrences.

2. **Climate change is a natural occurrence on this planet.**
   Human activity is burning more carbon into the atmosphere and changing the normal warming rate of the planet. Consequences include melting polar ice caps, rising sea level, expanding desert areas, disturbances in established

weather patterns, and the increasing intensity of active weather. Larger and more powerful hurricane systems in the southern states are one example of this intensification.

3. **Global warming is a hoax perpetrated by the Chinese to keep America down.**

The global scientific community confirms the increase in carbon dioxide in our atmosphere and recognizes its warming blanket effect on the planet. Too much evidence exists to ignore, even if scientific thinking is systematically purged.

> *"We've ended the war on beautiful, clean coal, and it's just been announced that a second, brand-new coal mine, where they're going to take out clean coal—meaning, they're taking out coal. They're going to clean it—is opening in the state of Pennsylvania, the second one."*
> —DONALD TRUMP
> PHOENIX ARIZONA,
> AUGUST 22, 2017

4. **Any damage has already been done by now.**

This is a cumulative phenomenon. The planetary warming rate increases exponentially as more carbon-based materials are burned to produce energy.

5. **American coal is clean coal.**

All coal burning releases carbon dioxide and other contaminants into the atmosphere. All coal is, by nature, a dirty fuel. Furnace filters can be used to prevent some impurities from being released into the atmosphere but carbon dioxide is always created and needs to be stored underground or released into the atmosphere. The adjacent quote from the president indicates that he either does not know what "clean" coal technology is, or he is playing dumb for his audience. The "clean" coal process involves the filtering and safe storage of carbon dioxide underground. Surprisingly, the first Trump budget actually cut funding for this 'clean' technology by over 50 percent. In addition, he has rolled back environmental regulations. When the only "clean" component left is the nickname, this plan looks and smells suspiciously like an unsophisticated cover for the same old dirty coal technology of a bygone era.

6. **American coal miners have a right to work and feed their families.**

Coal based energy will have to be replaced by alternate forms of energy. Retraining programs will make American miners more employable and able to work in emerging industries, including the production of renewable energy. Exporting American coal to foreign power plants certainly provides work for American coal miners, but it makes America complicit in the further carbonization of the atmosphere. Data from the US Energy Information Administration suggests that American coal production will decline in the coming decades as alternative 'green' energy sources continue to become less expensive and more technologically viable. Trump may be able to save a few coal mining jobs, for the short-term, but he cannot buck global trends or the economic reality that coal is becoming an increasingly more expensive and problematic fuel source.

7. The switch to alternative energy sources will require expensive technology, high risk investments, and a long implementation period.

> *"There are jobs to be created on both sides of the climate argument. Whether we are investing in oil or sun, coal or wind, gas or algae, the economy will be stimulated by the investment. The economy, unlike each of us, is not swayed by ideology."*
> —EVANGELINE LILLY

The conversion to greener energy is long overdue. Immediate action is required. Delays only complicate and prolong the problem. There is little incentive to invest in renewable 'green' energy if carbon based and nuclear materials are still being preferred to generate power. Technological innovation will bring production costs down once 'green' energy is prioritized, promoted, and seen to be a workable alternative. It is important that the investment pendulum is made to swing in the direction of more sustainable practices. This is where government leadership should come in, to serve and support the greater good.

Simply put, one cannot achieve progress by taking and promoting giant steps backward. This is not an indicator of visionary leadership. This new America has become a laughing stock for discerning people around the globe. Luckily, by perpetuating the problem, the denial movement has triggered counter reactions from angry Americans defiantly contributing to the real solution.

It would be unfair to land all anti-Earth activity on Trump's doorstep. Long before the advent of *The Donald*, additional short-sighted behaviours can be recognized as environmentally harmful. Perhaps the greatest example is the dumping of nuclear waste, potentially harmful for thousands of years to come, off the New Jersey/Maryland coast. Concrete lined steel barrels were used to sink the primarily military nuclear waste down to the ocean floor.

Inexplicably, when some barrels did not sink, they were shot full of holes by Navy fighter jets to make them sink. This was all done to avoid the expensive construction of a safe disposal site somewhere in America. This practice was officially stopped in 1970, but by then, an estimated 34,000 barrels had been dumped in the Atlantic Ocean and 57,000 barrels off the California coast, in the Pacific Ocean.

This short-sighted series of decisions will remain a ticking time bomb for thousands of years to come. On a blue planet where life requires clean water to survive, using the oceans for waste disposal is an ultimate attack on life itself. No dollar savings can ever justify these decisions. The naiveté of the "out of sight, out of mind"

> *"In the electronic age, we wear all of mankind as our skin."*
> —MARSHALL McLUHAN

mentality needs to be shaken to its fundamental core. This applies to nuclear waste disposal, hazardous waste disposal in private garbage cans, and toxic waste disposal by industry and hospitals.

We need to hold ourselves, our elected officials, and our community leaders accountable for the choices made in the name of profit, expediency, or human progress. Given our potential legacy of debt, toxicity, worker exploitation, and resource depletion, the ultimate critical questions for discerning thinkers are:

Does the current generation have a moral right to inflict substantial burdens on those that follow?

Can current leaders be trusted to do the right thing relative to sustainable practices?

What can I do to make sure that my actions contribute to the solution rather than the problem?

Ultimately, sustainability comes down to a question of ethical decision making and standing on the moral principles of:

- Eliminating waste and overconsumption;
- Protecting the environment from further damage;
- Equitable and fair treatment of all members of the human family, regardless of race, nationality, age, gender, wealth, or influence.

"Not only are labour standards the ethically correct policy, they are also the economically right one. Labour standards represent a "win-win" situation for workers in both the developing and the developed world. They are necessary to shift global economic development onto a path that is stable, sustainable, and fair."
—JOHN SWEENEY

"You have to hold yourself accountable for your actions, and that's how we're going to protect the Earth."
—JULIA BUTTERFLY HILL

"Yet all is not lost. Human beings, while capable of the worst, are also capable of rising above themselves, choosing again what is good, and making a new start."
—POPE FRANCIS

In the end, truth will ultimately prevail over ignorance and diversion. Under the spotlight of truth, people will be challenged to do the right thing, both individually and collectively. More sustainable practices must be one end result. The only variable will be whether sustainable practices result from human wisdom and enlightenment, or through the human instinct to overcome and survive crises. Let's hope we smarten up before it is too late to recover from our stupidity.

Just like the spontaneous heroic and altruistic efforts following devastating natural disasters, human goodness and decency tends to become more animated and prevalent during life-threatening crises. Hurricanes Harvey, Irma and Maria are three recent examples.

Responding positively to the immediate needs of their endangered fellow passengers on Spaceship Earth, many ordinary American heroes set aside personal differences, and other plans, to lend a helpful hand to those in need. All that is needed is the enlightened recognition that unsustainable practices are an equal, if not immediate, threat to the survival of life on Earth.

An Experience Worth Noting: Ecology and Sustainability

★ ★ ★ ★ ★ ★

From the start of my teaching career in 1974, two of my favourite subjects were geography and economics. Since my specialization was in economic geography, I was able to effectively integrate geographic and economic thinking into what I hoped would be valuable life lessons for my students. Throughout my teaching career, I searched for visual resources that would help students to understand complex realities. This was long before the advent of the VHS tape, the DVD, and the Internet.

Among my first finds was a short documentary film produced by the National Film Board of Canada, entitled *The Rise and Fall of the Great Lakes*. This film featured a canoeist (Bill Mason) simultaneously travelling through time while canoeing across the Great Lakes. These lakes provide the drinking water for millions of Americans and Canadians, including my students. The film used slapstick humour to effectively illustrate the significant changes the Great Lakes have undergone through geological history. The final message, a plea for environmental stewardship, was that none of these changes have been as damaging to the lakes as the more recent consequences of human activities, including water pollution.

To focus discussion on sustainability, I used this film in both my Grade 9 geography and Grade 13 economics classes. In geography, an understanding of air, land, and water pollution was part of the mandated curriculum. In economics, externalities (or costs of production not assumed by producer or consumer, but passed on to innocent third parties) were a new part of the mandated curriculum. I focused on such topics because I believed they made my classes relevant and progressive.

To be completely honest, I was also feeling a bit guilty about an incident that occurred while I worked in the sanitation department at Christie's Bakery, along west Toronto's lakeshore. On my second night on the job, along with an experienced veteran, we were ordered to clean out the numerous grease traps around the plant. The job required climbing down into tight pits and steaming away the built-up grease deposits. Apparently, this messy job was an initiation rite for new employees. We were instructed to never remove the final trap door from each grease trap, but we discovered that the job became a lot less messy when we did. So, we quickly removed and replaced the final trap door on all remaining traps.

Figure 9.2: Christie's Bakery circa 1990. (Courtesy of the City of Toronto Archives, Fonds 200, Series 1465, File 175, Item 5).

By the time we completed the task, we were totally drenched in grease, luckily it was all edible grease used in the baking process. The other workers found this sight quite funny, but we were glad to be finished in record time. Within a few days, however, Christie's received a formal complaint (and fine) from the Ministry of the Environment because of a grease slick in Lake Ontario that had been traced back to the plant. Needless to say, we were severely reprimanded for our actions, but we were never assigned to grease trap duty again. I felt bad about contributing to the lake's already poor water quality.

In time, I found a more recent, thorough, and serious documentary to use with my students, entitled *H2Overview*. Originally shown on the educational channel (TVO), this documentary provided a scathing indictment of human activities leading to water pollution. In one scene, fish taken from Lake Ontario were shown to have giant and protruding tumours. I decided to use this powerful new film.

First, I showed the documentary to my economics students. They were very interested in the subject matter and an excellent soul-searching conversation ensued regarding the ethics of externalities, and the need for more responsible consumerism and more socially responsible profit taking. As I had hoped, some students became active outside the classroom to raise awareness of these problems.

When I showed the documentary to my Grade 9 class, the students were quite upset. Days later, I was informed by the school's guidance counsellor that a few girls had drastically cut back their water intake and had become dehydrated and sick. Since I was after activism and not martyrdom, I revisited the issue, careful to protect the identity of the affected students. I reinforced that human bodies are at least 75 percent water, and that without water our bodies would slowly die.

I then clarified that the best solution was to stop harmful practices to allow nature to reverse our negative effects on water quality. A guest speaker was invited to explain how treatment plants make our drinking water safe. A political cartoon/ poster activity was used to engage students in the creation of informative messages raising awareness and promoting responsible treatment of fresh water resources. The most effective student cartoon, created by Paola Biagi, was eventually adapted in a teacher's resource produced by the school board. I went back to using the original film with my Grade 9s.

The Trump experience provides discerning thinkers with ample opportunity to reflect on the tenements of responsible stewardship for our fragile environment. Trump's complete denial of the global warming reality, and his contempt for environmental agencies that protected the environment at

POLITICAL CARTOONS

Cartoonists are often drawing public attention to serious global problems.

Make a scrapbook of your favorite political cartoons with a global message. Be sure to include a brief explanation of each cartoon.

In your scrapbook, draw a cartoon about a current global problem. Be sure to include a brief explanation of your cartoon.

Figure 9.3: Activity card from the curriculum support document *Let's Explore Canada*. (Courtesy of the Toronto Catholic District School Board).

the cost of reduced corporate profits, reveal a shallow, self-serving, and myopic vision. His apparent ignorance of 'clean coal' technology, the subsequent boasting about raising American coal exports, and the opening up of national parklands to economic exploitation, reveal a contempt for all things that inconveniently stand in the way of corporate profits.

Human sustainability on our fragile planet must be rooted in *economy* (the wise use of limited resources), *equity* (the fair treatment of all stakeholders), and *ecology* (protecting our fragile environment). Responsible stewardship is a global imperative that must extend to business, labour, government and consumers, as principal stakeholders in a common future. Allowing unbridled capitalism and corporate greed, at this critical turning point, can only further compromise human existence on our battered planet. Today's callous profiteers, void of any social conscience, are the "robber barons" of our post-modern age. Most regrettably, what they are robbing from us is our future. The POTUS should be a steadfast and progressive role model in this regard. He should serve as part of the solution and not as part of the persistent problem. There can be no future in pig-headed entrenchment. Humans can never come out ahead when they harm their environment.

The Parable of the Fishy National Pastime

★ ★ ★ ★ ★

The following post-modern parable depicts the counter-productive implications of climate change denial. Steadfast denial, despite a sea of evidence to the contrary, can accelerate the very reality being ignored.

Denial By Executive Order

Figure 9.4: By editorial cartoonist Paul Fell (www.CartoonStock.com).

Climate Change Denial

Figure 9.5: *Clay Bennett Editorial Cartoon* used with the permission of Clay Bennett, the Washington Post Writers Group and the Cartoonist Group. All rights reserved.

A billionaire misogynist spent his charmed life wrapped up in himself. He loved himself so much that he hated anyone who refused to include him in their special circles. In time, he realized that many people were 'outsiders' just like him. So, he promised the disenchanted outsiders the moon and they made him leader of their outsiders' club. Shrewd and cunning, he conscripted everyone into his club, by first refusing them admission and then drafting them into the fold as previously rejected outsiders.

Thus, he became undisputed leader of everyone that mattered. Since he was all that really mattered, he thought the leader's job would be relatively easy. When extreme weather brought flood waters, he told his members to stand on their tippy toes. When a massive hurricane swept across the land, after several days, he visited a devastated community to sign autographs and remark about the great turnout.

One day a reporter asked about climate change. He had the reporter thrown in jail as an enemy spy. When asked a second time he tweeted his club members "How can there be global warming when snow shovel sales are still climbing?" When confronted a third time, he used his influence to make climate change denial the national pastime. This angered all the baseball fans, but many other members were relieved to not have to worry about the terrible hoax any longer.

As it turned out, all the hot air emitted by the climate change denial camp caused the planet to warm up even faster. With sea level rising, flooding became a big problem. At first, men and women were told to wear high heels. When heels proved useless, they were told to walk on stilts. When stilts were no longer helpful, they were told to grow fins and gills. He thought this was a reasonable request. After all, club members had been acting like fish for a long time.

The billionaire did not have any personal worries because, by now, he believed he could walk on water. The last that was seen of him was his golden mop of hair, floating on the water's surface. This departure left the scientific community totally baffled. They were all convinced that anything that full of hot air could float indefinitely.

CHAPTER TEN

THE SMOKE SCREEN OF ORCHESTRATED DISTRACTION AND MISDIRECTION

★.★.★.★.★.★.★.★

REGRETTABLY, **POST-MODERN** life has become all about distraction. Some diversions, like watching sporting events with friends, are quite healthy. However, many other distractions provide potentially harmful diversions. Distracted drivers, intent on instant texting, voluntarily assume the risk of injury to themselves and others. Distracted consumers are enticed to keep the wheels of consumerism and materialism effectively greased, at the cost of personal debt. Distracted workers are willing to assume more job risks, to pay bills and manage growing debt. Distracted bankers and financial advisors advocate higher risk tolerance to reap greater rewards. Distracted voters often confuse hype with reality.

Ultimately, these confused voters can support politicians with ulterior motives and dubious plans. As the pace of life continues to pick up velocity, it becomes easier to fall victim to distractions. Unscrupulous politicians know this and they use it to full advantage.

The following analogy is helpful to better understand the political arena that has emerged in our post-modern world of mass media and social messaging. Ironically, the most apt analogy comes from the make-believe world of professional wrestling. This is an analogy Trump himself has used in meme to present himself as the people's champion against the evil media hordes, most specifically the "dishonest people" at CNN. By now, most television viewers in North America are familiar with the concealed "foreign object" wrestling routine.

> *"Our normal human tendencies are distraction and dissipation. We begin one task, then get seduced by some other option, and lose our focus. We drift away from what is difficult and we know to be true, to what is comfortable and socially condoned."*
> —DANIEL PINCHBECK

In this classic scenario, one combatant (usually a heel or villain) suddenly produces a concealed small item from under his/her tights. The villain then proceeds to use this object to harm the opponent (usually the good guy or fan favourite). Everyone in the arena has seen the object, except for the hapless referee. The incensed crowd goes nuts! The television cameras have caught this despicable act as well. But some accomplice (usually a tag-team partner or manager) is effectively distracting the referee. And so, the heel gets away with blatantly breaking the rules, without disqualification.

In the bitterly partisan politics of today, "shiny foreign objects" are often used to distract the referee. In this case, the referee is the voting public—the people responsible for deciding the outcome of the political contest. The "shiny foreign objects" used are figurative devices providing distraction, outrage, and ultimately misdirection. Because deception is a proven form of persuasion, the political arena has always involved deceptive distraction, to some degree.

> "We live in such an age of chatter and distraction. Everything is a challenge for the ears and eyes."
> —REBECCA PIDGEON

The advent of television, and then, the even more distracting Internet, have certainly increased the potential for mass distraction. These media have been used effectively to distort and dramatize fears and to raise the profile of fringe issues. In the process, viewer concentration, attention spans, and critical thought have all been effectively shrunk.

In 1964, during his presidential election campaign against Republican Barry Goldwater, Lyndon Johnson's "Daisy" ad was devastatingly effective. This loaded message featured a small girl picking petals off a daisy with the sudden explosion of a bright, shiny mushroom cloud. Johnson won the election handily over his more hawkish opponent.

> "America is addicted to wars of distraction."
> —BARBARA EHRENREICH

In 2003, George Bush Jr. used "weapons of mass destruction" to justify a second war in Iraq. It was later determined that the dictator of Iraq had no arsenal of destructive nuclear weapons, as originally feared. In the end, the bloody military campaign employed weapons of mass distraction to protect American oil interests in the region. The leadership vacuum left behind enabled radical Islamic groups to seize control in pockets of the region.

One of the problems leading to greater voter distraction is saturation. There are too many elections. Elections tend to drag on too long and become easily side-tracked on marginal issues and dubious claims. Too much election coverage is wasted on marginal matters. With the electorate almost constantly in election mode, overwhelmed voters can become de-sensitized to critical issues and their full array of implications and consequences. Alternatively, voters can become complacent, frustrated, or disillusioned and waste their voice. Both of these eventualities can compromise the quality of the government being empowered and the ultimate leadership provided.

When historian Daniel J. Boorstin published *The Image: A Guide to Pseudo-events in America*, in 1962, he accurately drew attention to the coming "age of contrivance," where staged happenings and spectacles he called "pseudo-events" are fabricated to convey a tightly controlled political narrative. For example, a proud mayor might cut the ribbon at the grand opening of a new shopping mall; the American president might pardon a Thanksgiving turkey; or a congresswoman might organize a press conference to announce a proposed job creation initiative in the state.

These 'photo ops' can be easily mistaken by viewers as real and full news stories. In reality, they can be nothing more than televised promotional events drawing the attention of journalists needing to fill valuable airtime. They provide incumbent politicians with a safe opportunity to show themselves as competent public servants. Dissenting voices are kept distant and difficult questions can be easily deflected without appropriate discussion. These events often orchestrate monologue, rather than the constructive dialogue needed to focus and direct the political process.

Boorstin also argued that American political leaders were starting to be seen as media stars. It has often been postulated that John Kennedy ultimately won the close presidential election of 1960 because of his carefully manicured television appeal, relative to the less appealing appearance of his opponent Richard Nixon. Like many, I believe that the 'superstar' media spotlight is what attracted Trump to politics.

Given the increasing demand for televised news material, much reporting remains under-analyzed by journalists and under-digested by busy viewers who demand concise coverage. With competing news services readily available, viewers will switch channels to find what they want. Therefore, short "quick hits" have become the norm and thought provoking analysis has been restricted. Newspapers once provided this more thorough analysis, but readership has been declining significantly in recent years. Politicians and political campaigns are happy to concoct concise and "shiny" messaging with limited details. This may not always involve deliberate misrepresentation of the truth, but at very least, it entails a very selective and limited account of the reality. For the sake of getting a story and meeting deadlines, the news media inadvertently collude with politicians, to further advance this culture of diversion. In the process, the line between news and entertainment can become blurry.

The sleight of hand trickery that has served magicians well for centuries has also proven useful for some contemporary politicians, who have become equally adept at misdirection. The skilful magician focuses audience attention on one specific thing, while something else is secretly being done that the audience is not allowed to see. When the audience suddenly sees what has happened, the result is considered a feat of magic. Trump has become a master of distraction and misdirection.

> *"Oh, what a tangled web we weave, When first we practise to deceive!"*
> —SIR WALTER SCOTT

Ironically, the distraction strategies used by politicians bear a remarkable resemblance to the techniques employed by lobbyists in attempting to influence politicians. Some of the more common strategies of the politics of distraction are listed below.

1. Monopolize the conversation.

To direct the conversation, politicians speak authoritatively and repeat the same message often. Exaggeration and hyperbole are used to accentuate the message and to make it memorable. A forum is conveniently provided for all favourable commentary. Opposing voices are drowned out and frustrated, by a steady stream of supportive messaging. *Trial balloons* are floated to gauge voter reaction and malleability, and to focus conversation favourably. *Trial balloons* are then reworked as required to secure the compromise of opponents and to grow political support.

2. Vilify the enemy.

Attack ads and negative messaging are used to demean opponents. Gaffes and weaknesses are exaggerated to expose the shortcomings of opponents and the limitations of their ideas. Once opponents are depicted as weak, inept, or bad, any harsh treatment becomes "fair game" and the tactics of 'dirty' politics become more acceptable to the public. By painting opponents as villains, their messaging can be dismissed as dangerous. Upset opponents are easily thrown off their game plan.

3. **Manipulate the media.**

A strong Internet presence is needed to flood the web with loaded messaging. This can overwhelm opposing messaging. By attacking the flaws of opposing arguments, there is less need to explain the details of favourable arguments. Safe photo ops and orchestrated events can be used to influence media reporting in your favour. By providing interesting sound bites, journalists may use them in their reports. Messages are kept simple and repeated often. Misdirection can be used to focus attention away from stories a politician does not want the media to cover or prioritize. By antagonizing unsupportive reporters, *pugilistic journalism* can be instigated. Once unsupportive journalists lose objectivity they can become sucked into the story instead of merely reporting it. Journalists can become more combative and invest more energy in an antagonistic contest of one-upmanship, aimed at forcing in the last word. Ultimately, this can mean paying less attention to the bigger issues and reporting can become more entertainment than news.

4. **Use fear mongering to grow support.**

Politicians invest time in finding out what voters fear most. Then, voter fears are used to make sure that messaging hits home. Often, a scenario is created where "the homeland is under attack," followed by an urgent call for decisive action on identified fears. Exaggeration and dramatization can be used to incite more fear. Dwelling on negativity can exhaust voters and discourage investigation into the claims being made or the remedies being proposed. Other voters will be relieved that their fears are being taken seriously, and willingly accept remedies at face value, without the due diligence of further investigation.

5. **Focus on the immediate.**

Crafty politicians focus on what people want to hear now. Implementation realities and complications are saved for later. Promises that entail instant results can have the most political mileage. Since politicians are elected for a short term, a focus on short term thinking is not surprising. A concise vision statement is developed, to repeat as needed, but a *dazzle me now* approach to politics is used to build currency and support. Hot buttons like immigration, health care, job creation, and reduced taxes can be pushed to attract voter interest. The 'shiny objects' being offered are shown off regularly to consolidate voter interest. Shiny objects can be tangible items, with perceived political value, such as a new local history museum, tax breaks for small merchants, and a retraining program for unemployed workers.

6. **Exploit populism and patriotism.**

By presenting as a reform candidate, interested in making the system better, a politician can cater to those disillusioned by the political process. By showing a willingness to challenge and confront the political establishment, a politician can successfully appeal to frustrated voters, who are upset with the sense of entitlement demonstrated by many career politicians. By waving the flag at every opportunity, patriotism can be confirmed. Then, those with opposing ideas can be safely branded as unpatriotic.

7. **Confuse issues and priorities.**

Crafty politicians gloss over or conceal inconvenient issues and truths, and draw attention to issues where the most gains can be achieved. A crisis or orchestrated confrontation can be manufactured to create sufficient distraction. This can help take attention away from issues that do not play into a particular agenda. Unfavourable issues can also be clouded with extraneous facts and details to confuse voters. Misdirected voters can be enticed into making more uninformed and emotional decisions.

It is important to note how Trump has employed the craft of distraction, misdirection, and camouflage, first to win election, and then, during his first several months in office. This will provide insight into the man and his cynical, opportunistic approach to contemporary politics.

How Trump Monopolizes the Conversation

* * * * * *

Donald Trump has spoken forcefully and constantly repeated his message. The following are all key parts of his memorable message stream or mantra. This is by no means intended as a complete listing.

Bad trade deals, by inept politicians, have stolen jobs away from Americans.
Lower taxes will create jobs in America.
Global warming is a hoax perpetrated by the Chinese to hold America back.
We are going to produce "clean coal" and get our coal miners back to work.
Borders need to be secured and illegal aliens need to be expelled.
We will build a great border wall and Mexico will pay for it.
We are being too soft on criminals.
The political elite are a spoiled and entitled lot.
We are going to drain the swamp when we get to Washington.
Together, we are going to Make America Great Again.

Clearly, exaggeration and hyperbole have been used to make his messaging memorable. Trump has tweeted a steady stream of caustic messages humouring his fan base and angering critics. Opponents have been frustrated by the lack of detail and proof he provides for his outrageous claims. Trump rarely provides sufficient detail to show that his plans can realistically achieve the desired results in the short turnaround time promised. The voices of critics have been drowned out or effectively discarded as noise from "sore losers" or from an elitist establishment interested only in perpetuating the status quo.

As for floating *trial balloons*, Trump has strategically used the Deferred Action for Childhood Arrivals (DACA) program as a kind of lead balloon. Early in September of 2017, Trump ended the program started by his predecessor some five years earlier. DACA had protected some 800,000 young undocumented immigrants from deportation. Often called "Dreamers," they were brought to America, as children, in the hope of a better life. Trump blamed Obama for creating the DACA program through executive order and urged Congress to come up with an appropriate political solution.

Congress was allegedly given a window and mandate to save or replace the program. In the meantime, Trump began discussions with leading Democrats to

> *"Does anybody really want to throw out good, educated and accomplished young people who have jobs, some serving in the military? Really!......"*
>
> —DONALD TRUMP
> TWEETED ON
> SEPTEMBER 14, 2017

strike a deal to legislate an amnesty like bill for *Dreamers*, in return for tax cuts and other concessions. If the bipartisan discussions were not fruitful, the DACA program would remain terminated. This gave Trump the upper hand in any negotiations and deal making. At the same time, some of his staunch supporters started to burn their "Make America Great Again" caps in protest over what was perceived as betrayal.

How Trump Vilifies the Enemy

★ ★ ★ ★ ★ ★

Trump strategists have brought the demeaning use of attack ads and negative messaging to new levels. Along the way, his opponents became "Lying" Ted Cruz, "Little" Marco Rubio, "Dumb as a Rock" Jeb Bush, John "the Disgusting Eater" Kasich, John "Not a Real Hero Because He Got Captured" McCain, Barack "the Founder of ISIS" Obama, and the mother of all villains "Crooked" Hillary Clinton. The gaffes and weaknesses of opponents were exaggerated and never forgotten. They were falsely used as indicators of incompetence and poor leadership ability.

> *"The last thing our country needs is another BUSH! Dumb as a rock!"*
>
> —DONALD TRUMP
> TWEETED ON
> SEPTEMBER 18, 2015

As the consummate 'anti-politician,' Trump can afford to be extremely harsh with all opponents. He is equally harsh with staffers who do not demonstrate absolute loyalty to him. Attorney general Jeff Sessions was referred to publicly as an "idiot" for recusing himself from the formal investigation into Russian pro-Trump tampering during the American elections. This recusal led to the naming of former FBI director Robert Mueller as special prosecutor. Trump wanted someone in the position who was more controllable.

How Trump Manipulates the Media

★ ★ ★ ★ ★ ★

Trump has proven to be a prolific tweeter, able to steal attention away from political issues and controversies through a seemingly endless stream of caustic tweets. His strategists have effectively flooded the Internet with favourable accounts to help offset criticism. Ultra conservative news agencies like *Fox News* and *Breitbart News* continue to provide strong support. Steven Bannon amicably left his White House post as chief strategist, to return to *Breitbart News,* where it was hoped he could be a much more forceful and uncensored media presence. However, five months later, the ultra-right, caustic, and venomous Bannon had become a political liability and was forced to resign.

In office, Trump continued to use the rally format that served him so well during the election campaign. Clearly, debate and dialogue were not his strong suits, although he arrogantly claims to have won all presidential debates. Rallies are used to safely communicate an uncontested message, to energize supporters, and to draw extensive media coverage. With a backdrop of energetic supporters celebrating his every word, Trump fabricates the perception that legions of Americans, from all walks of life, support his leadership. This is intended to counter negative data, from national polls, showing Trump's popularity to be in sharp decline.

One supporter, who calls himself "Michael the Black Man," has been a regular at many Trump rallies. He is often seen holding up a sign behind Trump that reads "Blacks for Trump." Quite often, he is the only African American visible in the camera shot of the large crowd immediately behind Trump. Token Latinos, proud war veterans and dedicated working class Americans can be seen to be strategically placed in the wildly cheering crowd. This creates the impression of extensive support.

Especially when he departs from the written script, Trump provides an endless stream of sound bites to help frame the news stories about his events. When Trump does not want media to cover a particular story thoroughly, such as reports that ultimately confirm Russian tampering in the election he won, his $25 million-dollar payout to settle the lawsuits against Trump University, massive anti-Trump protests by women and immigrant workers, or his inability to get the Republican Congress to replace *Obamacare* with a lame "we'll fill in the details after the bill is approved" replacement, Trump merely uses a stream of distracting tweets or public confrontations to divert attention.

> *"North Korea best not make any more threats to the United States... They will be met with fire, fury and frankly power the likes of which this world has never seen before."*
> —Donald Trump
> August 8, 2017

Specific examples of this diversion include ridiculing his attorney general, ridiculing and firing the FBI director, exchanging threats with the dictator of North Korea, and pulling America abruptly out of the Paris Accord on climate change. The adjacent quote was made during a photo op at the Trump National Golf Club in New Jersey. I will leave it for you to decide how fitting the venue was for such dangerously aggressive and conflict escalating rhetoric. You can well imagine what the lead story was that night, and for several nights to follow.

Trump is a master at inciting *pugilistic journalism* to antagonize unsupportive reporters, or "fake news media" with "very failing ratings," into combative responses to his insults. In response, some traditional journalists have bent over backwards to pick on every misstatement or gross exaggeration contained in Trump's endless stream of messaging. According to the Washington Post (one of Trump's designated media targets) the president made over 2,000 misstatements in the first year of his presidency. By drawing attention to so many exaggerations, errors, and misinterpretations, the significance of the most egregious statements can be effectively diminished in the public's mind.

For example, dwelling on the suspect grammar in the adjacent tweet, can take attention away from the deliberate and unwarranted labelling of unsupportive media outlets as un-American and failing enterprises. Instead of trying to hold

> *"The FAKE NEWS media (failing @nytimes, @NBCNews, @ABC, @CBS, @CNN) is not my enemy, it is the enemy of the American people."*
> —Donald Trump
> Tweeted on
> February 17, 2017

Trump accountable for everything, it is important for professional journalists to hold him accountable for all serious transgressions without drawing further attention to distractions. When a confrontational news reporter becomes part of the story, this can serve to add another level of distraction, by further confusing the line between objective journalism and entertainment.

How Trump Uses Fear Mongering to Grow Support

★ ★ ★ ★ ★ ★

Trump strategists accurately determined the fears most concerning Americans and made sure to address each fear in their successful campaign strategy. This created a prevailing sentiment that "America is under attack." Border security, strict immigration policy, job security, lower taxes, fighting establishment elitism, and entitlement, and affordable health care choices became the pillars of Trump's political agenda. All of this was expressly intended to return America to greatness. Late in 2016, *Rolling Stone Magazine* named Trump "Fearmonger in Chief."

Because all their fears were recognized, Trump's supporters were content to not have many details. The terrorist agenda of extremists was used to promote strict immigration controls and to incite Islamophobia. The drug wars in Mexico were used to justify a wall to keep rapists, criminals, drug pushers, and other illegals out of America. The aggressive communist agenda of the North Korean dictator was used to justify America's strong military presence in the region. The fear of the resurgence of radical Islamic militia was used to extend the American presence in Afghanistan and other vulnerable regions. The fear of losing more jobs to Asian factories was used to justify pulling out of badly "one-sided" trade deals, and climate change concessions, made by "incompetent" predecessors.

Since Americans historically have demonstrated a tendency to not change presidents in the middle of wars and serious conflicts, inciting conflict with Iran and North Korea can work to Trump's political advantage. Despite the inherent dangers of nuclear war, heated confrontations with declared enemies of America can work to strengthen Trump's base of support and consolidate his White House tenure.

> *"Refugees from Syria are now pouring into our great country. Who knows who they are—some could be ISIS. Is our president insane?"*
>
> *"Eight Syrians were just caught on the southern border trying to get into US, ISIS maybe? I told you so. WE NEED A BIG & BEAUTIFUL WALL!"*
>
> —DONALD TRUMP
> TWEETED ON
> NOVEMBER 17 AND 19, 2015

How Trump Focuses on the Immediate

★ ★ ★ ★ ★ ★

Trump masterfully built his entire presidential campaign around the immediate concerns of the American people. He promised immediate solutions to long term problems. By keeping details scarce, concerns of feasibility were never an obstacle. The efforts of predecessors were often depicted as "failures" needing immediate correction. The shiny objects he constantly paraded included the great border wall (which Mexico would pay), restrictive immigration policy, job creating tax cuts, pulling out of job killing trade deals, promoting "clean" coal, making better choices available in health care, and draining the swamp of entitled politicians. Trump's concise vision statement (borrowed from Ronald Reagan) was "Make America Great Again." MAGA baseball caps were seen to permeate the landscape in conservative communities across America.

How Trump Exploits Populism and Patriotism

★ ★ ★ ★ ★ ★

Trump presented himself to the American people as a reluctant politician. He entered the race only because other candidates were unacceptably bad for America. He successfully harnessed, and rode to victory, the American stream of a global wave of populism. Being an anti-establishment candidate, Trump could afford to bash and smear all opponents with impolite and insensitive rhetoric that would have crippled a more traditional politician. Instead, the more outlandish Trump became, the more attention he drew, and the more previously disillusioned voters he converted to his populist cause.

The ultimate promise of his populist movement focused on the reforms necessary to give the government back to the people. In return, Trump greatly enjoyed basking in the huge spotlight afforded to the leader of the free world. The Trump approach to inter-

> "We will stop apologizing for America, and we will start celebrating America... That flag deserves respect, and I will work with the American Legion to help to strengthen respect for our flag. You see what's happening. It's very, very sad. And, by the way, we want young Americans to recite the pledge of allegiance [in schools]."
>
> —DONALD TRUMP
> SPEECH TO AMERICAN LEGION
> IN CINCINNATI,
> SEPTEMBER 1, 2016

national politics unashamedly puts America first, at all times. If American interests cannot be guaranteed, Trump has shown a tendency to pull out of international trade and climate change agreements.

As a veteran reality TV star, Trump is careful to always stay in character as an anti-establishment, anti-traditional politician, and master dealmaker. He goes out of his way to present himself as a proudly patriotic American, at every opportunity. This is done, in full bold face, in spite of having successfully avoided compulsory military service and having constantly sought to avoid paying his rightful share of income taxes to the nation. His companies also buy cheap foreign products, effectively taking jobs away from Americans workers. He has steadfastly accused his opponents and critics of being un-American, perhaps the single most offensive label in the American lexicon. Trump has been able to further pepper his rhetoric by conveniently suggesting anti-American conspiracies both domestically and abroad.

How Trump Confuses Issues and Priorities

★ ★ ★ ★ ★ ★

Right at the start of his administration, Trump and his staff stirred up a silly debate over the size of the crowd attending his inauguration. Many believe this was orchestrated to deflect media attention away from woman's rights protest marches going on in Washington and other major cities in America. Similar protests were held in other democratic countries. This smoke screen strategy effectively deflected some news headlines away from the many protest marches of January 21, that were aimed at Trump's aggressively misogynistic, homophobic, and racist tendencies.

Almost a month later, Trump used a stream of harsh tweets and rambling news conferences (before, during and after) to deflect attention away from "A Day Without Immigrants," a one-day (February 16, 2017) national strike/boycott organized by immigrant workers across America to protest Trump's anti-immigrant policies. Many immigrants stayed away from work to demonstrate their impact on the national economy. Several small businesses across America showed their solidarity with immigrant workers. For example, many restaurants closed their kitchens for the day and posted signs to publicly announce their support of immigrant labour. Trump used a steady stream of tweets as weapons of mass distraction, deflecting attention away from all these protests.

To protect American jobs, Trump embarked on a climate change denial campaign which attempted to discredit a mountain of scientific evidence to the contrary. He chose instead to embrace a handful of reports that suggested no absolutely conclusive proof. Trump painted global warming as a Chinese "hoax" orchestrated to conspire against American industry. He appointed Scott Pruitt, a long time anti-EPA advocate to head and systematically neuter the Environmental Protection Agency. To keep his promise to unemployed coal miners, Trump has advocated the production of "clean coal" technology but he has simultaneously cut funding for the same technology. He has pushed for the re-opening of American coal mines and the exporting of "clean American coal" abroad.

This confusing and contradictory public position effectively removes from the scientific community the mandate to conduct research to discover and confirm objective truths about the natural world. More dangerously, Trump activates a right for politicians to dabble in science. In Trump's America, politicians are free to cherry pick which scientific truths are believable and which are fake. Regrettably, this right is assumed with absolutely no body of knowledge and no accountability for long-term environmental consequences. Jobs have selfishly been made a priority over the long-term health and welfare of the planet. This contempt for science has effectively promoted uninformed and emotional decision-making by a good number of American voters, and their elected politicians. But many Americans have also forcefully acted to defy Trump's withdrawal from the Paris Accord on climate change.

> *"Before we discuss the Paris accord, I'd like to begin with an update on our tremendous, absolutely tremendous economic progress since Election Day on November 8. The economy is starting to come back, and very, very rapidly."*
> —DONALD TRUMP
> PRESS CONFERENCE
> ON JUNE 1, 2017

In Trump's America, the reproductive rights of women and the equality rights of homosexual and transgendered citizens have effectively been ignored to favour the conservative views of the religious right, staunch Trump supporters. This position is difficult to justify in our post-modern world, enlightened by scientific understanding and a progressive sense of civility. Using the smokescreen of distraction, Trump has effectively blocked organizations performing abortion related services from receiving federal funding, without drawing much attention to this policy change.

On Friday June 2, 2017, as Trump proudly boasted about the great progress being made in job creation under his watch, the Bureau of Labour Statistics job report indicated that the American economy was still sluggish. The economy added 138,000 jobs, significantly less than the 180,000 expected by economists. Average hourly earnings grew slightly, but still less than projected, and still less than pre-recession levels.

By mid-June, a sharp decline in American auto sales was confirmed, after seven years of strong growth. Even with looming layoffs at GM, Chrysler, and Ford, Trump proudly boasted about a healthy economy and the creation of many jobs. Once again, this confirms Trump's belief that just by saying something, he can will it into existence. This might reflect remarkable confidence and/or cunningness. But at the same time, a clear ignorance of basic principles and indicators of economic growth is also evident. Conversely, this strategy reflects the clever political use of misdirection to drown out the negative political fallout from the abrupt withdrawal from a key international climate change accord, ostensibly to protect American jobs.

By exchanging hostile threats with North Korean Dictator Kim Jong-un, Trump can focus attention away from unfavourable happenings on the domestic front. However, antagonising a madman may lead to bloody confrontation. It is important for the American president to show no signs of weakness when confronting a paranoid villain, who has already murdered members of his own family. However, this nuclear chess game can backfire if the paranoid opponent senses an imminent strike and decides to be proactive. Equally foolish is the arrogant

> *"Spoke with President Moon of South Korea last night. Asked him how Rocket Man is doing. Long gas lines forming in North Korea. Too bad!"*
> —DONALD TRUMP
> TWEETED ON
> SEPTEMBER 17, 2017

strategy of taking all credit for any peace overtures made by North Korea, as the direct result of crippling American sanctions. This conveniently ignores ongoing diplomatic efforts to bring the two warring halves of the small Korean peninsula together peacefully. If anything, Trump's antics threatened this peace process.

Mocking an opponent with an extremely large military force at his disposal, and an emerging nuclear capacity, is not a wise strategy as well. But it can easily serve to take attention away from a sluggish domestic economy and ongoing bipartisan negotiations to strike a political compromise on the emotionally charged *Dreamer* issue.

The delicate political question of how to best deal with illegal immigrants is potentially upsetting to hard core elements in Trump's support base. This has been even more emotionally charged by the president's often promised treatment (no-amnesty, no-compassion) of illegal immigrants who have broken the rules to sneak into America. Trump can use the *Dreamer* issue to secure political concessions on other priorities, such as tax cuts, border security, and health care, but he runs the risk of alienating a sizeable and core element of his support base. The political contest will come down to the following test.

Will this strategy gain Trump more support than he loses, to ultimately create a positive flow?

The task of growing support might have been effectively compromised by his bombastic and contemptuous treatment of political opponents. Those holding out an olive branch now might be seen by their hard-core constituents as holding out a white flag. Only time will tell. I would suggest erring on the side of caution and not counting on tweets until they hatch tangible results. After all, such talk is cheap, cheep, cheap! Fruitful actions and actual achievements speak much louder than weasel words.

If nothing more, the Trump experience will teach the American people valuable lessons about their ailing democracy, their precarious dream, and the need to work cooperatively to revitalize both. Luckily, America has shown great resilience in the past. This occasion certainly calls for it once again. Not only has Trump lowered the bar for what passes as acceptable behaviour by elected politicians to an all-time low, but other politicians have now started to profess to be more Trump than Trump himself. These dangerous individuals must not be allowed to gain momentum and power.

Death by a Thousand Cuts

★ ★ ★ ★ ★ ★

It has often been said that "He who lives by the sword, dies by the sword." In the case of Donald Trump, he has proudly demonstrated a propensity to use cutting tweets as his weapon of choice, in the political wars. To that end, he tweets a steady stream of caustic messaging at all hours of the day or night. Trump has

proven both unpredictable and uncontrol-
lable, and he has proudly boasted about his
keen ability to use the medium to influence
thinking. Clearly, Trump has shown limited

> *"In politics, nothing good ever comes from the unexpected."*
> —CHRIS MATTHEWS

ability to use debate and dialogue to communicate effectively. He has also shown
limited ability to stick to the written script when speaking in public. The problem
is that he may start believing his own distractions. An even greater problem is
that his continued use of "alternative facts" and questionable exaggerations of
the truth suggest that he believes he can will things into existence. This is an
almost god-like quality.

Trumpian tweet storms often reveal a contempt for both the subject and the
audience of his messages. As presented, they can only be effective on gullible,
ignorant, or mesmerized people. This is a high-risk venture that can quickly
become counterproductive. The end product may be a cynical view of the world
and a pessimistic view of potential outcomes. Another outcome may be an abrupt
backlash, when staunch supporters feel they have been duped and betrayed.

Because of its ultimate lack of integrity, authenticity, and transparency, the
Trump strategy has only short-term staying
power. Smoke and mirrors can obfuscate the
political environment for a while, but not
indefinitely. It is only a matter of time before
truth and reason prevail. Boxed into a political corner, Trump will one day be forced
to use one of the carefully crafted exit strategies he keeps in cold storage. This strategy
will be used to affect what he will undoubt-
edly claim as a triumphant departure after
a job well done, leaving nothing left to prove.

> *"Distraction leaches the authenticity out of our communications. When we are not emotionally present, we are gliding over the surface of our interactions and we never tangle in the depths where the nuances of our skills are tested and refined."*
> —MARIAN DEEGAN

Trump has already tipped his hand. No scenario must ever depict him as
having lost a contest, having been outmanoeuvred in a transaction, or having
shown bad judgement. These weaknesses are simply not good for his carefully
manicured brand. As the 2016 election day approached, with polls indicating
that he was running behind his rival, Hillary Clinton, Trump began to lay out
his face-saving exit strategy. He publicly and repeatedly expressed his belief that
the election was rigged against him and that Obama had bugged his Trump

Tower offices. When he lost the popular vote, but secured the Electoral College vote, he had to abruptly abandon his exit strategy to plan his coronation strategy.

Eventually, after a thorough investigation by the Justice Department, the claim about wiretapping was found to be groundless. To date no apology has been made to Obama for the false accusation. But then, using Trumpian logic, why should he apologize for something he honestly believed? After all, he never stated it as fact, only as an honest belief or feeling. If stupid people assume it to be fact, that is not something for which he needs to apologize. In fact, I believe he has never apologized for anything. Again, this is a key element of the carefully crafted Trump brand.

> *"I know for sure that what we dwell on is who we become."*
> —OPRAH WINFREY

In office, Trump surrounded himself with like-minded individuals who were attracted to power like moths to a burning light. He had promised to "drain the swamp" but in the end, he merely replaced one opposing set of swamp creatures (sometimes referred to as the entitled political elite) with a more supportive cast of carnivorous swamp creatures. Ironically, swamp creatures, like alligators, rarely see themselves as swamp creatures, but merely as well adapted survivors of a very competitive natural environment.

In time, some of his hand-picked swamp creatures grew tired of the nonsense and realized the full extent of what they had got themselves into. Some might have conscientiously realized that they had sold their soul in the pursuit of power. But few had the courage to confront the problem. Instead, they dutifully supported their leader in affecting the program cuts needed to support his agenda. To avoid further public debt, spending cuts would have to precede the promised tax cuts. And so, funding was systematically cut to organizations providing abortion related services, public education, healthcare (to facilitate the demise of *Obamacare*), the arts, scientific research, and the Environmental Protection Agency, to name a few key targets.

In the end, the kind of leadership demonstrated by *The Donald* is terminal by nature. Instead of building bridges of consensus and compromise, walls of isolation were advocated as the American way. In fact, compromise became a dirty word. This conclusion required the arrogant assumption that one had nothing left to learn from different and diverse perspectives. Politics is supposed to be about support building through persuasive dialogue, but not in Trump's America.

Seeing himself as the consummate deal-maker, to get what he wants, Trump prefers to wheel and deal in hardball fashion. He likes to come on strong, them allow opponents to talk him down from his deliberately lofty position. Opponents will be relieved by his settlement for less than what he originally demanded. Meanwhile, the dealmaker-in-chief will get what he really wanted all along. Such is the artful theory! It remains to be seen, what the actual outcomes will be. By burning bridges and building walls, very few opportunities remain for growing support. Any return to more conventional political practices is bound to seriously upset hard core supporters.

> *"Leadership is about making others better as a result of your presence and making sure that impact lasts in your absence."*
> —SHERYL SANDBERG

While Trump is busy orchestrating the many program cuts needed to fund his promised tax cuts, and also to bankrupt *Obama-care*, his aggressive and spiteful demeanour has also resulted in numerous self-inflicted cuts to both his ego and his brand. Triggered by a case of steadfast denial, each self-inflicted cut appears a bit deeper than the previous one. For example, Trump has resorted to creating bolder new distractions to direct public attention away from earlier distractions gaining too much momentum. For example, on

> *"The president of the United States took time out—while, it is worth noting, over 3 million American citizens in Puerto Rico are without power—to call Colin Kaepernick a son of a bitch... Even NFL commissioner Roger Goodell denounced the president's comments. And when you have lost the moral f---ing high ground to Roger Goodell, something is horribly wrong."*
> —JOHN OLIVER

September 22, 2017, Trump began a foul-mouthed attack on professional football players who choose to take a knee during the playing of the national anthem. When the partisan crowd reacted positively, he dug in and made it a key focus for the entire weekend. All of this was done while 3 million American citizens in Puerto Rico were digging out from the most destructive hurricane in decades.

Some football players, like Colin Kaepernick, symbolically go down on one knee to protest an apparent disrespect for black lives in various American communities. Eventually, Trump also turned on weak-kneed NFL owners who will not fire professional athletes who disrespect America. He also ridiculed their declining television ratings. For Trump, declining ratings are the ultimate insult.

There was no mention of the suffering in Puerto Rico, or words of encouragement for the survivors. Instead the president focused on the NFL problem to help deflect growing fears about an imminent attack by North Korea.

Ironically, Trump chose to pick a fight with the madman dictator of North Korea to distract the attention of Americans from an FBI investigation into election tampering by Russian agents. As the investigation got closer to the possible involvement of Trump campaign leadership, a great distraction was needed and North Korea's rogue missile program provided a convenient opportunity for confrontation. With escalating tensions between the two nations, a new distraction was now needed to distract from the original distraction. This new distraction also served to conveniently take attention away from another failed attempt to defeat *Obamacare*, effectively stalling another major campaign promise.

Discerning Americans can no longer deny the harmful rhetoric being systematically spewed by the Trump message machine. There was a time when one could claim that Trump was not given a fair chance by sore losers. That time has long passed. With mounting evidence, discerning Americans are now challenged to do the right thing. The NFL community showed their solidarity against abusive treatment, and an unprecedented presidential assault on freedom of speech, by protesting together during the playing of the national anthem on the following Sunday. Trump dug in and continued to claim that the issue had nothing to do with race, but only patriotism.

> *"What you think, you become. What you feel, you attract. What you imagine, you create."*
>
> —BUDDHA

A visionary leader cannot afford to resort to crudeness, insult, and defamation. A visionary leader cannot afford to dwell on the negative, dragging the political narrative down into the gutter. At least, these things cannot be done while still claiming the moral high ground. Just like how you can never sell chicken shit as chicken soup, or pass off a sow's ear as a silk purse, you cannot fabricate a huge triumph out of a self-inflicted clusterfuck!

Both the Republican Party and the Democratic Party must engage in deep soul searching, and honest reflection, to recover and move forward from the many cuts inflicted by the Trump experience. Their continued existence will depend on it.

Christopher Wylie, the Canadian whistle-blower who recently exposed the deviously mercenary work of Cambridge Analytica, as "Steve Bannon's psychological warfare mind fuck tool," did the post-modern digital world a big favour.

The exposed weaponization of a supposedly neutral Facebook® platform is by no means an isolated or unique case. This public admission serves as a cold, hard revelation of new realities. When there is no product to purchase or rent, the user becomes the product and user data becomes a resource advertisers and other shrewd manipulators (like Cambridge Analytica's pro-Trump election strategists) will be eager to acquire. At first glance, the selling of supposedly anonymous user data to advertisers may appear to be innocuous. When this data is used to deliver custom messaging to a target audience, thinking, purchasing, and voting patterns can be effectively manipulated.

Politicians, and their representatives, employing cyber mercenaries to mine data containing the personal interests, fears, and lifestyle choices of potential voters, and then using it to manipulate voter thinking can effectively bypass normal safeguards and campaign restrictions. When misinformation is used to manipulate thinking, this can quickly become an act of cyberwarfare against the democratic process. In a combative arena where one person's weaponization ceiling quickly becomes the next person's floor, the argument that rivals and predecessors have engaged in similar practices should never be considered as acceptable reasoning.

HandLing by Trump and Putin

charles weissart.com

Figure 10.1: A gripping editorial cartoon courtesy of Charles Weiss. (© Charles Weiss).

This rapid escalation can only lead to manipulated election results that reflect the will of the people about as much as the sham 'free' elections conducted under totalitarian regimes in Russia, Iran, and China. Not surprisingly, Trump was quick to congratulate Putin on his decisive victory against skeleton opposition, while totally ignoring the attempted murder of a Russian defector and his daughter on

> *"They [Russians] bailed him out, set him up and made him their stooge. With Trump in the White House, Putin may win the 3rd World War without firing a shot. #PuckerUpPOTUS."*
>
> —JIM CARREY
> (TWEETED ON
> NOVEMBER 12, 2017)

British soil, using a deadly Soviet-era nerve agent known as *Novichok*. Once again, alarm bells have been triggered, signalling a potential conflict of interest. In a scathing tweet, actor-comedian turned artist Jim Carrey boldly depicted Trump puckering up to kiss Vladimir Putin's ass. This graphically represented Putin's apparent hold on Trump.

Technology today is growing faster than our collective ability to regulate it and render it safe. When Russian hacks boast about attempting to remotely shut down the American power grid, the potential for weaponization of Internet technology can no longer be dismissed as pro-censorship fearmongering. Allowing cyber assaults to go by unchallenged only serves to embolden foreign rival powers eager to cripple those who dare to oppose them. Conceivably, the next global conflict may well be a great cyberwar.

In any manifestation, undermining democracy can only be seen as the act of a traitor, and never as the act of a patriot, regardless of how long this perpetrator holds his hand over his heart while reciting the *Pledge of Allegiance*. When agents of a rival power are encouraged to exploit the democratic process in support of a favourable candidate, national security can be further compromised, regardless of the steady stream of "witch hunt" accusations and a constant return to "Crooked Hillary" musings that always play well to a bitterly polarized core support base.

One of Trump's most masterful distractions involved the moving of the American Embassy from Tel Aviv to Jerusalem, days after his former national security advisor, Michael Flynn, pleaded guilty to secret dealings with Russians, and agreed to cooperate with the special counsel investigating Russian meddling in the U.S. presidential elections. Without consultation, or regard for consequences, Trump boldly announced his controversial decision to move the embassy. By siding with Israel in recognizing Jerusalem as the true Israeli capital city, this slight to Palestinians in the contested "Holy City" was met with protests and marches around the world, including violent anti-Zionist demonstrations in East Jerusalem, Gaza and other parts of the Islamic world.

The Trump team's claim that he was merely keeping an election promise to his base constituted a weak rationalization, given *The Donald's* previously expressed belief that he could shoot someone and still not lose any votes from his loyal base. Trump's highly controversial decision, Israel's elation, and the numerous international protests that followed, dominated news headlines for several news cycles, until the Flynn story effectively became "old" news.

Critical Questions for Discerning Minds: Dealing with Distraction and Misdirection

★ ★ ★ ★ ★ ★

1. What is my attention being drawn toward?

2. What strategies are being used to draw and hold my attention?

3. What proof do I have that this is worth my undivided attention?

> *"Do the best you can until you know better. When you know better, do better."*
> —MAYA ANGELOU

4. What exactly am I being told? What evidence do I have to confirm this as believable?

5. What am I not being told? What evidence do I have to confirm this as equally important?

6. What is my attention being drawn away from?

7. What strategies are being used to distract or misdirect my attention?

8. Why is my attention being distracted?

9. What needs further research or investigation before I can form a sound conclusion?

10. What evidence can I use to support my conclusion?

> *"The illiterate of the 21ˢᵗ century will not be those who cannot read and write, but those who cannot learn, unlearn, and relearn."*
> —ALVIN TOFFLER

11. What has this experience taught me about specific politicians?

12. What has this experience taught me about the political process?

13. What has this experience taught me about myself?

An Experience Worth Noting: Orchestrated Distraction and Misdirection

★ ★ ★ ★ ★ ★

I found working as a part-time lecturer at Niagara University quite rewarding. Through my teaching methods courses, I was able to help many candidates obtain their teaching qualifications, while passing on my experienced knowledge to a fresh group of teachers entering the profession. What I found most gratifying was the overwhelmingly positive feed-back from most graduates. But over my seven years at Niagara, there were a handful of students who saw things differently.

Figure 10.2: Identification card for Niagara University faculty. (Supplied by the author).

One particular student went well out of the way to come after me. This person consistently sat at the back of the classroom. Beyond personal opinions, very little of substance was contributed to class discussions, preferring to type away on a laptop. Most assignments submitted reflected a minimalist approach to coursework.

In an attempt to send a subtle message, I started to wander by, whenever I saw this student working attentively on the computer. As I approached, the laptop would be closed shut. With each passing class, I made my routine more obvious. Finally, the student approached me during a class break. Without mincing words, I was bluntly told that after paying some $20,000 for this degree, what the candidate chose to do with available class time was none of my business. I did not agree with this assessment or demeanour, but I elected not to engage.

A few classes later, this student made an uninformed comment in class and this time I invited a rethinking of the position taken, in light of the contents of the readings I had previously assigned. The views expressed reflected minimal evidence of having studied this assigned material. Eventually, I was able to guide this student's articulated thinking to a more supportable conclusion, relative to research findings and curriculum policy. During this entire discussion, the student remained seated at the back of the class, while I was writing on the white board at the front. Once the student reached a supportable conclusion, I congratulated the student from across the room. Shaking my head, I went on to foolishly say: "Sometimes I could just strangle you! You have so much potential when you care to apply it."

To my shock, a few days later, I was called in by the program director, who told me that I had been accused of assault by a student and that the student wanted to press charges. The program director had known me for many years and found this accusation completely out of character. I admitted to a poor choice of words and proceeded to explain the frustrating circumstances. The program director must have interviewed classmates and their observations must have been consistent with my account.

In the end, the assault claim was found to be groundless. A threat was made to go to the police anyway, but nothing ever came of it. In a closing salvo, the student's strategy was finally revealed by suggesting: "This exercise of my rights, and genuine fear for my safety, had better not affect my final grade in this course." The opportunist speculated that this distraction would tie my hands and force me to assign a more favourable grade. This thinking revealed the cardinal error of perceiving grades as something a teacher gives, rather than being something the student earns through demonstrated achievement.

I eventually figured out what this crafty person was up to. Because this student consistently did the bare minimum to scrape by, the accumulated grades were among the lowest in a very high achieving cohort. As the mid-term point was now behind us, the student wanted to fabricate a narrative of misinformation to foster the mistaken impression that my assessment was personal. As a result, I was deliberately undervaluing the quality of this student's fine work.

The final grade earned was among the lowest in my course. When the course director noticed the result, I was asked if I could safely document the determination of this final grade. Since the educative assessment of student achievement was one of the areas of concentration for my master's degree in education, this brought the conversation directly into my wheelhouse. I was in the habit of keeping copies of all completed assessments, for all underachieving students. This was done to help diagnose avenues to improved learning and performance. On this one occasion, it served to confirm the accuracy and validity of my professional judgement. After the program director looked at my assignments and assessments, the final grade was no longer questioned.

At the end of the course, the university invites students to anonymously complete a course evaluation based on their experience. All of my students responded. There was a lone dissenting voice in a sea of positive feedback. The other students recognized my course as one of the most practical, interesting, and highly appreciated experiences in the program. The mean score resulting from individual student assessments was 4.53 out of 5, for a 91 percent overall rating. A good number of these students remained as friends well after their graduation. I was proud to be asked for letters of reference by more than a quarter of this high achieving class. As you might have guessed, this crafty individual was not one of them. But then, the attempt at misdirection had not achieved the intended result. My letter would have thanked this student for teaching me to choose my words much more carefully, even in jest.

The Trump experience provides discerning thinkers with ample opportunity to reflect on orchestrated distraction and misdirection. Rather than building up the quality of his character, Trump has spent a lifetime meticulously crafting and portraying a fictitious public persona. As the FBI probe into wide scale Russian meddling in the American elections expanded its scope, Trump fabricated a series of distractions to deflect the national narrative away from the probe he clearly feared. He also embarked on a campaign to discredit the FBI, the chief investigator, and the Department of Justice, in a vain attempt to undermine the investigation and to cast doubt on its eventual findings. In my view, such behaviour can only become a top priority for a self-serving POTUS with much to hide from the American people, as his impotent Helsinki Summit performance confirmed.

Casting doubt on national institutions of law enforcement and intelligence can only weaken America from within. In the scathing words of Republican senator John McCain: "We are doing Putin's job for him." All the while, Russian funded cyber robots continue to assault American democracy through a series of widely distributed falsehoods circulating the Internet as factual accounts that Americans should trust over traditional media allegedly reporting only "fake news."

The arch-villains of America are not the DACA dreamers, but the DC schemers, the bold faced liars eager to dupe Americans for personal gains and bitterly partisan interests. All human relationships, including the relationship between a leader and the led are based on trust. Only a POTUS with integrity can be seen as honest and trustworthy. Where there is integrity, there should be no need to deny, conceal, or revise the past to better manipulate the present and influence the future.

To pretend infallibility is a de-humanizing enterprise, often negating the capacity to learn and adapt. Such behaviour can never be a God-loving pilgrim's legacy. To act in a self-serving and abusive manner, at the expense of national security and prestige, can never be a true patriot's legacy.

Critical Thinking Checkpoint Four

★ ★ ★ ★ ★ ★

Reflect on the following probing question to apply your critical thinking skills.

What are the most important long-term implications of Trump's manipulation of contemporary American politics?

JUDGEMENT CRITERIA On what would a reasonable and objective person base this decision?	MY DECISION
☐	
☐	
☐	
☐	
☐	
SUPPORTING EVIDENCE What evidence can be used to confirm this decision as sound?	**RELIABILITY** How do I know my sources are objective, accurate and trustworthy? Can I find other sources to independently corroborate the facts?

The Parable of the Great Distractor

★ ★ ★ ★ ★ ★

The following post-modern parable depicts some of the dangers of orchestrated distraction and misdirection, in a political world increasingly pulled away from moderation and consensus.

The Great Distractor-in-Chief

Figure 10.3: By editorial cartoonist Paul Sharp (www.CartoonStock.com).

Distracted From Draining the Swamp

Figure 10.4: By editorial cartoonist Paul Sharp (www.CartoonStock.com).

A billionaire misogynist spent his charmed life on the lookout for beautiful young women. He was so self-obsessed that he believed everything he touched turned instantly into gold. He bought himself a gold toilet to remind him of his prowess. When he saw how inept all politicians were, he entered politics. As a ruthless tycoon, he knew he had many skeletons in his closet. But, as a modest celebrity he relished the opportunity to become a supernova. So, he proceeded carefully in his new role as supreme commander.

Being an honest servant leader, he took credit for the good work of his predecessors and staff. Being an ethical person, he blamed his predecessors and staff for everything that went wrong. Being a genius, he used every opportunity to distract his followers from what he did not want them to know. As an international tycoon, he had many things to keep secret. When an investigation into foreign influence on his election got too close for comfort, he called it "a witch hunt." Then he fired the director who would not end it.

To distract the nation, he picked a fight with an evil dictator, who was eager to try out new and deadly weapons. When the nation became afraid of impending war, he criticized his military, justice, and border security people, once again, to create alternative headlines. But still the witch hunt continued to come closer.

When people feared for their security, he cut spending on the environment, education, and health care to distract them from earlier distractions. But the witch hunt still continued. To distract the headlines, he next accused professional football players of not being patriotic. But the witch hunt still kept getting closer to him, his closest advisors, and his family. So, he publicly endorsed a controversial choice for the capital city of a foreign nation. This endorsement generated violent protests around the world, effectively monopolizing the nightly news. But still the witch hunt continued to get closer.

In the end, the witches got really angry at all the bad publicity and they turned him into a horny toad. This allowed him to effectively hide away in the very swamp he had long promised to drain, but never did. Lucky for him, he never felt the obligation to keep his word, or most of his grandiose promises.

CHAPTER ELEVEN

FUTURE PROSPECTS: THE SAVING GRACE OF CAUTIOUS OPTIMISM

AND SO, it comes down to this. Distracted and frustrated people may do insensitive things. This is not so much a conspiracy of evil, as a set of misguided self-indulgences. Guided by cautious optimism, the continued evolution of the human positivist spirit can affect movement towards more enlightened and sustainable decision-making. This can apply to both individual and collective decisions. Where progress is seen to happen, it needs to be recognized, celebrated, and used as a building block for further growth and development.

On the other hand, negativity needs to be overcome at every opportunity. Dwelling on the negative can only diminish, never enhance, our humanity. Cynicism and pessimism must be held in check to allow the positive to prevail. A modicum of pessimism can be helpful in keeping things grounded in reality. A modicum of skepticism can

> *"In any given moment, we have two options: to step forward into growth or to step backward into safety."*
> —ABRAHAM MASLOW

stimulate the honest and thorough self-reflection needed to enable the cautious and calculated risk taking required to propel progress. But pessimism and skepticism must always be held to a functional level. The result is a cautious optimism that can fuel a progressive movement forward, into uncharted territory.

Trump is ultimately leading America to step backward into safety. A modicum of this rear-view thinking can be helpful to consolidate origins and ideals. But, in the exaggerated approach favoured by *The Donald*, backward thinking can only serve to douse

> *"No problem can be solved by the same consciousness that created it. We need to see the world anew."*
> —ALBERT EINSTEIN

the flames of positivity and collective progress. At times, Trump seems bent on taking Americans back to an America that never was. This 'America' only seems great through the rosy coloured glasses of nostalgia and privilege.

Since only shared prosperity is sustainable prosperity, putting America first must mean putting all Americans first, and not just 'first-class' Americans. Internationally, putting America first does not mean putting everyone else last. Over the years, America has made great friends, partners, and allies. Despite inherent imperfections, these relationships should not be allowed to be compromised by excessively regressive thinking.

Cautious optimism is driven by a healthy mix of creative and critical thinking. Creative thinking enables the transformation of problems into opportunities to achieve progress. Thinking outside-the-box will help find new solutions for contemporary problems, rather than attempting to retrofit what clearly has not worked in the past. This inventive problem solving requires vision.

> *"Failure is not an objective reality. Failure means that you have merely stopped trying."*
> —NORMAN KUNC

Functional vision includes a sense of the next possible growth step and a clear path to *imagineer* its realization—a mindful transition from vision to reality. Creative thinking also requires calculated risk-taking, and a propensity to embrace 'failure' and 'error' as parts of the learning curve, on the winding road to success.

Critical thinking is equally useful in affecting positive change. Critical thinking must always be informed, rational, reflective, and constructive. Too often, critical thinking is wrongfully associated with criticism and negativity. In reality, critical thinking involves making judgements based on reasoned criteria and supporting evidence. The soundness of this kind of thinking is based on the appropriateness of the criteria used to base any judgement, and on the evidence used to confirm the wisdom of what has been determined.

> *"When one engages in high-quality thinking, one functions both critically and creatively; one produces and assesses, generates and judges, the products of his or her thought."*
> —RICHARD PAUL AND LINDA ELDER

In our post-modern digital age, critical thinking has become an essential skill. When bombarded by loaded and often conflicting messages, it is of paramount importance that a discerning recipient be able to accurately process each message to determine what to accept and what to discard. When people can accurately assess the quality of message contents, they can make more responsible choices. They can also hold their elected officials accountable for the choices they make in serving the common good.

Each of the previous chapters has invited critical reflection to better understand and more accurately judge what is most believable and authentic in the two-sphered, and sometimes two-faced, world of politics. As Noam Chomsky suggests, it is important to always question the assumptions inherent in what passes for conventional wisdom. This discernment is absolutely essential to maintain honesty and accountability in an increasingly more complex political world.

> *"I try to encourage people to think for themselves, to question standard assumptions... Don't take assumptions for granted. Begin by taking a skeptical attitude toward anything that is conventional wisdom. Make it justify itself. It usually can't. Be willing to ask questions about what is taken for granted. Try to think things through for yourself."*
> —NOAM CHOMSKY

The political world simultaneously functions on two distinct yet interrelated spheres—one public, one private. The public side of politics involves what the politicians want constituents to know and see, as a matter of public record. This public record constitutes the body of work upon which politicians prefer to be judged. The private sphere of politics involves the secretive side that is intentionally kept hidden from public view. This side can include matters of public security, secrets kept to reduce public anxiety, and secrets enabling confidential negotiations and difficult trade-offs. Often, this is done behind the scenes to make priority securing deals.

Some secrecy is required to expedite the process of political decision making, especially in controversial matters where public opinion is greatly divided. Discerning citizens must learn to recognize the telltale sounds of silence from their elected officials. In a political world, where brownie points can mostly be achieved in the public sphere, prolonged silence can mean that delicate and crucial discussions are going on, behind closed doors, to break a political impasse or to move the discourse forward.

Citizens have a right to insist on maximum transparency from elected officials. This is especially the case for government leaders. The disclosure of tax returns and business holdings can reveal personal ties and potential conflicts of interest. Subject to an impartial adjudication, potential conflicts of interest must be effectively removed. This is the price one must agree to pay for the privilege of public service.

Greater scrutiny is needed to find appropriate new candidates with a progressive agenda and a positive disposition. This search may have to transcend party lines and traditional alliances. These traditional alliances have often contributed to the political impasse presently curtailing forward movement. Ugly internal politics, within both Democrat and Republican camps, have rendered each party dysfunctional at times. Any party propping up weak leaders, for the sake of clinging to power, should be held accountable for all outcomes by a discerning electorate. When the electorate is not sufficiently discerning or engaged, then it deserves the kind of government it ultimately gets.

> *"Our liberty depends on freedom of the press, and that cannot be limited without being lost."*
> —THOMAS JEFFERSON

Elitism, and the sense of entitlement that easily grows from it, can create dysfunction in any democratic system. Political elitism must be dealt with to maximize the benefits of democratic government while minimizing waste. Entitled political elites exist on all sides of any legislature, parliament, or congress. In fact, elitism can be found in every professional occupation. In politics, elitist motives and actions need to be exposed and their influence removed from the political arena. Since it would be naïve to expect politicians to completely clean up their own houses, the critical role of an impartial and free press is essential in facilitating this long overdue transformation. A free press is absolutely essential for keeping voters informed and aware. Any attack on the free press is an attack on democracy itself.

The power inherent in politics bestows great privilege and simultaneously great obligation on all elected officials. It is important to monitor this privilege to ensure that it does not become entrenched as self-serving entitlement, providing a disservice to ordinary citizens. By maintaining a spirit of cautious optimism, long standing problems (like transparency and entitlement) can be tackled and overcome through collaborative effort. This effort must be marked

> *"[It] is of fundamental importance that justice should not only be done, but should manifestly and undoubtedly be seen to be done."*
> —GORDON HEWART

by civility and a steadfast vigilance against further infractions.

When the conduct of elected officials does not meet articulated standards, swift and decisive action must be seen to be taken. Optimistically, we assume the best service from our elected officials, but cautious optimism requires vigilance and accountability. To date, we have been too lax about such matters, to the detriment of dream fulfilment for some of the most vulnerable citizens.

In my mind, anyone siding with rival foreign powers in attempting to influence thinking and voting domestically is a traitor to the nation being manipulated. Anyone mining the Internet usage data of rival politicians for personal gain, or hiring foreign hacks to find incriminating evidence to target adversaries, is guilty of a conspiracy to compromise the democratic process. Anyone hiring computer mercenaries to manipulate the truth to promote a self-serving, morally dishonest narrative is guilty of cyberwar crimes against the nation being manipulated. These new violations require new laws and appropriate penalties.

Trumping *The Donald*

★ ★ ★ ★ ★ ★

A year into his mandate, some Americans remain loyal supporters of Donald Trump. For many others, the level of frustration with Trump's antics continues to escalate. For non-Americans observing from a 'safe' distance, after Trump's long and threatening speech at the United Nations (on September 19, 2017), it should have become clear that there is no safe viewing distance. Ironically, the only rival nation not taken to task by *The Donald* was Russia. This would be the same Russian state that is confirmed to have systematically attempted to influence the outcome of the American election in Trump's favour. This covert meddling constitutes an assault on American democracy.

Some might say, Hillary Clinton among them, that ongoing Russian hacking and strategically timed allegations of uncovered criminal activity by the Clinton camp, ultimately cost her the election. In a tight political contest, the hastily called FBI investigation, which ultimately found nothing wrong, came too late to undo the damage caused by the allegations. At the UN, Trump came down hard on the leaders of North Korea, Iran, Cuba, and Venezuela, but he gave Vladimir Putin a free pass. This left some Americans wondering what secrets Putin knows that Trump does not want to be made public.

For those concerned about the net impact of Trump's presidency, both in

America and abroad, the following theories provide interesting perspective on potential impact and plausible remedies.

The Boomerang Effect

In social sciences (including politics and psychology), sometimes forceful attempts to influence one specific result can end up achieving the opposite. In a democratic

> *"The game of life is a game of boomerangs. Our thoughts, deeds, and words return to us sooner or later with astounding accuracy."*
> —FLORENCE SCOVEL SHINN

society, people sensing an attempt to restrict their freedom of choice may react by not conforming and defiantly doing the opposite. For example, Trump's climate change denial, and his pulling out of the Paris Accord, resulted in many influential Americans doing something positive about climate change. It can

be argued that those Americans feeling that Trump's agenda has been forced upon them, without sufficient consultation or dialogue, will resist its implementation and limit its ultimate impact.

The Right-of-Way Effect

Giving him the benefit of the doubt, Trump believes that he is doing the right things for himself and his country. However, being in the right does not grant any special power or extra privilege to those in the right, to be held over those with

> *"When virtue is lost, benevolence appears, when benevolence is lost right conduct appears, when right conduct is lost, expedience appears. Expediency is the mere shadow of right and truth; it is the beginning of disorder."*
> —LAO TZU

opposing views. This includes those with clearly 'wrong' views. Even they deserve to be treated with decency and respect. If anything, being in the right creates an obligation to educate others, not a right to abuse them. Trump's obvious contempt for critics, unsupportive media, and opposing views is inexcusable, and ultimately, counterproductive.

Given the exaggerated and harsh comments Trump loves to fire at his critics and rivals, he demonstrates a remarkable inabil-

ity to take any criticism fired back at him. In the end, his harsh and condescending treatment of others will adversely affect his ability to accomplish his political agenda. Trump can become his own worst enemy with minimal provocation. This tendency appears to have escalated as more of his attempts to force through his political agenda have been blocked or derailed. The more Trump falters, the more desperate he becomes for a win, any win. The politics of desperation have rarely yielded edible fruit. Impeachment is a more likely scenario than reconciliation or consensus building.

The Strongman/Bully Effect

Trump loves to come on strong. He needs to be in control and at the centre of every situation. This includes petty symbolic gestures like when to let a hand shake go. Strongman tactics might impress some, but they can cause alarm bells to ring for many other observers. Trump's over-the-top strongman persona has embraced right-wing, law and order inclinations from time to time. Early in 2016, he retweeted the following quote, a favourite of fascist dictator Benito Mussolini. "It is better to live one day as a lion than 100 years as a sheep." When questioned, he admitted knowing the origin of the quote and explained he always liked to share interesting quotes. Trump's ultra-strong positions, amounting to decrees banning Muslims and building border walls to keep out dangerous Mexicans, resemble fascist rhetoric and propaganda. His reluctance to unequivocally blame profascist agitators for their key confrontational role in the Charlottesville riots indicates a potential soft spot for aspects of the ideology, and the propaganda machine needed to sustain it.

Based on the tactics used, Trump is often seen as a schoolyard bully. This is a revealing analogy. Bullies are essentially cowards who pick on the most vulnerable targets they can find in the schoolyard. In Trump's case, Muslims, Mexicans, illegal immigrants, homosexual and transgendered individuals, and women appear to be the most vulnerable, in the contemporary American schoolyard.

The other known reality about bullies is that, when confronted, they tend to back

> [Republicans in Congress should go on television, confront Trump] *"and say, Listen, you crazy, lunatic 70-year-old man-baby, stop it! You are now the president of the United States, the commander-in-chief, and you need to stop acting like a mean girl."*
> —ANA NAVARRO

down and move on to other victims. By not confronting the bully, as Ana Navarro strongly suggests, his demeaning and mean spirited tactics have been enabled and allowed to continue unchallenged by his own political party. Even more regrettably, racially charged bullying incidents have increased in American schools. In defense of their children, some parents have boldly argued that behaving like the president always constitutes appropriate behaviour. This too will become an undeniable part of the Trump legacy. It can be argued that under his watch and influence, America has become a more openly mean spirited place.

The Bad Karma Effect

Notwithstanding the political polarization in Washington, Trump has gone out of his way to engage in mean spirited politics. His stern, brooding facial expression has become a trademark for his angry political persona. He treats opposing politicians and critical media with absolute contempt and invites confrontation. He tweets with an aggressive arrogance. These intentional strategies attempt to throw critics off their game. The intent is to solicit a more negative and emotional response from opponents. With Trump there is no middle ground, you either love him or hate him.

As a political opportunist, Trump is not completely comfortable in the Republican fold, nor would he be more comfortable with the Democrats. He rode a fear-anger-hate driven populist wave into the White House and he continues to play to his core constituency with fear-anger-hate rhetoric. The problem is that dwelling on negativity colours one's perception of the political reality.

> "I denounce Donald Trump for not denouncing the kind of vitriol, the kind of violence that he has perpetrated with his angry rhetoric, and he knows exactly what he is doing."
> —DONNA BRAZILE

Negativity can render a politician less capable of transforming the issues and crises being confronted into opportunities for growth and lasting change. Dwelling on negativity invites bad karma. Opportunities for constructive dialogue can be scuttled or bypassed. The growing of a support base, an absolute essential in the world of politics, is effectively compromised. Any promise Trump represented, to do some good things for the American people, has been darkened and compromised by his brash and ultra-negative behaviour. Trump ran successfully as a disturber and divider, not as a *uniter* of the American people. He has consciously chosen to govern divisively. This divisive strategy includes sowing seeds of fear, anger, and distrust and playing on lingering racial resentment in America.

Trump's political shtick is terminal. In the end, there will be no need to bring him down. He will accomplish this completely on his own, by dwelling on negativity. Trump's propensity to embrace and promote extreme views limits his appeal among progressives and has effectively locked him into a group with dark and potentially explosive company. Adapting a more conventional political tone and approach may be taken as a seismic shift by his most extreme supporters.

The Cold Fish Effect

Trump's political shtick of choice involves the sporting of a perpetual scowl. Unlike his mentor, Ronald Reagan, who smiled almost constantly, Trump presents as quite cold and distant. This does not bode well for building trust and voter confidence outside his hard-core base of support. To further alienate some voters, Trump presents as secretive, hyper-sensitive, and insecure. These can be very difficult qualities for political leaders to overcome. The public is constantly exposed to the Trump persona, but very few people are allowed to experience the real Donald Trump. These secrets are as carefully guarded as the secrets of Fort Knox.

The adjacent tweet, in response to criticism connected to his reality TV series, reveals the very insecurity and feeblemindedness he accuses his critics of showing. It presents as the classic primary school retort: "I know you are but what am I?" The claim of possessing "one of the highest" IQs is inconsistent with the language and content of much of his uncensored messaging. If he is content to bring this cold fish act into the White House, Trump should not be upset when he is seen as a cold-hearted prick with nothing nice to say about anyone other than himself and his cronies. This insensitivity

> "Sorry losers and haters, but my I.Q. is one of the highest —and you all know it! Please don't feel so stupid or insecure, it's not your fault."
> —DONALD TRUMP
> TWEETED MAY 8, 2013

does not bode well for building support in many parts of America. After Hurricane Maria destroyed most of Puerto Rico's infrastructure, Trump chastised residents for wanting "everything to be done for them," instead of helping themselves.

The Transformative Effect of Positivity

Dealing with the positive and engaging in promising dialogue can re-direct the political process into more fruitful directions. Obama was a master at promoting hope and recognizing the potential for good to prevail in overcoming existing issues. Trump's political behaviour to date, on the other hand, suggests a fixation on the negative. According to *The Donald*, nothing done by predecessors has been good, and therefore, everything needs a complete overhaul—trade policy, military spending and strategy, taxation levels, spending on social programs, education, funding scientific research, border security, immigration policy, foreign aid, fighting terrorism, stacking the Supreme Court with liberal judges, medical insurance, etcetera, etcetera.

By being so entrenched in the darkness of negativity, Trump fails to draw any illumination or benefit which a spirit of optimism, progressive thinking, solidarity, and human goodness would provide. Negative is as negative does. Once again, this takes away another opportunity to grow personally, or as a political leader. One of the most telling observations about the Trump experience is the reaction of senior staff and key advisors as Trump is speaking.

> "Turning points, while they often come from moments of darkness, can steer us in the direction of great light—light bulb moments."
> —RICHARD BRANSON

When you see the White House chief of staff, John Kelly, hanging his head or covering his face, while Trump is addressing the United Nations General Assembly, you can tell that this extreme negativity originates from and resides in the president himself. Equally revealing is the facial expression and body language of the chief of staff, as Trump kept voluntarily going back to his ultimately pro-fascist rhetoric, after the Charlottesville riots. As Trump continued to argue that there was never anything wrong with his original words, until the dishonest media twisted them, you saw a man clearly unhappy with what his boss had decided to keep bringing up.

Trump appears willing to commit repeated errors, and dig himself deeper into a big hole, in order to not admit or acknowledge his original bad judgement. He even resorts to selectively twisting his original verbiage to make his convoluted point. Ultimately, one can only conclude that Trump will most probably never benefit from the transformative power of positive thinking while in office.

The Integrity Effect

The ultimate result of these manifestations by Donald Trump is the sad confirmation that the man, as he presents himself to the American people, lacks integrity. Without the moral compass of integrity, any politician (veteran or novice), cannot hope to pass any internal consistency test comparing what is preached to what is actually practiced. This moral inconsistency will preclude any lasting effect on the American political landscape. That is, of course, except

> *"If you have integrity, nothing else matters. If you don't have integrity, nothing else matters."*
> —ALAN K. SIMPSON

for the effect of achieving the opposite of the intended result. The American presidency will survive the Trump experience, and quite possibly emerge stronger in the end. Discerning Americans can use the experience to recognize the dangers of unscrupulous populists employing divide and conquer strategies, and concerted fearmongering to assume power and the public trust.

After Trump, the American people will no longer be able to deny that, in spite of a gruelling and costly two-year process, someone almost totally ill-equipped for the job can orchestrate his/her way into the White House. America's reputation abroad may have taken a big hit, but this will be slowly reversed as people see the resilient return of

> *"Non-violence is the greatest force at the disposal of mankind. It is mightier than the mightiest weapon of destruction devised by the ingenuity of man."*
> —MAHATMA GANDHI

the kind spirit the American Dream is long famous for. Americans and non-Americans will be relieved to see the world-famous dream being once again brought on course, and possibly even re-energized.

To achieve this, Americans will not have to compromise their rugged individualism. They will have to show the prevailing quality of their collective character. One of the most powerful manifestations can be the return to non-violent protest and non-violent resistance against perceived injustice and darkness.

It is important that the non-violence movement, used effectively to secure civil rights for all Americans, during the turbulent 1960s, be used again to affect the badly needed transformation in our post-modern times. The temptation to fight aggressive behaviour with further aggression must be resisted at all times. It is most alarming to read about surveys of university students showing almost one-in-five students condoning the use of violence to challenge what is determined as socially and politically unacceptable. Violence breeds reciprocal violence and brings an abrupt end to constructive dialogue. This can only hasten the sad degeneration into savagery.

Extremist groups want nothing more than to bring any confrontation down

> *"Non-violence leads to the highest ethics, which is the goal of all evolution. Until we stop harming all other living beings, we are still savages."*
> —THOMAS A. EDISON

to the gutter where they excel. Neither the extreme left nor the extreme right should be allowed to violate the right to peaceful protest. This propensity to embrace violence, even among educated citizens, speaks volumes about the need to refocus and prioritize the teaching of civics in American schools.

Equally disturbing is the recent trend to prevent controversial speakers from exercising their right to freedom of speech, especially on university campuses. This constitutionally protected right should only be forfeited by speakers promoting hatred, racism, and violence. Protest and boycott should be used to publicly demonstrate rejection of a controversial message. But a controversial speaker should not be prevented from speaking, even when presenting a bitterly partisan political message. At the same time, commencement speeches, with a captive audience, should not be turned into a forum for the dissemination of partisan rhetoric. This too reflects a calculated abuse of decision-making power.

Free speech is an important pillar of American democracy that needs to be protected. Requesting and providing rebuttal time might be one way to bring together radically opposed viewpoints. Challenging the process used to select appropriate

> *"My father used to say, 'Don't raise your voice; improve your argument."*
> —DESMOND TUTU

speakers might be another useful dialogue. University campuses should be one place where radically different thought is discussed and assessed. Preventing free speech is less productive than asking the difficult questions

that hold speakers accountable. Intellectual confrontation always trumps physical confrontation. Any battle should be between opposing ideas.

To confront perceived injustice, the more Americans are seen to actively embrace non-violent protest and non-violent resistance, the sooner the healing process will begin. To succeed domestically, non-violence must be accompanied by honest

> *"The greatness of a community is most accurately measured by the compassionate actions of its members."*
> —CORETTA SCOTT KING

dialogue to redirect the American Dream in a direction that supports and benefits all Americans. Clearly, the status quo of both pre-Trump and post-Trump America needs careful and honest assessment, and a far more equitable recalibration.

To succeed internationally, Americans need to confirm their commitment to support the spread of democracy, social justice, and fair trade. Once again, preserving the status quo is not an option, given existing complications resulting from the skewed globalization currently favouring rich and powerful transnational corporations. What is needed is a renewed humanism—promoting economy, ecology, and equity in all endeavours, across our fragile planet.

> *"Successful people have a social responsibility to make the world a better place and not just take from it."*
> —CARRIE UNDERWOOD

What is needed is a sustainable politico-economic order based on socially conscious and ecologically responsible enterprise. What is needed is a renewed ***social contract*** between nations, corporations, and citizens to respect each other and to work collaboratively to share and sustain our fragile planet. The same humanitarian spirit that is seen to prevail in times of devastating earthquakes, hurricanes, and tsunamis needs to be harnessed and used to move a united humanity forward. As the people's collective voice, government must be seen to embrace and respect this *social contract*, as well as the inherent social obligations of shared prosperity.

The future of life on earth depends on this *social contract*. At the economic heart of this *social contract*, consumers must insist on demonstrated *corporate social responsibility* (CSR) from each company they choose to reward through their purchasing power. Every corporation and its executive leadership and senior management team need to be held accountable for all consequences of their actions and economic choices, as good corporate citizens.

The time for safely sleepwalking through economically induced planetary calamity has long passed. Both individually and collectively, all decisions must be mindfully made to enable sustainability. To help make this possible, citizens must insist on a standard of demonstrated integrity from all elected representatives. Every politician must then be held accountable to the people she has been elected to serve. This too, is a key component of this *social contract*.

> *"In terms of power and influence... there is no more powerful institution in society than business... The business of business should not be about money, it should be about responsibility. It should be about public good, not private greed."*
> —ANITA RODDICK

Revitalizing the Dream

★ ★ ★ ★ ★ ★

There is little doubt that the American Dream has taken a substantial hit over time. There is even less doubt that the Trump experience will set American dreaming even further back. But the end result of this slippage need not be terminal. In fact, by refocusing priorities and redirecting the collective effort on sustainable goals based on equity, economy, and ecology, the noble dream can be revitalized and disenchanted dreamers can be reinvigorated.

Only an inclusive and empowering approach will affect lasting progress towards common social, political, and economic goals. In the end, all dreamers want the same things out of their American experience: the freedom to imagine bolder dreams; the opportunity to pursue their dreams; the privilege to enjoy the fruits of their labour in peace and harmony; the right to rework their dreams after careful self-reflection; and the wisdom to leave the world in better shape than they found it. Only a truly visionary and humanist spirit will allow all these stars to align in a way that enables peaceful and shared prosperity. A true visionary does not predict the future, but rather enables it into existence.

> *"Follow effective action with quiet reflection. From the quiet reflection will come even more effective action."*
> —PETER DRUCKER

Fuelled by cautious optimism the American spirit can still achieve amazing things, both domestically and internationally. Americans can serve as positive role models and responsible stewards of the many gifts of creation entrusted to them. This may require carrying some negatively charged compatriots along for the ride. All along the way, some might even be yelling, kicking, and screaming about what is being done to 'bastardize' their America. But the end result will be worth the aggravation. And along the way, a more enlightened humanity will slowly be seen to emerge and prevail.

> *"Never doubt that a small group of thoughtful, committed citizens can change the world; indeed, it's the only thing that ever has."*
> —MARGARET MEAD

This will require a substantial investment in goodness. And as Henry David Thoreau has so aptly pointed out: "Goodness is the only investment that never fails." This will also require a courageous leap of faith, that others will respond in kind. For guidance, we need look no further than Muhammad Ali. Reflecting back on key turning points in his life, he noted that: "He who is not courageous enough to take risks will accomplish nothing in life." Guided by cautious optimism, Americans will be required to take calculated risks to move their dreams forward. This pursuit of goodness has the potential to simultaneously move humanity forward.

> "Rats and roaches live by competition under the laws of supply and demand; it is the privilege of human beings to live under the laws of justice and mercy."
> —WENDELL BERRY

Each chapter has attempted to contribute insight into the revitalization of the noble American Dream. At the core of the noble dream is the relationship between free individuals and their government. Each chapter has also addressed this core theme. The more government is allowed to grow and tax, the more individual freedoms and choices are eroded away. This reality is at the heart of the great American political debate. Almost since its inception, America has debated the right blend of individual freedom and government control. Perhaps the greatest philosophical divide between Republican and Democratic parties is their

> "I respect and value the ideals of rugged individualism and self-reliance. But rugged individualism didn't defeat the British, it didn't get us to the moon, build our nation's highways, or map the human genome. We did that together. This is the high call of patriotism."
> —CORY BOOKER

innate view of the most productive balance. Republicans traditionally favour smaller government. This generally entails lower taxes, less dependence on government, and more individual self-reliance. Democrats traditionally favour more socially responsible government to address disparities. This generally entails more government intrusion into private lives and more taxation to support social programs.

Given the partisan politics that have emerged in America, by peacefully alternating turns in power, a more moderated balance has emerged. Unfortunately, the provision of more choice to people is not a sustainable reality if some people cannot afford the choices made available to them. While wealthy and healthy Americans can adequately look after themselves, it is painfully clear that others need social assistance to work towards self-reliance. If this assistance could come from a spirit of humanism, then there would be no need for government intrusion. Except in response to natural disasters, humanity does not appear to have evolved to the point where such government intrusion can be safely dismissed as redundant.

At present, the American playing field is not level. Some are favoured while others are disadvantaged. Widening disparity between 'have' and 'have not' Americans increases the need for some mechanism to share prosperity more equitably. The current approach can only end up perpetuating class distinctions and socio-cultural divisions. Hence, the political landscape must rise above partisan alliances to enable the realization of diverse dreams, each contributing to the collective American Dream. In any functional democracy, every elected official becomes the representative of not just those who elected her but also those who did not. Honest, fair, and transparent representation is owed to both groups.

To revitalize both the dream and the dreamer, a concerted effort is needed to address mitigating factors. Each chapter has attempted to touch on these obstacles individually. Each chapter has also exposed current behaviours compromising the process of dream realization for many Americans. Critical thinking skills are developed and remedies are considered to address counterproductive behaviours.

The following serves as an executive summary of chapter foci and the requisite discernment. For each chapter summary, the first focus question is dream based. The second focus is discernment based.

1. **Thinking with Discernment**

    In the first chapter the need for discernment is established, in light of the circus atmosphere being created to confuse, divert, and pollute voter attention. Citizens are encouraged to become more discerning consumers of the truth.

    How can my thinking be manipulated, by self-serving tricksters, to have me question what I can see with my own eyes and hope with my own heart?

    How and by whom is the truth ultimately defined?

2. **Truth Seeking**

    In the second chapter, the need to consciously focus on seeking out the truth was examined. Citizens are encouraged to become more discerning pursuers of the truth.

    How can the beauty and goodness of my dreams be enabled?

How can evidence, logic, objectivity, and reason guide the truth-seeking process?

243

FUTURE PROSPECTS: THE SAVING GRACE OF CAUTIOUS OPTIMISM

3. **Fact Finding and Reality Checking**

In the third chapter, the pursuit of the truth was focused on the need to develop functional crap detectors to sort out disingenuous messaging. Discerning thinkers are encouraged to consider pretext, context, and subtext to develop a fuller understanding of the significance and implications in messages.

How can my dream withstand prejudice and racially motivated injustice?

What evidence can I use to confirm truthfulness, accuracy and motive?

4. **Testing for Integrity and Internal Consistency in Leadership**

In this instalment, the importance of personal integrity and the consistent staking of the moral high ground are addressed. Discerning thinkers are encouraged to compare what is preached to what is actually practiced, to determine personal integrity and the internal consistency of what is proposed.

What hope and growth does my dream enable or inspire?

Can I see evidence of integrity at work in what is being promised relative to what is actually done?

5. **Challenging Conventional and Populist Thinking**

In the fifth chapter, the myths of populism are exposed and the need for an effective counterbalance is established. Discerning thinkers are invited to question conventional wisdom to ensure accuracy. In effect, Americans are all invited to be honorary citizens of Missouri, "the show me state."

What factors most influence and shape my dream?

What am I being sold? What am I not being told? What are the benefits and costs of different options?

6. **Promoting Fair Play and Decency**

In the sixth instalment, the current politics of mean spirt are contrasted with the historical American spirit of fair play. Discerning thinkers are invited to reflect on the spirit and fairness of the political strategies being implemented or proposed.

Who stands to gain from my dream? Who stands to lose? How can
    harm be mitigated?
How do I know that what is being sold is not an over-simplification
    of complex realities? What proof is there that the matter has been
    carefully studied and diverse stakeholders have been consulted?

7. Disarming Divisiveness Through Constructive Dialogue

The seventh chapter investigates the effects of extreme political polarization plaguing American politics and looks at ways to remedy the current bitterly partisan impasse. Discerning thinkers are challenged to look for and promote honest, inclusive, and constructive dialogue.

How do I know that my dream is not divisive or politically partisan?
What evidence of a bias towards honesty, diversity, reconciliation,
    objectivity, empathy, independent critical thinking, integrity,
    and ethical considerations are evident in this strategy or
    proposal? How can constructive dialogue be promoted?

8. Fostering Fair Trade and Social Responsibility

The eighth chapter investigates the economic realities emerging from the golden age of the transnational corporation, as created by the current globalization movement. Discerning thinkers are challenged to consider the changes needed to transform free trade into fair trade.

How do I know that my dream does not contribute to exploitation
    and dehumanization?
How can government social responsibility, corporate social
    responsibility, and consumer social responsibility enable social,
    economic, and political justice in current trade and business
    practices?

9. Enabling Sustainable Choices and Practices

The ninth instalment investigates the standard of responsible stewardship and the need to assess the sustainability of all actions and choices. After exposing false assumptions related to climate change, discerning thinkers are challenged to think globally, as they act locally to reduce waste, environmental damage, and harmful impact on future generations.

How do I know that my dream is economically, ecologically, and
ethically sustainable?

How can my choices as a voter, worker, and consumer enable
greater sustainability?

10. Overcoming Distraction and Manipulation

This tenth chapter focuses on the critical thinking required to overcome
strategies intended to deliberately distract and misdirect voters and to confuse
issues and priorities.

What is distracting me from achieving my dream? How can I fix
this problem?

To what is my attention being directed? Why? What is not being
given sufficient attention? Why? What have I learned from this
experience?

11. Imagineering Dreams

This final chapter synthesizes reflections from previous chapters to focus
thinking on the power of cautious optimism, hope, and positivity, in order
to revitalize dreams and re-energize dreamers.

How does my dream reflect cautious optimism, hope, and positivity?

How can creative and critical thinking be used to transform
contemporary problems into opportunities for growth and
shared prosperity?

The most noble dreams are purveyors of
hope and goodness. Dreams enable goodness and positivity to prevail in our busy and
sometimes frightening world. Framed in
positive thinking, dreams help overcome fear
and protect against despair.

Those who dare to dream, dare to change
the world. But this result is not automatic.
First, the dreamer must have the courage to
dream big. Then, the dreamer must have the
stamina to work hard to make it happen.

> "Consult not your fears but
> your hopes and your dreams.
> Think not about your
> frustrations, but about your
> unfulfilled potential.
> Concern yourself not with
> what you tried and failed in,
> but with what it is still
> possible for you to do."
> —SAINT POPE JOHN XXIII

Perhaps Harriet Tubman addressed the first part best. She said: "Every great dream begins with a dreamer. Always remember, you have within you the strength, the patience, and the passion to reach for the stars to change the world." Colin Powell addressed the second point most succinctly, when he said: "A dream doesn't become reality through magic; it takes sweat, determination and hard work."

An Experience Worth Noting: Significance and Impact — So What?

★ ★ ★ ★ ★

Figure 11.1: The Toronto skyline from Centre Island, in 2014. (Photo by the author).

When teaching photographic arts, I have always planned as many field trips as possible to provide students with supervised opportunities to apply the techniques learned in class. On one memorable occasion, I took my summer school class of eighteen students to photograph cityscapes in downtown Toronto. In the afternoon, we took the ferry to the Toronto Islands, to work on skyline photos.

While we were on Centre Island, the cloud cover began to rapidly change, making for some rather dramatic photos. As more and more dark clouds filled the sky, my thoughts slowly shifted away from the artistic and to the pragmatic. If the sky opened up on us, and the sudden gusts of wind made that possibility anything but remote, we would have no shelter in our present location.

I asked the students to note where they left off and then to quickly proceed to the nearest sheltered picnic area. I explained that given the day's high temperatures, the rapid buildup of clouds, and the darkness of their colour, it was going to be a very heavy downpour. By the time we got to the shelter, the rain had started to come down. The shelter was already crowded, but since the rainfall was intensifying, people made room for us. With the sky rumbling and crackling above us, I cleaned up my glasses and proceeded to take a head count. Two of my students were missing.

A quick survey revealed that Enza and Susan had found a large plastic sheet, left behind by one of the park's workers. With this sheet for protection, they had decided to stop under a large tree to take pictures of the storm. I could barely see them in the distance, but the storm made communication impossible. I waved to them to come join us, but they just waved back. So, I borrowed an umbrella and a windbreaker and ran out into the monsoon to bring them back. Needless to say, I was not pleased!

By the time I reached them, I was out of breath. So, I kept my words simple: "Get your assets under the shelter immediately, if not sooner!" Enza, the more talkative of the two students responded with: "It's okay, sir! It's just as dry under here, really!" I sternly snapped back: "It's not okay and it's not up for discussion! So, let's start moving right now!"

Walking towards the shelter, we all huddled under the plastic sheet. In a much more civil tone, I eventually asked: "Didn't you learn anything in geography class?" Enza's quick response was priceless. With a big smile on her face she said: "Yeah, sir, don't you remember? You gave me an 'A'! So what?"

I barely had enough time to repeat "So what?" when a lightning bolt cut through the sky and instantly split a large willow tree in half well behind us. We turned in response to a cracking sound, and watched as the smaller half of the tree came crashing down to the ground. The part that remained standing was smouldering as the rain drops came in contact with the parts of the tree burned by the lightning strike. This tree was not really that far from the tree my two intrepid photographers had decided to wait under.

It has often been said that a good teacher knows when to talk and that a great teacher knows when to shut up. In this case, I could not have said anything, even if I had wanted to. In our section of the shelter, nobody had much to say. People were just staring in the distance, at what used to be a large and healthy tree. In one corner, a group of elderly ladies were saying the Rosary in what appeared to be Portuguese.

The storm did not last much longer, but its effects have lasted a lifetime. In our geography classes, we had discussed all of the weather facts that contributed to our perfect storm experience. Yet, Enza could not apply them effectively, to her current situation, to make the important connection when it counted most. For me, the most fundamental question of geography was no longer 'what is where?' or 'why there?' but rather 'so what?' In more precise wording: "What is the full significance of this geographic phenomenon, and how does it affect my life or the lives of other people?"

Without this question, geography can become interesting but trivial. As educators, it is imperative that we not get upset by students asking the 'so what?' question. Instead, we should encourage learners to constantly ask this important question. More importantly, we should develop in lifelong learners the thinking skills required to accurately determine significance and relevance on their own. Years after graduation, I met Enza at a school reunion. As she approached me, she did not say hello or use any of the more customary greetings. She simply smiled, looked into my eyes and said, "So what?" As we hugged, no other words were necessary.

The Trump experience provides discerning thinkers with ample opportunity to assess the full significance of what is taking place in the name of returning America to greatness. Trump's pandering to populist sentiments, and his solemn promise to rid the political landscape of entitled and self-serving political elites, is a noble sentiment. But his actions speak louder than his empty rhetoric.

While POTUS, Trump has systematically pursued his own agenda, furthered his own interests, and worked deviously hard to discredit anything that might reflect negatively on him, such as Mueller's investigation into Russian activities. In responding to the 'so what?' question, discerning Americans must look past the various smoke screens created to see and understand the full significance of the harsh reality now before them. This kind of honest, critical thinking is not un-American, but rather, it is the only thinking that can help save the promise and prestige of America.

There is an interesting comparison to be made between Trump's political tactics and those described by Niccolò Machiavelli, the diplomat, political philosopher, and writer of the Florentine Renaissance. Machiavelli is often considered by scholars to be the father of modern political science. Written in 1513, Machiavelli's *The Prince* outlines how a despot can seize and hold power by being ruthless and immoral. The end justifies the means. Electrifying in its frankness, almost diabolical in its analysis of power, this unethical code of political conduct was only meant to outline the political reality, not as an overall philosophy of life. For Machiavelli, all was seen as fair in war, and politics was just another form of warfare. Ruthless and immoral behaviour was presented as normal and effective behaviour in politics.

The following Machiavellian principles provide a tangible example:

> *It is not necessary for a prince [leader] to be faithful, merciful, sincere, or religious, for this will make him dangerously weak. He must seem to do good, but at the same time, he must know how to do wrong when it becomes necessary ... A prince must lie and be able to do it well ... A prince must be both a lion and a fox — a lion in order to frighten the men around him, and a fox to avoid their plots ... It is better to be loved and feared by your subjects, but since the two are virtually impossible, it is better to be feared.*

In time, two schools of thought emerged in response to Machiavelli's most important work. At first, it was recognized as a political science treatise advocating whatever necessary to gain, consolidate, and hold power in an Italy badly fractured by regional territorial interests, including those of the Pope. Later, a second group saw Machiavelli's work as a biting satire on despotism, by a lifelong republican deeply concerned about recent un-democratic trends. More than 200 years later, philosopher Jean-Jacques Rousseau wrote: "While pretending to give lessons to kings, he [Machiavelli] gave great ones to peoples."

It can also be said of Trump that in pretending to be the people's only realistic choice, his time as POTUS will provide great learning

Figure 11.2: Machiavelli's tomb in Santa Croce Basilica bears the Latin inscription, "So great a man has no adequate eulogy." (Photo by the author).

opportunities for the American people — at present politically, racially, economically, and regionally fractured. In claiming to be the consummate anti-politician, Trump's callously divisive antics have clearly exposed the dark side of American politics, for all to see. A true prince was supposed to be more deviously competent.

Based on what is already known, there should be no safe place left for Trump's supporters and enablers to hide from the political fallout.

Figure 11.3: One of many protest signs openly questioning Trump's agenda as not a good fit for the majority of Americans. This clever poster presents an interesting twist on the proverbial loaded question about how a particular dress makes its wearer look. (B. Christopher / Alamy Stock Photo).

Interestingly, Americans have put a clear limit on the number of years an individual can serve as their president. Given the ugly nature of partisan politics, this same protection should be applied to many other elected positions. This would help prevent the entrenchment of self-serving, career politicians. Fresh faces would have the opportunity to receive a focused mandate, get the job done, take their victory lap, and then move on to another career. To further advance 'so what?' thinking, given the ugly realities of the political world, additional checks and balances need to be put in place to quickly address actions found detrimental to the common or greater good of the American people. If nothing more, the Trump experience should underscore this as necessary protection for a fragile and easily exploitable democracy. All democracies are exploitable, when people choose to look the other way.

The following reality is clearly focused on the 'so what?' question. In a dysfunctional and bitterly divided political arena, the president is supposed to be the caring adult in the room—the forward-thinking servant leader, shaping constructive dialogue to effectively address existing problems with new solutions. Thinking clearly, the resurrection of old solutions, that have not worked in the past, is not evidence of wise leadership. More than anything else, doing the same old things and expecting different results is a sure sign of insanity.

Instead of this caring adult and purveyor of hope, frustrated Americans seem to have empowered a class clown, schoolyard bully, and self-serving narcissist. Instead of building bridges of reconciliation, this president appears to take great delight in furthering existing divisions. Instead of healing a divided nation, this president appears interested in furthering the great divide, content to rely exclusively on the diehard followers that constitute a whopping 33 percent of the nation.

Instead of stopping the downward slide into intolerance and insensitivity, this president appears interested in demonizing the purveyors of any dissenting opinions, making them targets of public ridicule. In this sad case, the 'so what?' response becomes rather staggering, like a lightning bolt flashing through the sky. Instead of reversing the nation's downward slide, this president appears content to lead it proudly into mediocrity and irrelevance, as long as the spotlight remains focused on him and his every musing.

A further 'so what?' can be easily drawn from the new and more viciously nasty normal being defined for America. Instead of chastising and challenging this degradation, many Americans have accepted it as the new normal. This sad decline needs to be reversed for any sustainable return to decency and honour to be possible.

The truth is often messy, especially in today's post-modern information age. Ironically, the more technology advances to permit instant and global communication, the less willing people appear to be to listen attentively and actively to the thoughts of others. Since no person or group holds a monopoly on truth, listening skills must be improved and made less selective, to break the shackles of indoctrinated privilege, complicit parroting, and comfortable conformity.

As a further tragedy, a growing number of people today are ill-equipped to assess the credibility of the ideas they read or hear. There must be a call for more critical thinking, and a concerted effort to develop critical thinking skills in and out of schools. The proliferation of these skills is the only safeguard against being bamboozled by computer hacks and robots bent on reshaping the thoughts of the gullible masses.

There is now great concern about malicious Russian meddling in the American thought process. The messy truth is that unscrupulous Americans are also engaged in the same dirty 'mind control' tactics. Otherwise, for one disgusting example, claims that the Sandy Hook school massacre was a government hoax to promote the gun control agenda would not have had the legs that these ridiculous stories ultimately acquired. Only a heartless opportunist who perceives his victims to be malleable, ill-informed, and ill-equipped would attempt such a dastardly strategy. But then, this is not the only 'snake oil' this wealthy merchant sells to gullible Americans.

March 24, 2018 marked a watershed moment for many distraught dreamers across America. Building on the momentum of a successful *National School Walkout* the previous week, survivors of the senseless February 14th massacre at Marjory Stoneman Douglas High School, in Parkland, Florida, led well over a million Americans in a *March for Our Lives*. Though the main event was held in Washington, D.C., more than 800 sister marches were held in major cities and concerned communities across America, and around the world.

These public demonstrations represent a powerfully cumulative response to a lingering 'so what?' question. Students, teachers, parents, survivors of school shootings, and celebrities took their defiant message against escalating gun violence and an unrelentingly manipulative gun lobby to the seats of government. That's what! The impassioned warning that Washington's inaction on the scourge of gun violence is no longer acceptable could not be ignored or diminished, even by condescending NRA backed politicians pre-emptively complaining that children should not be listened to because only adults have the right to make laws.

Some of the more foolish supporters of the gun lobby even went as far as to declare the turnout smaller than organizers expected and underwhelming. Most crowd estimates by police confirm a very different reality. I will leave it to the reader to judge which of the following messages about the *March for Our Lives* is full of hope and which is full of poisonous fearmongering.

Marjory Stoneman Douglas survivor, David Hogg, boldly told the standing-room only gathering in Washington: "To those politicians supported by the NRA that allow the continued slaughter of our children and our future, I say get your resumes ready." The planned Washington march turned into a thunderous, tightly packed, and peaceful gathering when the anticipated draw of 400,000 participants almost doubled on the day of the march. This student-led gathering became one of the largest protests in America since the Vietnam War era.

> *"Michelle and I are so inspired by all the young people who made today's marches happen. Keep at it. You're leading us forward. Nothing can stand in the way of millions of voices calling for change."*
> —BARACK OBAMA
> TWITTER, MARCH 24, 2018

Hopefully, as former president Obama suggests, this is not just a moment in time, but part of a concerted movement—a sustained forward movement where young dreamers can inject the voice of reason into a long-polarized debate. These courageous students are all traumatized survivors of a death defying nightmare where 17 of their fellow students and teachers were violently executed by a former student with serious mental health issues. This sick and violent individual used assault weapons he was able to purchase legally in Florida. Common sense is badly needed in the gun control debate, badly skewed after years of acquiescing to the NRA's escalating Second Amendment demands.

> *"Today's protests aren't spontaneous. Gun-hating billionaires and Hollywood elites are manipulating and exploiting children as part of their plan to DESTROY the Second Amendment and strip us of our right to defend ourselves and our loved ones."*
> —National Rifle Association (NRA) Facebook, March 24, 2018

After each new episode of gun violence in American schools, the NRA's response of choice has been to reenergize its long-standing campaign to have armed security and armed teachers in every American school, thus proliferating the existing gun culture! The survivors of the Parkland massacre are now boldly saying to America: "Enough is enough." The senseless carnage in Parkland took place while the school's armed security guard cowardly hid to avoid confrontation with a well-armed murderer.

Speaking of cowardly responses, right after Melania's nicely crafted speech about the importance of courage in America today, she and the POTUS quickly retreated from Washington for a quiet weekend in Mar-a-Lago, as protesters continued to flood into Washington. Apparently, the presidential Twitter fingers suffered a case of temporary paralysis as not a single mention was made of the growing movement started by these passionate dreamers, waking up from their personal nightmare and serving notice that their generation will not sit back silently while the NRA continues to buy lawmakers, repeating the deadly mistake their parents and grandparents made.

Distraught dreamers everywhere can find solace in the tenacity of the young dreamers from Parkland, Florida. If they continue their mission to not let their classmates die in vain, they may achieve unprecedented gains that many others before them were unable to realize. This may go down in American history as a key turning point in a bitterly polarized gun debate. All because they cared enough to make a difference in the gun riddled world they inherited. And their generation is only now starting to become eligible to vote! As a career educator, I have always taken great comfort in trusting students to become the responsible stewards of our better tomorrows.

Once again, the fate of the American Dream rests squarely on the shoulders of the American people. As it should, the fate of all dreams rests squarely on the shoulders of their dreamers.

And so, it all comes down to this. Dreamers must be willing to pay the price to make their dreams a reality. They must be driven by the desire to make a positive difference. No matter how bleak the future may seem at times, never underestimate the power of dreamers and their dreams.

> *"The positive thinker sees the invisible, feels the intangible, and achieves the impossible."*
> —WINSTON CHURCHILL

By all means, dream big, beautiful dreams and then work hard to make them happen. Cynics and pessimists may say, "Why bother?" For me, the best response has always been, "Why not?" If we cannot be bothered to engineer our own futures, then what can we ever be bothered to do?

And so, dear daughters, and other distraught dreamers, dream big and work hard. Don't let the Trump experience darken your outlook. After all, that is exactly what *The Donald* is trying to do. In time, he will sow the seeds of his own downfall, and achieve the very opposite results from what he intended.

Whatever you decide to do, know that I will be deeply proud of you. Be sure to lead with your beautiful hearts, to see that goodness prevails. But, always remember to take your head along for the adventure of your lives.

Critical Thinking Checkpoint Five

★ ★ ★ ★ ★ ★

Reflect on this final probing question to consolidate your critical thinking. Consider organizing your thinking around two distinct question parts, focusing on American politics and on American society. You can broaden your reflection by adding a third focus on international politics and relations.

Assessing the Trump experience as both a helpful and harmful influence on American politics, and American society, what will Trump's ultimate legacy be?

JUDGEMENT CRITERIA On what would a reasonable and objective person base this decision?	MY DECISION
☐	
☐	
☐	
☐	
☐	
SUPPORTING EVIDENCE What evidence can be used to confirm this decision as sound?	**RELIABILITY** How do I know my sources are objective, accurate and trustworthy? Can I find other sources to independently corroborate the facts?

The Parable of the Slick Psychic

★ ★ ★ ★ ★ ★

The following post-modern parable illustrates some of the fallout when citizens fail to use critical thinking to discern what is believable and supportable in an increasingly more contrived political world.

On the Good Ship Lies and Distraction

Figure 11.4: By editorial cartoonist Chris Weyant. (Courtesy of Cagle Cartoons).

The Real Ringmaster?

Figure 11.5: By editorial cartoonist Paul Fell. (www.CartoonStock.com).

A billionaire misogynist was so vain that he believed just by predicting something, he could make it happen. Since he knew more about everything than anyone else, he felt the world should pay for his genius. He was so smart that he predicted his own IQ. There was a constant bitterness in his heart because with all his wealth and brilliance, the people had never seen fit to make him their undisputed king. And so, he foretold the demise of all other contenders to the throne.

When he threw his over-sized hat into the ring, he predicted a populist wave would sweep him to power. Then, he went on a campaign of fearmongering and poisoned tweeting to rally the populist cause. He hired cyber hacks to help secretly wage cyberwar on his last opponent. Right after his coronation, he predicted great and immediate economic gains. To help his subjects understand the truth, he explained that the economy was growing so fast the growth was invisible to the naked eye. To silence his critics, he predicted that only enemies of the state would dare contradict him. As a great contrarian, the more his advisers warned against something, the more he did it anyway.

When forward thinking proved complicated, he became especially adept at predicting the past. He proudly foretold of a triumphant return to the "golden age of laundromat democracy," where whites and coloureds were kept apart to avoid staining the fabric. The king liked to use riddles, convoluted hyperbole, and clichés, when talking to his peasants. This made his predictions as clear as mud.

The psychic king predicted great trade deals where only exports would grow exponentially. He chastised all trading partners for being selfish and dishonest. He predicted foreign goods were cheap junk. Finally, he banned imports to keep all the jobs in his kingdom.

To keep his subjects in line, he always predicted a rosy future for his fans and a gloomy future for his detractors. Remarkably, even with great psychic powers, he never foresaw his own demise. His harsh predictions made it difficult to win over new supporters. In fact, the more he tried wooing new supporters, the more he angered his diehard followers.

Eventually, there were few able minded subjects left who actually believed his predictions and other musings. His ministers secretly plotted to position themselves for a safe landing after the psychic king's demise. Nobody bothered to warn the king, because they all figured he already knew everything.

ANSWER KEY FOR PAGE 24

Spoiler Alert: *Do not read the following page until you have completed the activity on page 24 for yourself.*

SEPARATING FACT FROM OPINION

The purpose of this activity is to test your ability to separate fact or direct observation from inference or opinion. Read the story and then assess the 10 statements that follow to determine whether each is true or false. If you cannot determine whether a statement is true or false relative to the facts presented, check the Don't Know box. You must not make any inferences, form unsubstantiated assumptions, or form any opinions.

THE STORY

A storekeeper had just turned off the lights in the store when a man appeared and demanded money. The owner opened a cash register. The contents of the cash register were scooped up, and the man sped away. A member of the police force was notified immediately.

	True	False	Don't Know
1. A man appeared after the owner had turned off **his** store lights. **[sex assumed]**			■
2. The **robber** was a man. **[robbery assumed]**			■
3. The man did not demand money. **[factually incorrect]**		■	
4. The **man** who opened the cash register was the owner. **[sex assumed; owner and storekeeper can be different individuals]**			■
5. The store **owner scooped** up the contents of the cash register and sped away. **[identity of scooper assumed]**			■
6. Someone opened a cash register. **[factually correct]**	■		
7. After the man who **demanded** the money **scooped** up the contents of the cash register, he ran away. **[same person assumed to demand money and scoop contents]**			■
8. While the cash register contained money, the story does not state how much. **[exact contents assumed]**			■
9. The story concerns a series of events in which **only three persons** are referred to: the owner of the store, a man who demanded money, and a member of the police force. **[storekeeper and owner cannot be assumed to be the same person]**			■
10. The following events were included in the story: someone demanded money, a cash register was opened, its contents were scooped up, and a man sped away. **[factually correct]**	■		

How well did you do in this activity?
More importantly, what does this activity reveal about human nature?

APPENDIX TWO

LIST OF SUPPORTING QUOTES

About the Author

Born in the village of Carpanzano in Calabria, Italy in 1951, **Angelo Bolotta** emigrated to Canada in 1955. He graduated from the University of Toronto with an Honours B.A. in economic geography in 1973, and a Bachelor of Education (in geography and economics) in 1974. He also obtained a Master of Education in Curriculum and Assessment in 1988 from the Ontario Institute for Studies in Education. Angelo is a career educator, curriculum leader, administrator, consultant, university instructor and author with over 40 years of experience in public education. He started teaching with the Toronto Catholic District School Board in 1974, and retired in 2009, after serving his last 18 years as a secondary school principal and curriculum leader. He continued his teaching career as an instructor and supervisor with Niagara University from 2007–2014. In 2012, Angelo received the Chief Justices' Award, from the Ontario Justice Education Network in recognition of his "significant contribution to the establishment of a civil society through education and dialogue." Angelo is the author of numerous textbooks and educational publications about civics, Canadian history, economics, the immigrant experience, and student assessment.